CT/F/ E12.50
7/11/84 T

THE COLLISION REGULATIONS

THE COLLISION REGULATIONS

The application and enforcement of the Merchant Shipping (Distress Signals and Prevention of Collisions) Regulations 1983

By

R. H. B. STURT

M.A. (CANTAB)
Solicitor of the Supreme Court

Illustrations by **Ann L. STURT**, B.Sc.

SECOND EDITION

LONDON

LLOYD'S OF LONDON PRESS LTD.

Legal Publishing & Conferences Division,
26-30 Artillery Lane, Bishopsgate, London, E1 7LX

1984

©

R. H. B. STURT

1984

ISBN 0-907432-67-0

Printed in Great Britain by
Holmes & Sons (Printers) Limited, Andover, Hampshire

PREFACE TO THE SECOND EDITION

In the first edition of this book I described my rude awakening to the dangers of collisions at sea when, in the safety of my bed near Dover on 11th January 1971, I was awoken by an explosion following the collision of the *Texaco Caribbean* and the *Paracas*. There followed much international discussion and eventually, on 15th July 1977, the Collision Regulations and Distress Signals Order 1977 came into force as regards British ships. This has now been replaced by the Merchant Shipping (Distress Signals and Prevention of Collisions) Regulations 1983, which came into force on 1st June 1983.

Since the publication of the first edition there have been numerous prosecutions for breaches of the Collision Regulations and the maximum fine for breach of the regulations has been increased in one instance to £50,000 and in all other cases to at least £1,000. The obligation to obey the regulations has been made stricter and it has become even more important for ships' masters to know the extent of their duty with regard to the regulations and for owners to ensure that their masters are fully informed. There have also been numerous changes in the law, particularly with regard to Department of Transport inspectors and investigations, as well as some alterations to the Collision Regulations themselves.

As in the previous edition, the main legal principles are expounded in the text, with detailed discussion, authorities and cross-references in the footnotes. In order to make this edition more useful to mariners, I have included in an Appendix a number of Department of Transport "M" Notices, which set out the Department's guidance on various aspects of the regulations. For lawyers, there are over 60 new cases and numerous new statutes and statutory instruments. The Collision Regulations and Distress Signals Order 1977 contained rules which had been agreed internationally in 1972. In many cases these were derived from previous rules agreed in 1960 and contained in an Order of 1965. I have referred to the rules agreed in 1972 (with the recent amendments to them) as the 1972 Rules and the rules agreed in 1960 as the 1960 Rules and included a detailed destination table of the 1960 Rules showing which 1960 Rule became which 1972 Rule. In Appendix 1 the two sets of rules are printed side by side. I hope this treatment will make the book equally useful to mariners and lawyers. The law is stated as at 1st October 1983.

I am grateful for much assistance given to me by Mr R. M. Malbey, of the Department of Transport; Captain R. K. N. Emden, D.S.C., O.B.E., R.N., of H.M. Coastguard; and The Legal Office of the IMO Secretariat. Appendices I and III are reproduced by permission of H.M. Stationery Office and Appendix II reproduced by permission of The Ministry of Defence.

Dover
November 1983

RICHARD STURT

CONTENTS

CHAPTER ONE
HISTORY AND APPLICATION OF COLLISION REGULATIONS

PARA.

1.01 History of collision regulations
1.02 Conventions and English law
1.03 The International Maritime Organization (IMO)
1.04 The *ultra vires* principle
1.05 Power for the Secretary of State to make regulations
1.06 Power to extend regulations to foreign vessels
1.07 Application of the regulations to United Kingdom vessels
1.08 Application of the regulations to non-United Kingdom vessels
1.09 Interpretation of regulations
1.10 Duty to obey regulations
1.11 Duty of vessel to assist in case of collision
1.12 Obligation to assist vessels in distress
1.13 Duty to log and report casualties, etc.
1.14 Duty to obey the rules of good seamanship

CHAPTER TWO
COLLISION REGULATIONS—STEERING AND SAILING RULES

Sect. (1) *Conduct of vessels in any condition of visibility*

PARA.

2.01 Look-out—Rule 5
2.02 Safe speed—Rule 6
2.03 Risk of collision—Rule 7
2.04 Action to avoid collision—Rule 8
2.05 Narrow channels—Rule 9
2.06 Traffic Separation Schemes—Rules 1(d), 10
2.07 Separation Schemes currently in force

Sect (2) *Conduct of vessels in sight of one another*

PARA.

2.08 Sailing vessels—Rule 12
2.09 Overtaking—Rule 13
2.10 Head-on situation—Rule 14. Crossing situation—Rule 15
2.11 Action by give-way vessel—Rule 16. Action by stand-on vessel—Rule 17
2.12 Responsibilities between vessels—Rule 18

APPENDIX I

SCHEDULE ONE TO THE MERCHANT SHIPPING (DISTRESS SIGNALS AND PREVENTION OF COLLISIONS) REGULATIONS 1983

(INTERNATIONAL REGULATIONS FOR PREVENTING COLLISIONS AT SEA 1972 —AS AMENDED BY IMO RESOLUTION A.464 (XII))

APPENDIX II

ADMIRALTY NOTICE TO MARINERS No. 17 of 1983

(TRAFFIC SEPARATION SCHEMES—INFORMATION CONCERNING SCHEMES SHOWN ON ADMIRALTY CHARTS)

APPENDIX III

DEPARTMENT OF TRANSPORT MERCHANT SHIPPING NOTICES

LIST OF ABBREVIATIONS

A.C. (preceded by date)	Law Reports, Appeal Cases, House of Lords Council, since 1890 (e.g., [1891] A.C.)
A.-G.	Attorney General
All E.R. (preceded by date)	All England Law Reports, 1936-(current)
All E.R. Rep.	All England Law Reports Reprint, 36 vols., 1843-1935
App. Cas.	Appeal Cases 1875-1890
art.	article
Asp. M.L.C.	Aspinall's Maritime Law Cases, 22 vols., 1870-1943
B.	Baron
B. & Ald.	Barnewall and Alderson's Reports, King's Bench, 5 vols., 1817-1822
B.F.S.P.	British and Foreign State Papers
B.I.L.C.	British and International Law Cases
C.	Chancellor
C.A.	Court of Appeal
C. & P.	Carrington and Payne's Reports, Nisi Prius, 9 vols., 1823-1841
C.C.A.	Court of Criminal Appeal
cf.	compare
C.L.R.	Commonwealth Law Reports, 1903-(current)
Cmd.	Command Paper (1919-1956)
Cmnd.	Command Paper (1956 to date)
Ch. (preceded by date)	Law Reports, Chancery Division, since 1890 (e.g., [1891] 1 Ch.)
Ch. App.	Law Reports, Chancery Appeals, 10 vols., 1865-1875
Ch. Rob.	Christopher Robinson's Reports, Admiralty, 6 vols., 1798-1808
col.	column
Cox, C.C.	E. W. Cox's Criminal Law Cases, 31 vols., 1843-1941
Cr. App. Rep.	Cohen's Criminal Appeal Reports, 1908-(current)
Crim. L.R. (preceded by date)	Criminal Law Review, 1954-(current)
C.R.O.S.S.	Centre Régionel Opérationel de Sauvetage et Surveillance
D.C.	Divisional Court
Dods.	Dodson's Reports, Admiralty, 2 vols., 1811-1822
E. & B.	Ellis and Blackburn's Reports, Queen's Bench, 8 vols., 1852-1858
Edn.	Edition
F. (Ct. of Sess.)	Fraser, Court of Session Cases (Scotland), 5th series, 8 vols., 1898-1906
F. & F.	Foster and Finlason's Reports, Nisi Prius, 4 vols., 1856-1867

H. & N.	Hurlstone and Norman's Reports, Exchequer, 7 vols., 1856-1862
H.L. Cas.	Clark's Reports, House of Lords, 11 vols., 1847-1866
Hag. Ad.	Haggard's Reports, Admiralty, 3 vols., 1822-1838
H.C.	High Court
H. of C.	House of Commons
H.L.	House of Lords
Holt. Ad. Ca.	Holt's Admiralty Cases, 1 vol., 1863-1867
ibid.	ibidem
IMCO	Inter-Governmental Maritime Consultative Organization
IMO	International Maritime Organization
J	Justice
J.P.	Justice of the Peace, 1837-(current)
Jur.	Jurist Reports, 18 vols., 1837-1854
K.B. (preceded by date)	Law Reports, King's Bench Division, 53 vols., 1900-1952 (e.g. [1901] 2 K.B.)
L.C.	Lord Chancellor
L.C.J.	Lord Chief Justice
L.J.	Lord Justice
L.J. Ad.	Law Journal, Admiralty, 1865-1875
L.J.C.P.	Law Journal, Common Pleas, 1831-1875
L.J.K.B. or Q.B.	Law Journal, King's Bench or Queen's Bench, 1831-1946
L.J.P.	Law Journal, Probate, Divorce and Admiralty, 1875-1946
L.R.A. & E.	Law Reports, Admiralty and Ecclesiastical Cases, 4 vols., 1865-1875
L.R.C.P.	Law Reports, Common Pleas, 10 vols., 1865-1875
L.R.P.C.	Law Reports, Privy Council, 6 vols., 1865-1875
L.R.Q.B.	Law Reports, Queen's Bench, 10 vols., 1865-1875
L.T.	Law Times Reports, 177 vols., 1859-1947
Ll.L.Rep.	Lloyd's List Law Reports, 1919-1950
Lloyd's Rep. (preceded by date)	Lloyd's Law Reports, 1951-(current) (e.g., [1952] 1 Lloyd's Rep.)
Lush.	Lushington's Reports, Admiralty, 1 vol., 1859-1862
Marsd. Ad. Cas.	Marsden's Admiralty Cases
Mar. L.C.	Maritime Law Reports, (Crockford), 3 vols., 1860-1871
Moo. P.C.	Moore's Privy Council Cases, 15 vols., 1836-1862
Moo. P.C.C.N.S.	Moore's Privy Council Cases, New Series, 9 vols., 1862-1873
M. & M.	Moody and Malkin's Reports, Nisi Prius, 1 vol., 1826-1830
M.R.	Master of the Rolls
N.I. (preceded by date)	Northern Ireland Law Reports, 1925-(current) (e.g. [1925] N.I.)

Not. of Cas.	Notes of Cases in the Ecclesiastical and Maritime Courts, 7 vols., 1841-1850
Ord.	Order
P. (preceded by date)	Law Reports, Probate, Divorce and Admiralty Division, 1890-1971 (e.g. [1891] P.)
P.	President
para. (s)	paragraph(s)
P.C.	Judicial Committee of the Privy Council
P.D.	Law Reports, Probate, Divorce and Admiralty Division, 15 vols., 1875-1890
Plowd.	Plowden's Reports, fol., 2 vols., 1550-1580, and Plowden's Queries, Vol. I
Pt.	Part
Q.B.	Queen's Bench Reports (Adolphus and Ellis, New Series), 18 vols., 1841-1852
Q.B. (preceded by date)	Law Reports, Queen's Bench Division, 1891-1901; and since 1952 (e.g. [1891] 1 Q.B.)
Q.B.D.	Law Reports, Queen's Bench Division, 25 vols., 1875-1890
Quebec L.R.	Quebec Law Reports
r.	rule
reg.	regulation
R.S.C.	Rules of the Supreme Court
s.	section
S.C.	Supreme Court
S.C.(J.) (preceded by date)	Court of Justiciary Cases (Scotland), since 1906 (e.g. 1906 S.C.(J.))
S.L.T.	Scots Law Times, 1893-(current)
Sch.	Schedule
S.I.	Statutory Instruments published by authority
Sp.	Spinks' Prize Court Cases, 2 parts, 1854-1856
S.R. & O.	Statutory Rules and Orders published by authority
S.R. & O. Rev. 1904	Statutory Rules and Orders revised edition to 1903
S.R. & O. Rev. 1948	Statutory Rules and Orders revised edition to 1948
Sw.	Swabey's Reports, Admiralty, 1 vol., 1855-1859
T.L.R.	The Times Law Reports, 71 vols., 1884-1950
T.L.R. (preceded by date)	The Times Law Reports, 1951-1952 (e.g. [1951] 1 T.L.R.)
T.R.	Taxation Reports, 1939-(current)
T.S.	Treaty Series
VHF	very high frequency
W.L.R.	Western Law Reporter (Canada), 34 vols., 1905-1916
W.R.	Weekly Reporter, 54 vols., 1852-1906
W. Rob.	William Robinson's Reports, Admiralty, 3 vols., 1838-1850

TABLE OF ILLUSTRATIONS

TABLE OF STATUTES

Table of Conventions, Orders, Rules, Regulations, Codes, Resolutions, Notices, Instructions, Treaties and Command Papers

TABLE OF CASES

A

B

Destination Table of Rules in the Collision Regulations (Ships and Seaplanes on the Water) and Signals of Distress (Ships) Order 1965, S.I. 1965, No. 1525 ("The 1960 Rules") showing the destination of the 1960 Rules in the Merchant Shipping (Distress Signals and Prevention of Collisions) Regulations 1983, S.I. 1983, No. 708 ("The 1972 Rules").

The 1960 Rules	The 1972 Rules	Paragraph
PART A		
1(a)	1(a), 31	1.07, 3.10, 6.01, 6.31
(b)	20(a), (b), (c)	3.01, 6.20
(c)(i)	3(a)	1.09, 6.03
(ii)	3(e)	2.12, 6.03
(iii)	3(b)	2.06, 6.03
(iv)	3(c)	2.06, 6.03
(v)	3(i)	2.12, 6.03
(vi)	Annex 1.1	3.01, 6.39
(vii)	3(j)	2.06, 6.03
(viii)	—	—
(ix)	3(k)	2.08, 6.03
(x)	—	—
(xi)	32(b)	4.02, 6.32
(xii)	32(c)	4.02, 6.32
(xiii)	32(a)	4.01, 6.32
(xiv)	3(d)	2.05, 6.03
PART B		
2(a)(i)	22(a), 23(a)(i)	3.02, 3.03, 6.22, 6.23
(ii)	23(a)(ii)	3.03, 6.23
(iii)	23(a)(ii), Annex 1.2(f), 1.3(a)	3.01, 3.03, 6.23, 6.39
(iv)	21(b), 22(a), 23(a)(iii)	3.02, 3.03, 6.21, 6.22, 6.23
(v)	21(b), 22(a), 23(a)(iii)	3.02, 3.03, 6.21, 6.22, 6.23
(vi)	Annex 1.5	3.01, 6.39
(b)(i)-(iii)	—	—
3(a)	24(a)(i), (ii), Annex 1.2(i)	3.01, 3.04, 6.24, 6.39
(b)	24(a)(iii)	3.04, 6.24
(c)	24(a)(v)	3.04, 6.24
(d)	—	—
4(a), (b)	27(a)(i), (ii), Annex 1.6(a)(i)	3.01, 3.07, 6.27, 6.39
(c)	27(b)(i), (ii), Annex 1.6(a)(i), (iv)	3.01, 3.07, 6.27, 6.39
(d)(i)	27(f), Annex 1.6(a)(i)	3.01, 3.07, 6.27, 6.39
(ii)	—	—
(e)	27(a)(iii), (b)(iii)	3.07, 6.27
(f)	—	—
(g)	27(h)	3.07, 6.27
5(a)	24(e), 25(a)	3.04, 3.05, 6.24, 6.25
(b)	25(c)	3.05, 6.25
(c)	24(f)	3.04, 6.24

The 1960 Rules	The 1972 Rules	Paragraph
(d)	24(e)(iii), Annex 1.6(a)(iv)	3.01, 3.04, 6.24, 6.39
6(a)	—	—
(b)	—	—
7(a)(i), (ii)	23(c), Annex 1.2(h)	3.01, 3.03, 6.20, 6.39
(b)(i),(ii)	—	—
(c)	—	—
(d)	25(b)	3.05, 6.25
(e)	—	—
(f)	25(d)(i), (ii)	3.05, 6.25
(g)	27(g), 30(e)	3.07, 3.09, 6.27, 6.30
8(a)(i), (ii)	29(a)	3.08, 6.29
(iii)	—	—
(b)(i)-(iii)	—	—
(c)	29(a)(iii)	3.08, 6.29
(d)	29(b)	3.08, 6.29
9(a)	26(e)	3.06, 6.26
(b)	26(a)	3.06, 6.26
(c)(i)	26(b)(i), (ii), Annex 1.2(j)	3.01, 3.06, 6.26, 6.39
(ii)	—	—
(d)	26(c)(i), (ii)	3.06, 6.26
(e)	26(b)(iii), (c)(iii)	3.06, 6.26
(f)	Annex 1.4(a)	3.01, 6.39
(g)	Annex II.2(b)(i)	3.06, 6.40
(h)	26(c)(i), (ii), Annex 1.6(a)(ii)	3.01, 3.06, 6.26, 6.39
10(a)	21(c), 23(a)(iv), 25(a)(ii)	3.02, 3.03, 3.05, 6.21, 6.23, 6.25
(b)	—	—
(c)	—	—
11(a)	30(b)	3.09, 6.30
(b)	30(a)	3.09, 6.30
(c)	30(a)(i), Annex 1.2(k)	3.01, 3.09, 6.30, 6.39
(d)	27(b)(iv), 27(d)(iii)	3.07, 6.27
(e)	30(d)	3.09, 6.30
(f)-(h)	—	—
12	36	4.04, 6.36
13(a)	1(c)	3.01, 6.01
(b)	1(e)	3.01, 6.01
14	25(e)	3.05, 6.25

PART C

Preliminary 1	—	—
2	—	—
15(a)	33(a), (b)	4.01, 6.33
(b)(i)-(iii)	—	—

The 1960 Rules	The 1972 Rules	Paragraph
PART F		
29	2(a), 5	1.14, 2.01, 6.02, 6.05
30	1(b)	1.07, 6.01
31(a)	37, Annex IV.1	4.05, 6.37, 6.42
(i)-(ix)	Annex IV.1(a)-(k)	4.05, 6.42
Note	Annex IV.1(l)-(n)	4.05, 6.42
(b)	Annex IV.2	4.05, 6.42
ANNEX		
(1)	7(c)	2.03, 6.07
(2)	6(b)(iv, (v)	2.03, 6.06
(3)	—	—
(4)	8(d)	2.04, 6.08
(5)	8(b), (c)	2.04, 6.08
(6)	—	—
(7)	8(b)	2.04, 6.08
(8)	8(e)	2.04, 6.08

CHAPTER ONE

HISTORY AND APPLICATION OF COLLISION REGULATIONS

1.01 *History of collision regulations*

For at least two hundred years, there have been rules for the navigation of ships. These rules have in many cases been no more than rules of good seamanship.[1] The first official regulations, reciting three recognized rules for sailing vessels and promulgating two new rules for steamships, were published on 30th October 1840, by the London Trinity House.[2] Although they had no statutory authority, the Admiralty Court enforced them in civil actions arising out of collisions.[3] In 1847 a statute came into force giving statutory effect to the steam navigation rules; and a starboard side rule for ships navigating in narrow channels was introduced.[4] Lights regulations were made in 1848.[5] A penalty was imposed for disobedience to the navigation and lights rules.[6] In 1851 the statutory rules for steamships were repealed and substantially re-enacted with application to both steam and sail.[7] The 1851 rules were replaced by new statutory rules in 1854, by which the port to port rule was applied to all ships, while the starboard side rule in narrow channels was retained for steamships only.[8] Regulations as to lights for vessels under way were made in 1852,[9] and also in 1858 when regulations were made as to fog signals, lights for pilot vessels and vessels at anchor.[10]

In 1862 all existing regulations were repealed[11] and a mandatory obligation to stand by after collisions was introduced.[12] A new code of regulations was promulgated in 1863[13] which, after numerous alterations and additions, was replaced by new regulations in 1910.[14] The 1910 regulations were revoked and replaced in 1953 by new regulations[15] implementing international rules of navigation agreed in London in 1948.[16] The 1953 regulations were replaced in turn in 1965[17] by regulations implementing rules agreed at the International Conference on Safety of Life at Sea 1960.[18] The 1965 regulations, which generally applied, like those of 1953, to seaplanes on the water as well as ships, clarified the mariner's responsibility as to the use of radar in reduced visibility or fog.[19] The 1965 regulations also made changes in the requirements for navigational lights, sound signals and to the steering and sailing rules.[20] In 1972 the regulations of 1965 were made applicable to hovercraft[21] and in the same year an order provided for compulsory traffic separation schemes in the Dover Strait and elsewhere.[22]

The regulations of 1965 and the order of 1972 were revoked and replaced by the Collision Regulations and Distress Signals Order 1977, which came into force on 15th July 1977.[23] This order has been revoked and replaced by the Merchant Shipping (Distress Signals and Prevention of Collisions) Regulations 1983[24] which came into force on 1st June 1983.[25] The 1983 Regulations incorporate the International Regulations for Preventing Collisions at Sea 1972 as amended by IMO Resolution A.464 (XII) of 19th November 1981.[26] These International Regulations of 1972 (as amended) are referred to throughout this book as "the 1972 Rules", to avoid confusion with the 1983 regulations to which they are scheduled. The international background and the extent of application of the 1983 regulations and of the 1972 Rules are described in the following paragraphs.[27]

[1] See, e.g., the rule that a ship which has the wind at large may go either to leeward or to windward; *Handaysyde* v. *Wilson* (1828) 3 C. & P. 528. For a history of collision regulations see "Two hundred years of collision regulations" by John F. Kemp, "Journal of Navigation", Vol. 29, No. 4, October 1976.

[2] See 1 W. Rob. 488. The Trinity House still exercises many functions in such matters as pilotage, lighthouses and buoys. The address of the London Trinity House is Tower Hill, London EC3.

[3] See *The Duke of Sussex* (1841) 1 W. Rob. 274; *The Unity* (1856) Sw. 101; *The Hope* (1840) 1 W. Rob. 154; *The Immaganda Sara Clasina* (1850) 7 Not. of Cas. 582; 8 Moo. P.C. 85; *The Friends* (1842) 1 W. Rob. 484; on appeal 4 Moo. P.C. 314.

[4] See the Steam Navigation Act 1846 (repealed).

[5] See the Admiralty Regulations as to Lights, 1848; "London Gazette", 11th July 1848; 29th May 1849. As to the power to make these regulations see the Steam Navigation Act 1846, s. 10 (repealed).

[6] See ibid., s. 9 (repealed).

[7] See the Steam Navigation Act 1851 (repealed).

[8] See the Merchant Shipping Repeal Act 1854; and the Merchant Shipping Act 1854 (repealed).

[9] See Admiralty Notice respecting Lights 1852, "London Gazette," 4th May 1852; Sw. App. p. i.

[10] See Admiralty Notice respecting Lights and Fog Signals, 1858, "London Gazette," 24th February 1858; Sw. App., p. vi.

[11] See the Merchant Shipping Act Amendment Act 1862 (repealed).

[12] See ibid., s. 33 (repealed). This Act also introduced a statutory presumption of fault where a collision was occasioned by non-observance of a regulation; see s. 29 (repealed).

[13] See Order in Council of 9th January 1863, "London Gazette," 13th January 1863; Lush. App., pp. i and lxxii (revoked).

[14] See Order in Council of 13th October 1910, S.R. & O. 1910, No. 1113; Rev. XIV, p. 515; 1910 p. 457 (revoked). As to intermediate collision regulations see, e.g., Orders in Council, dated 30th July 1868, 14th August 1879, 11th August 1884, 30th December 1884, 24th June 1885, 18th August 1892, 30th January 1893, 27th November 1896, 23rd October 1905, 4th April 1906.

[15] See the Collision Regulations (Ships and Seaplanes on the Water) and Signals of Distress (Ships) Order 1953, S.I. 1953, No. 1557 (revoked).

[16] The agreement was reached at the International Conference on Safety of Life at Sea, held in London from 23rd April 1948 to 10th June 1948.

[17] See the Collision Regulations (Ships and Seaplanes on the Water) and Signals of Distress (Ships) Order 1965, S.I. 1965, No. 1525 (revoked).

[18] See the International Conference on Safety of Life at Sea 1960—Final Act; Cmnd. 2956; T.S. 23 (1966).

[19] See the Collision Regulations (Ships and Seaplanes on the Water) and Signals of Distress (Ships) Order 1965, Sch. 1, r. 16, Annex (revoked).

[20] See ibid., Sch. 1, Parts B, C, D.

[21] See the Hovercraft Act 1968, s. 1; Hovercraft (Application of Enactments) Order 1972, S.I. 1972, No. 971, art. 4, Sch. 1, Parts A, B, which incorporated extra rules (since revoked) for hovercraft. The order provides that the specified enactments and instruments are to have effect as if any reference therein in whatever terms to ships, vessels, boats or activities or places connected therewith included a reference to hovercraft or activities or places connected with hovercraft; see art. 4. "Hovercraft" means a vehicle which is designed to be supported when in motion wholly or partly by air expelled from the vehicle to form a cushion of which the boundaries include the ground, water or other surface beneath the vehicle; Hovercraft Act 1968, s. 4(1).

[22] See the Collision Regulations (Traffic Separation Schemes) Order 1972, S.I. 1972, No. 809; (amended by S.I. 1974, No. 1890) (revoked).

[23] See the Collision Regulations and Distress Signals Order 1977, S.I. 1977, No. 982, art. 1(1), (3) (revoked).
[24] S.I. 1983, No. 708. See also the Merchant Shipping (Distress Signals and Prevention of Collisions) (Overseas Territories) Order 1983, S.I. 1983, No. 762, which makes equivalent provision for certain British overseas territories; and the Hovercraft (Application of Enactments) (Amendment) Order 1983, S.I. 1983, No. 769, which applies the 1983 regulations to hovercraft; and the Collision Rules (Seaplanes) Order 1983, S.I. 1983, No. 768, which applies to seaplanes the 1972 Rules (referred to in the text to note 27, *infra*.)
[25] See the Merchant Shipping (Distress Signals and Prevention of Collisions) Regulations 1983, reg. 1(1).
[26] See ibid., reg. 1(2)(a); and the Resolution to amend the International Regulations for Preventing Collisions at Sea 1972, Cmnd. 8500; Cmnd. 8846.
[27] See paras. 1.02-1.10, *post*.

1.02 *Conventions and English law*

International conventions are multilateral treaties or agreements between States. Their status in international law needs careful consideration owing to their importance in the field of shipping. International co-operation in maritime matters has a long history and the United Kingdom has always been in the forefront of movements to agree by conventions on such matters as fisheries,[1] whaling,[2] territorial waters,[3] maritime ports[4] and collision regulations.[5]

Although in English law the power to enter into conventions is vested in the Crown by virtue of the royal prerogative, the Crown cannot, in time of peace at any rate, create a criminal offence or otherwise interfere with the liberty of the Crown's subjects, without the sanction of Parliament.[6] Therefore in most cases an Act of Parliament (or regulations authorized by an Act of Parliament[7]) is required to implement the provisions of a convention in English law and make those provisions binding upon the citizen.[8]

When Parliament enacts legislation for the purpose of implementing the provisons of a convention in English law, special rules apply for the construction of such legislation, or of any regulations authorized by such legislation.[9] If the meaning of a particular provision in the legislation is clear, then the English courts will apply that meaning, even where it conflicts with the wording of the convention.[10] There is, however, a presumption against an interpretation which breaks the terms of an international convention, so that ambiguities are resolved in accordance with the provisions of the convention where that is a plausible construction.[11] If the wording of the relevant provision of the convention is itself ambiguous or differs as between two equally authentic translations, reference may, it seems, be made to previous international practice and to the *travaux preparatoires* of the convention itself.[12]

It is against this background that the Merchant Shipping (Distress Signals and Prevention of Collisions) Regulations 1983[13] must be construed. The 1983 regulations were made under statutory powers by the Secretary of State, for the purpose of implementing in English law the provisions of the Convention on the International

Regulations for Preventing Collisions at Sea 1972 as amended by subsequent International Resolution,[14] and for the purpose of making those International Regulations binding upon Her Majesty's subjects. The 1972 convention was the result of a conference held in London in October 1972, at the invitation of the Inter-Governmental Maritime Consultative Organization.[15] Forty-two States, including the United Kingdom, were represented at the conference by delegations and another five States, together with Hong Kong, were represented by observers.[16] The convention was signed by the United Kingdom Government[17] (on behalf of the Crown) and entered into force on 15th July 1977,[18] upon which date the United Kingdom became bound to implement its provisions.[19] The convention is established in a single copy in the English and French languages, both texts being equally authentic.[20] The subsequent amending Resolution entered into force on 1st June 1983.[21]

[1] See, e.g., the Convention of London concerning Fisheries and Boundaries (London, 20th October 1818; 6 BFSP3; Cmd. 3262).
[2] See, e.g., the Convention for the Regulation of Whaling (Geneva, 24th September 1931; T.S. 33 (1934); Cmd. 4751).
[3] See, e.g., the Convention on the Territorial Sea and the Contiguous Zone (Geneva, 29th April 1958; T.S. 3 (1965); Cmnd. 2511).
[4] See, e.g., the Convention and Statute on the International Regime of Maritime Ports (Geneva, 9th December 1923; T.S. 24 (1925); Cmd. 2419).
[5] See, e.g., The Collisions Convention 1910 (Brussels, 23rd September 1910; Parliamentary Paper, Miscellaneous, No. 5 (1911)). The Maritime Conventions Act 1911 implemented the 1910 Convention in English law.
[6] See *The Parlement Belge* (1879) 4 P.D. 129, 3 B.I.L.C. 305, on appeal (1880) 5 P.D. 197, 3 B.I.L.C. 322, C.A.; *Walker* v. *Baird* [1892] A.C. 491, 6 B.I.L.C. 465, P.C.; *Republic of Italy* v. *Hambros Bank Ltd. and Gregory* [1950] Ch. 314, [1950] 1 All E.R. 430, 6 B.I.L.C. 525; *Blackburn* v. *A.-G.* [1971] 2 All E.R. 1380 at p. 1382 [1971] 1 W.L.R. 1037 at p. 1039, C.A.; *Pan American Airways Inc.* v. *Department of Trade* [1976] 1 Lloyd's Rep. 257, C.A.; *Laker Airways Ltd.* v. *Department of Trade* [1976] 3 W.L.R. 537.
[7] As to such delegated legislation see para. 1.04, *post.*
[8] There are some fields in which the Crown may make law without the sanction of Parliament. For example, the Crown may, by an exercise of the royal prerogative, extend its sovereignty and jurisdiction to areas of land or sea over which it has not previously claimed or exercised sovereignty or jurisdiction; see *Post Office* v. *Estuary Radio* [1967] 3 All E.R. 663 at p. 680. The prerogative may be exercised by entering into a convention or by Order in Council. For an example of such an Order in Council see further para. 1.08, text and notes 19-26, *post.*
[9] As to the construction of delegated legislation generally see para. 1.09, *post.*
[10] See *Mortensen* v. *Peters* (1906) 8 F. (Ct. of Sess.) 93, 3 B.I.L.C. 754. See also *Polites* v. *The Commonwealth* (1945) 70 C.L.R. 60 (Aust. H.C.).
[11] See *The Le Louis* (1817) 2 Dods. 210, 3 B.I.L.C. 691; *Madrazo* v. *Willes* (1820) 3 B. & Ald. 353; *The Annapolis* (1861) Lush. 295; *Bloxam* v. *Favre* (1883) 8 P.D. 101, 104; (1884) 9 P.D. 130. See also *Cheney* v. *Conn* [1968] 1 All E.R. 779, per Ungoed-Thomas, J., at p. 781; and *Corocraft Ltd.* v. *Pan American Airways Inc.* [1969] 1 Q.B. 616, *per* Lord Denning, M.R., at p. 653; and *Salomon* v. *Comrs. of Customs and Excise* [1966] 3 All E.R. 871; [1967] 2 Q.B. 116. See also *Buchanan and Co.* v. *Babco Shipping* [1977] 2 W.L.R. 107, C.A.
[12] See *Post Office* v. *Estuary Radio* [1968] 2 Q.B. 740; [1967] 3 All E.R. 663 at p. 679; *Fothergill* v. *Monarch Airlines Ltd.* [1980] 2 All E.R. 696.
[13] As to the Merchant Shipping (Distress Signals and Prevention of Collisions) Regulations 1983, S.I. 1983, No. 708, see Chapters 2-4, *post.* As to the power to make such regulations see para. 1.05, *post.*
[14] (London 20th October 1972; Misc. 28 (1973); Cmnd. 5471); Misc. 8 (1982); Cmnd. 8500; Misc. 10 (1983); Cmnd. 8846.

[15] As to IMO see para. 1.03, *post*.
[16] See Cmnd. 5471, p. 3.
[17] Nineteen other States signed and all signatures were subject to ratification, acceptance or approval by the States concerned.
[18] The convention provided that it should enter into force 12 months after the date on which at least 15 States, the aggregate of whose merchant fleets constitutes not less than 65% by number or by tonnage of the world fleet of vessels of 100 gross tons and over have become parties to it, whichever was to be achieved first; see Convention on the International Regulations for Preventing Collisions at Sea 1972, art. IV, para. 1(a).
[19] See ibid., art. 1.
[20] See ibid., art. IX.
[21] See Cmnd. 8500, art. 2; Merchant Shipping (Distress Signals and Prevention of Collisions) Regulations 1983, reg. 1(1).

1.03 *The International Maritime Organization (IMO)*

The growth of international co-operation in many fields has led to the establishment of various permanent agencies. In 1948 the Inter-Governmental Maritime Consultative Organization (IMCO), as it was then called, was founded to promote co-operation in maritime matters between States.[1] Although founded in 1948, IMCO did not come into existence until 1957 when the convention setting it up came into force. It has its headquarters in London[2] and there are now 124 member States.[3] IMCO has been responsible for much work of international importance and in particular promoted the conference which resulted in the Convention on the International Regulations for Preventing Collisions at Sea 1972.[4] The United Kingdom Government is an active member.[5] IMCO changed its name to the International Maritime Organization (IMO) on 22nd May 1982.[6]

[1] See the Convention for the Establishment of the Inter-Governmental Maritime Consultative Organization (Geneva, 6th March 1948; T.S. 54 (1958); Cmnd. 589). See also Amendment (London, 15th September 1964; T.S. 92 (1967); Cmnd. 3463); Amendment (Paris, 28th September, 1965; T.S. 105 (1968); Cmnd. 3839); Amendment London, 17th October 1974; T.S. 67 (1978); Cmnd. 7262.
[2] The address of IMO is 4 Albert Embankment, London SE1 7SR. The premises and archives of IMO and its personnel enjoy special privileges, including freedom of communication and exemption from direct taxation; the accredited personnel also enjoy diplomatic immunity from suit and legal process. See the Agreement between the Government of the United Kingdom and the Inter-Governmental Maritime Consultative Organization regarding the Headquarters of the Organization (London, 28th November 1968; T.S. 18 (1969); Cmnd. 3964; amended by Exchange of Notes (London, 28th October to 1st November 1971; T.S. 25 (1972); Cmnd. 4917); and by Exchange of Notes (London, 13th to 25th February 1974; T.S. 133 (1975); Cmnd. 6340); and by Exchange of Notes (London, 20th January 1982; T.S. 30 (1982); Cmnd. 8623). See also the Inter-Governmental Maritime Consultative Organization (Immunities and Privileges) Order 1968, S.I. 1968, No. 1862 (amended by S.I. 1972, No. 118; S.I. 1975, No. 1209).
[3] A list of the member States may be obtained from the Secretary-General of IMO at the headquarters mentioned in note 2, *supra*.
[4] See para. 1.01, text and notes 18-26, *ante*. IMO also promoted the Third United Nations Conference on the Law of the Sea which produced the 1982 United Nations Convention on the Law of the Sea; as to which see para. 1.08, notes 17-27, *post*.
[5] An initiative by the United Kingdom Government, following the *Torrey Canyon* stranding in 1967, led directly to the International Convention on Civil Liability for Oil Pollution Damage (Brussels, 29th November 1969, to 31st December 1970; T.S. 106 (1975); Cmnd. 6183).
[6] See IMO Resolution 358.

1.04 *The ultra vires principle*

As has been explained, the Crown may not make laws which interfere with the liberty of the subject without the sanction of Parliament.[1] Although non-statutory rules, if generally accepted, may acquire the status of customs which the courts will recognize in civil cases,[2] no criminal sanctions could be applied to those guilty of contravening such customary laws.[3] Therefore it has become the practice to make collision regulations by, or under the authority of, an Act of Parliament. Where such regulations are expressly incorporated in an Act, no question of their validity can arise, since Parliament is sovereign.[4] Where, however, the regulations are made by a Minister or the Crown acting under powers delegated by an Act of Parliament, it is necessary to read the regulations in the light of the power contained in the Act, for if the regulations go beyond the power and purport to legislate in a way in which the Minister or Crown was not authorized to legislate, the regulations, or part of them, may be void on the ground that they are *ultra vires*.[5]

The *ultra vires* principle may invalidate regulations in more than one way. For example, regulations may purport to incorporate another, non-statutory, document.[6] Such incorporation will be valid if it is merely referred to in order to save words but if the regulations purport to incorporate the document "as varied from time to time" by a third party, the incorporation will usually be invalid as an *ultra vires* "sub-delegation", unless the enabling statute expressly authorizes the incorporation of a variable document.[7] This trap has been avoided in the Merchant Shipping (Distress Signals and Prevention of Collisions) Regulations 1983,[8] since although these regulations incorporate traffic separation schemes and codes of signals set out in published documents and documents amending them which are considered by the Secretary of State to be relevant from time to time,[9] the Secretary of State[10] is expressly empowered by statute to make regulations in this form.[11]

Another application of the *ultra vires* principle affects the construction of words used in regulations. Where, as is the case of the collision regulations, statute authorizes the Secretary of State to make regulations relating to "ships"[12] and the regulations themselves purport to apply to "vessels"[13] it may be necessary to restrict the interpretation of "vessel" to ensure that it is not wider than the meaning of "ship" in the enabling statute. "Ship" in the Merchant Shipping Acts includes every description of vessel not propelled by oars;[14] whereas "vessel" in the International Regulations for Preventing Collisions at Sea 1972[15] includes every description of water craft, including non-displacement craft and seaplanes, used or capable or being used as a means of transportation on water[16] (i.e. including rowing boats). Moreover "vessel" in the Merchant Shipping Acts includes any ship or boat or any other description of vessel used in navigation.[17] Thus the Merchant Shipping Acts do not empower the Secretary of State to make regulations for rowing boats, whereas the regulations would appear to legislate for them; and the regulations do not require a vessel to be used in navigation before it can be construed as a vessel, merely that it is capable of being used for transportation on water. The courts have gone some way to resolving these discrepancies by holding that vessels exclusively propelled by oars are not subject to the collision regulations;[18] and by suggesting that a vessel is "used in navigation" if she is designed for carrying passengers or cargo by water, whether or not she has any means of propulsion.[19] Statute has now given power to the Secretary of State to provide by order that a thing designed or adapted for use at sea is to be treated as a ship for certain purposes, including the Merchant Shipping Acts and regulations made under them.[20] In addition the Secretary of State has provided in the Merchant Shipping (Distress Signals and Prevention of Collisions) Regulations 1983 that the regulations apply to "United Kingdom vessels" which are defined as bearing the same meaning as "United Kingdom ships" in the Merchant Shipping Act 1979.[21] This, so far as United Kingdom ships are concerned, eliminates the discrepancy between "ship" and "vessel". However, the regulations also apply to "other vessels"[22] which are not defined except in the 1972 Rules which are scheduled to the regulations. Here "vessels" have the meaning mentioned above.[23]

[1] See para. 1.02, text and note 6, *ante*.
[2] See *The Resolution* (1789) Marsd. Ad. Cas. 332. See also *Handaysyde* v. *Wilson* (1828) 3 C. & P. 528; and *Jamieson* v. *Drinkald* (1826) 5 L.J.C.P. (o.s.) 30.
[3] Compare, however, the ancient common law crimes of murder and manslaughter.
[4] The courts will enforce an Act of Parliament even where this conflicts with international law; see *Mortensen* v. *Peters* [1906] 8 F. (Ct. of Sess.) 93, 3 B.I.L.C. 754; and para. 1.02, text and note 10, *ante*.
[5] See *Commrs. of Customs and Excise* v. *Cure and Deeley Ltd.* [1962] 1 Q.B. 340; *Ward* v. *James* [1966] 1 Q.B. 273; *Turner* v. *Midgley* [1967] 1 W.L.R. 1247; *Hotel and Catering Industry Training Board* v. *Automobile Proprietary Ltd.* [1968] 1 W.L.R. 1526; and see *The Anselm* [1907] P. 151. Nevertheless, a breach even of *ultra vires* regulations may amount to negligence; see *Thomas Stone Shipping Ltd.* v. *The Admiralty, The Albion* [1953] P. 117, C.A.; [1953] 1 All E.R. 978.
[6] See, e.g., the Merchant Shipping (Dangerous Goods) Regulations, S.I. 1981, No. 1747.
[7] See *Allingham* v. *Minister of Agriculture and Fisheries* [1948] 1 All E.R. 780; *Blackpool Corpn.* v. *Locker* [1948] 1 K.B. 349, 362, 369. A sub-delegation of purely administrative powers may be valid.
[8] S.I. 1983, No. 708. See also the Merchant Shipping (Distress Signals and Prevention of Collisions) (Overseas Territories) Order 1983, S.I. 1983, No. 762.
[9] See the Merchant Shipping (Distress Signals and Prevention of Collisions) Regulations 1983, S.I. 1983, No. 708, reg. 1(2)(b), (d); and paras. 2.07, 4.05, *post*.
[10] As to the Secretary of State and his functions, see para. 5.01, *post*.
[11] See para. 1.05, text and note 11, *post*.
[12] See the Merchant Shipping Act 1979, s. 21(1)(a).
[13] See the Merchant Shipping (Distress Signals and Prevention of Collisions) Regulations 1983, reg. 2.
[14] See the Merchant Shipping Act 1894, s. 742; Merchant Shipping Act 1979, s. 50(1).
[15] I.e. the 1972 Rules set out in the Merchant Shipping (Distress Signals and Prevention of Collisions) Regulations 1983, Sch. 1.
[16] See ibid., Sch. 1, r. 3(a).
[17] See the Merchant Shipping Act 1894, s. 742.
[18] See *Edwards* v. *Quickenden and Forester* [1939] P. 261. On the other hand a coble with auxiliary oars has been held to be a ship; *Ex parte Ferguson and Hutchinson* (1871) L.R. 6 Q.B. 280.
[19] *The Mac* (1882) 7 P.D. 126; *The Mudlark* [1911] P. 116. A dumb barge may be a "vessel used in navigation"; *The Lighter No. 3* (1902) 18 T.L.R. 322; see also *Gapp* v. *Bond* (1887) 19 Q.B.D. 200.

[20] See the Merchant Shipping Act 1979, s. 41(1). No such order had been made under this section at the date at which this edition states the law.
[21] See The Merchant Shipping (Distress Signals and Prevention of Collisions) Regulations 1983, regs. 1(2)(a), 2, and para. 1.07, *post*.
[22] See ibid., reg. 2; and para. 1.08 *post*.
[23] See the text and notes 15, 16, *supra*.

1.05 *Power for the Secretary of State to make regulations*

The Secretary of State[1] has been given extensive statutory powers[2] to make such provision by regulations as he considers appropriate[3] for securing the safety of United Kingdom ships[4] and persons on them and for giving effect to any provisions of an international agreement[5] ratified by the United Kingdom so far as the agreement relates to the safety of other ships or persons on them.[6] Safety regulations[7] made under this power may make provision, among other things,[8] for (1) the steps to be taken to prevent any collision involving a ship and in consequence of any collision involving a ship;[9] and (2) the steps to be taken, in a case where a ship is in distress or stranded or wrecked, for the purpose of saving the ship and its machinery, equipment and cargo and the lives of persons on or from the ship.[10] Safety regulations may make provision in terms of approvals given by the Secretary of State or another person and in terms of any document which the Secretary of State or another person considers relevant from time to time.[11] Thus the Secretary of State may incorporate by reference extraneous documents in safety regulations without acting *ultra vires*.[12] Safety regulations providing for any such approval must provide for the approval to be given in writing[13] and must also provide for the approval to specify the date on which it takes effect and the conditions, if any, on which it is given.[14] Safety regulations may provide for the granting by the Secretary of State or another person, on terms,[15] of exemptions from specified provisions of the regulations for classes of cases or individual cases and for the alteration or cancellation of exemptions granted in pursuance of the regulations.[16]

Safety regulations may provide that in prescribed cases[17] a ship is liable to be detained.[18] They may also provide that a contravention of the regulations is to be an offence punishable on summary conviction by a fine not exceeding the statutory maximum and on conviction on indictment by imprisonment for a term not exceeding two years and a fine.[19] Alternatively they may provide that any such contravention is to be an offence punishable only on summary conviction by a maximum fine of an amount not exceeding level 5 on the standard scale, or such less amount as is prescribed by the regulations.[20] The Secretary of State must consult[21] such persons as he considers will be affected, before making safety regulations or before he or another person gives an approval under safety regulations.[22] He may by regulations make such repeals or other modifications of the Merchant Shipping Acts[23] and of any instruments made under these Acts as he considers appropriate in consequence or in anticipation of the making of safety regulations.[24]

Regulations made under these provisions must be made by statutory instrument.[25] Safety regulations implementing an international agreement relating to the safety of non-United Kingdom ships[26] must not be made unless a draft of the regulations has been approved by resolution of each House of Parliament.[27] Other safety regulations and the other regulations mentioned above[28] are subject to annulment in pursuance of a resolution by either House of Parliament.[29]

The Secretary of State has no power under the Merchant Shipping Act 1979 to make safety or collision regulations in relation to seaplanes but the previous statutory power for Her Majesty to make collision regulations by Order in Council, now repealed as to ships and hovercraft,[30] still applies to enable collision regulations to be made for the prevention of collisions at sea between seaplanes on the surface of the water and between vessels and seaplanes on the water.[31]

[1] As to the Secretary of State, see para. 5.01, post.
[2] I.e. by the Merchant Shipping Act 1979, ss. 21, 22.
[3] As to the exercise of statutory discretions of this type, see Pyx Granite Co. Ltd. v. Ministry of Housing and Local Government [1958] 1 All E.R. 625; and Halsbury's Laws of England, 4th edn, vol. 1, paras. 60, 61.
[4] A United Kingdom ship "means a ship which is registered in the United Kingdom or a ship which is not registered under the law of any country but is wholly owned by persons each of whom is either a citizen of the United Kingdom and Colonies or a body corporate which is established under the law of a part of the United Kingdom and has its principal place of business in a part of the United Kingdom"; Merchant Shipping Act 1979, s. 21(2). For the meaning of "ship" see para. 1.04, text and note 14, ante. For the meaning of "the United Kingdom" see para. 1.08, note 16, post. "Colony" means any part of Her Majesty's dominions outside the British Islands except countries having fully responsible status within the Commonwealth, territories for whose external relations a country other than the United Kingdom is responsible, and associated States; Interpretation Act 1978, s. 5, Sch. 1. "The British Islands" means the United Kingdom, the Channel Islands and the Isle of Man; ibid., Sch. 1. "Associated State" means a territory maintaining a status of association with the United Kingdom in accordance with the West Indies Act 1967; Interpretation Act 1978 s. 5, Sch. 1.
[5] In the context of this work, this provision provides clear authority for the Secretary of State to implement in English law the conventions and resolutions of IMO relating to foreign ships. As to conventions and English law, see para. 1.02, ante. As to IMO, see para. 1.03, ante.
[6] See the Merchant Shipping Act 1979, s. 21(1)(a), (b). This power extends to hovercraft; see note 30, infra. As to the procedure for making regulations under s. 21(1)(b), see the text and note 27, infra. As to the power of Her Majesty by Order in Council to extend the statutory provisions to the ships of "relevant" countries, see para. 1.06, post.
[7] Regulations made under ibid., s. 21(1) are designated "safety regulations" by s. 21(3).
[8] The other matters for which safety regulations may provide include, design and construction, loading of cargo, carrying out of operations, use of machinery, manning, communications, access, ventilation, noise prevention, fire precautions, removal of danger on a ship, records, registers, information and payment of fees: see ibid., s. 21(3). The Secretary of State's powers of legislation by regulations are thus extremely wide.
[9] Ibid., s. 21(3)(k).
[10] Ibid., s. 21(3)(l). These steps include those to be taken by other persons for giving assistance in such a case; s. 21(3)(l). This power supersedes the power to prescribe distress signals which was contained in the Merchant Shipping (Safety Convention) Act 1949, s. 21(1) (repealed by the Merchant Shipping (Distress Signals and Prevention of Collisions) Regulations 1983, S.I. 1983, No. 708, reg. 1(5)(a), Sch. 2, Part I).

[11] Ibid., s. 21(4)(a). As to the exercise of this power, see para. 1.04, text and notes 8, 9, *ante.*

[12] As to this problem, see para. 1.04, text and notes 6-11, *ante.*

[13] "Writing" includes typing, printing, lithography, photography and other modes of representing or reproducing words in a visible form, and expressions referring to writing are construed accordingly; Interpretation Act 1978, s. 5, Sch. 1.

[14] Merchant Shipping Act 1979, s. 21(4)(c). Safety regulations may also provide for the cancellation of an approval given in pursuance of the regulations and for the alteration of the terms of such an approval; ibid., s. 21(4)(b).

[15] I.e. on such terms (if any) as the Secretary of State or other person may specify; see ibid., s. 21(5)(a).

[16] Ibid., s. 21(5)(a), (b). This provision is expressed to be without prejudice to s. 22(1)(b) which provides that safety regulations may be made so as to apply only in such circumstances are as prescribed by the regulations. Section 22(1) also provides that safety regulations may (1) make different provision for different circumstances and, in particular, make provision for an individual case (s. 22(1)(a)); (2) be made so as to apply only in such circumstances as are prescribed by the regulations (s. 22(1)(b)); (3) be made so as to extend outside the United Kingdom (s. 22(1)(c)); (4) contain such incidental, supplemental and transitional provisions as the Secretary of State considers appropriate (s. 22(1)(d)).

[17] I.e. in such cases as are prescribed by the regulations; ibid., s. 21(6)(a).

[18] Ibid., s. 21(6)(a). The safety regulations may also provide that the Merchant Shipping Act 1894, s. 692, is to have effect in relation to the ship with such modifications, if any, as are prescribed by the regulations; Merchant Shipping Act 1979, s. 21(6)(a). "Modifications" includes additions, omissions and alterations; ibid., s. 50(2). This power has been exercised; see para. 1.10, text and notes 14-20, *post.*

[19] Merchant Shipping Act 1979, s. 21(6)(b); Criminal Justice Act 1982, s. 49(3)(a)(i). "Contravention" includes failure to comply; Merchant Shipping Act 1979, s. 50(2). As to the statutory maximum, see para. 1.11, note 13, *post.*

[20] Ibid., s. 21(6)(c); Criminal Justice Act 1982, s. 49(3)(a)(ii).

[21] For authorities on what constitutes consultation; see *Rollo* v. *Minister of Town and Country Planning* [1948] 1 All E.R. 13 C.A.; *Re Union of Whippingham and East Cowes Benefices, Derham* v. *Church Commissioners for England* [1954] A.C. 245; [1954] 2 All E.R. 22, P.C.

[22] Merchant Shipping Act 1979, s. 22(2).

[23] "The Merchant Shipping Acts" means in this context, the Merchant Shipping Acts 1894 to 1977 and does not include the Merchant Shipping Act 1979; see ibid., s. 50(2). Thus, while the Secretary of State has wide powers to modify existing legislation by making regulations, he may not modify the Act of 1979.

[24] Ibid., s. 22(3)(a). The Secretary of State used this power first to amend, and subsequently to revoke the Collision Regulations and Distress Signals Order 1977, S.I. 1977, No. 982; see the Safety (Collision Regulations and Distress Signals) Regulations 1979, S.I. 1979, No. 1659 (revoked): and the Merchant Shipping (Distress Signals and Prevention of Collisions) Regulations 1983, reg. 1(5)(b), Sch. 2 Part III. The Secretary of State has also used this power to repeal (except as to seaplanes) the Merchant Shipping Act 1894, ss. 418, 419, under which former collision regulations were made and enforced; see the Merchant Shipping (Distress Signals and Prevention of Collisions) Regulations 1983, reg. 1(4)(a). The Secretary of State also has power by regulations to make such repeals or other modifications of provisions of any enactment passed and any instrument made before the passing of the Merchant Shipping Act 1979 as he considers appropriate in connection with any modification made or to be made under ibid., s. 22(3)(a); see s. 22(3)(b). In addition he may provide for anything done under a provision repealed or otherwise modified under s. 22(3)(a) or (b) to have effect as if done under safety regulations and he may make such other transitional provision and such incidental and supplemental provision as he considers appropriate in connection with any modification under s. 22(3)(a) or (b); see s. 22(3)(c).

[25] Merchant Shipping Act 1979, s. 49(1). As to statutory instruments see the Statutory Instruments Act 1946.

[26] I.e. safety regulations made under the Merchant Shipping Act 1979, s. 21(1)(b); see the text and notes 5, 6, *supra.*

[27] Merchant Shipping Act 1979, s. 49(3).

[28] I.e. safety regulations made under ibid., s. 21(1)(a) and regulations made under s. 22(3); see the text and notes 1-4, 23, 24, *supra.*

[29] Merchant Shipping Act 1979, s. 49(4). As to annulment of statutory instruments, see the Statutory Instruments Act 1946, ss. 5(1), 7(1).

30 See the Merchant Shipping (Distress Signals and Prevention of Collisions) Regulations 1983, reg. 1(4)(a); Hovercraft (Application of Enactments) (Amendment) Order 1983, S.I. 1983, No. 769, art. 3(a). The Merchant Shipping Act 1979 and instruments made under that Act may be applied to hovercraft; see ibid., s. 48. As to the exercise of this power, see para. 1.07, text and note 6, *post*.
31 Merchant Shipping Act 1894, s. 418(1); Civil Aviation Act 1982, s. 97(1). As to the exercise of this power, see para. 1.07, text and note 7, *post*.

1.06 *Power to extend regulations to foreign vessels*

As will be seen, regulations made by the Secretary of State[1] under his statutory powers[2] apply to United Kingdom vessels wherever they may be. They also apply to other vessels while they are within the United Kingdom or its territorial waters.[3] In addition, Her Majesty may by Order in Council[4] provide that any of certain specified provisions of the Merchant Shipping Act 1979[5] and instruments in force under them[6] are, with such modifications, if any, as are as specified in the order, to extend to a "relevant country"[7] specified in the order[8] as part of the law of that country; or are to apply to ships[9] registered in a specified relevant country[10] and to masters[11] and seamen employed in those ships, as they apply to ships registered in the United Kingdom[12] and to masters and seamen employed in them.[13]

There are powers to apply the regulations to hovercraft[14] and seaplanes[15] registered outside the United Kingdom.

1 As to the Secretary of State, see para. 5.01, *post*.
2 I.e. under the powers conferred by the Merchant Shipping Act 1979, s. 21; see para. 1.05, *ante*.
3 See paras. 1.07, 1.08, *post*. The power of the Secretary of State to implement an international agreement by making safety regulations relating to foreign ships has already been described; see para. 1.05, text and notes 5, 6, 27, *ante*.
4 The power to make Orders in Council is exercisable by statutory instrument; Statutory Instruments Act 1946, s. 1(1)(h). The statutory instrument is subject to annulment in pursuance of a resolution of either House of Parliament; Merchant Shipping Act 1979, s. 47(3).
5 The provisions in question include ibid., ss. 21, 22; see s. 47(2).
6 The instruments in force include the Merchant Shipping (Distress Signals and Prevention of Collisions) Regulations 1983, S.I. 1983, No. 708.
7 "Relevant country" means the Isle of Man, any of the Channel Islands, any colony and any country outside Her Majesty's dominions in which Her Majesty has jurisdiction in right of the government of the United Kingdom; Merchant Shipping Act 1979, ss. 15(1), 47(2).
8 Ibid., s. 47(1)(a).
9 For the meaning of "ship" see para. 1.04, text and note 14, *ante*.
10 I.e. a relevant country specified in the order.
11 For the meaning of "master", see para. 1.10, note 5, *post*.
12 As to the registry of ships, see the Merchant Shipping Act 1894, ss. 1-23; Merchant Shipping Act 1983. For the meaning of "the United Kingdom", see para. 1.08, note 16, *post*.
13 Merchant Shipping Act 1979, s. 47(1)(b). This power has been exercised. See para. 1.08, *post*. Compare the power of the Secretary of State to make regulations relating to the ships of "other countries"; in para. 1.05, text and notes 5, 6, *ante*.
14 See the Hovercraft Act 1968, s. 1(1)(h); Merchant Shipping Act 1979, ss. 21(1)(b), 48.
15 See the Civil Aviation Act 1982, ss. 97(1), applying the provisions of the Merchant Shipping Act 1894, s. 418(2), which enables the collision regulations to be applied to foreign seaplanes on the surface of the water within British jurisdiction; and see the Collision Rules (Seaplanes) Order 1983, S.I. 1983, No. 768, art. 2; and para. 1.08, text and note 5, *post*. As to the territorial waters of the United Kingdom, see para. 1.08, text and notes 16-26, *post*.

1.07 *Application of regulations to United Kingdom vessels*

The Merchant Shipping (Distress Signals and Prevention of Collisions) Regulations 1983[1] apply to United Kingdom vessels[2] wherever they may be.[3] The regulations do not apply to Her Majesty's ships,[4] although equivalent provisions have been made in relation to them.[5] The regulations apply to United Kingdom hovercraft[6] and the 1972 Rules apply (with the exception of the provisions as to distress signals) to seaplanes registered in the United Kingdom on the surface of the water, wherever they may be.[7]

The 1972 Rules are stated to apply to all vessels upon "the high seas and in all waters connected therewith navigable by seagoing vessels".[8] Nothing in the rules is to interfere with the operation of special rules made by an appropriate authority[9] for roadsteads, harbours, rivers, lakes or inland waterways connected with the high seas and navigable by seagoing vessels, although such special rules must conform as closely as possible to the rules.[10] Moreover any rules made under the authority of a local Act, concerning the lights and signals to be carried, or the steps for avoiding collision to be taken, by vessels navigating the waters of any harbour, river or other inland navigation, are fully effective notwithstanding anything in the Merchant Shipping Acts.[11]

While a vessel is within the territorial jurisdiction of a foreign State, the application of the rules would be subject to the municipal law of that State.[12] The international collision regulations are only applicable in so far as the law of the place of collision makes them so.[13]

[1] S.I. 1983, No. 708.
[2] "United Kingdom vessel" has the same meaning as "United Kingdom ship" (as to which see para. 1.05, note 4, *ante*); Merchant Shipping (Distress Signals and Prevention of Collisions) Regulations 1983, reg. 1(2)(a).
[3] Ibid., reg. 2. As to the power of the Secretary of State to make regulations, see para. 1.05, *ante*.
[4] See the Merchant Shipping Act 1894, s. 741; Merchant Shipping Act 1979, s. 50(1). This exemption appears to apply to all ships in the service of a Government department (see *Young* v. *S.S. Scotia* [1903] A.C. 501, 505) but not to ships chartered by the Crown.
[5] Her Majesty may by Order in Council provide for the registration of Government ships (other than naval ships) and for the application of the Merchant Shipping Acts to the ships so registered; Merchant Shipping Act 1906, s. 80. Regulations have been made with regard to such ships; see, e.g., the Regulations of 1921 affecting vessels in the service of the Department of Trade (S.R. & O. 1921, No. 1211); Merchant Shipping (Registration of Government Ships) Order 1978, S.I. 1978, No. 1533.
[6] See the Hovercraft Act 1968, s. 1(1)(h); Hovercraft (Application of Enactments) Order 1972, S.I. 1972, Sch. 1, Part B; Hovercraft (Application of Enactments) (Amendment) Order 1983, S.I. 1983, No. 769, art. 3(b). "United Kingdom hovercraft" means a hovercraft which (i) is registered in the United Kingdom or (ii) is not registered under the law of any country but is owned by persons any one of whom is ordinarily resident in the United Kingdom or is a body incorporated in the United Kingdom having its principal place of business in the United Kingdom or a firm carrying on business in Scotland; ibid., art. 3(b). For the power under which art. 3(b) was made see para. 1.05, note 30, *ante*. For the meaning of the United Kingdom see para. 1.08, note 16, *post*.
[7] See the Collision Rules (Seaplanes) Order 1983, S.I. 1983, No. 768, arts. 2, 4.

8 See the Merchant Shipping (Distress Signals and Prevention of Collisions) Regulations 1983 Sch. 1, r. 1(a). The collision regulations were formerly made under the Merchant Shipping Act 1894, s. 418 which authorized the making of regulations "for the prevention of collisions *at sea*"; see ibid., s. 418(1) (now repealed except as to seaplanes). There was thus a difficulty in determining whether the regulations could properly be applied in "all waters *connected with* the high seas", as well as on the high seas. The wording of the Merchant Shipping Act 1979, s. 21, removes any problem of *ultra vires* by referring to "the safety of . . . ships" and "the steps to be taken to prevent any collision involving a ship" without geographical limitation; see s. 21(1)(a), (k). There still remains the question of whether waters in any particular place are connected with the high seas. Estuaries, rivers and narrow channels have been held to be so connected; see *The Anselm* [1907] P. 151; *The Concordia* (1866) L.R. 1 A. & E. 93; *The Velocity* (1869) L.R. 3 P.C. 44; *The Ranger and The Cologne* (1872) L.R. 4 P.C. 519; *The Owen Wallis* (1874) L.R. 4 A. & E. 175; *The Voorwaarts and The Khedive* (1880) 5 App. Cas. 876. It was formerly held that the waters must be tidal (*The Carlotta* [1899] P. 223 at p. 226) but this may no longer be good law. However, it is still probably the case that the regulations cannot apply in land-locked artificial channels, such as the Manchester Ship Canal; *The Hare* [1904] P. 331; 9 Asp. M.L.C. 547.
9 "Appropriate authority" means in relation to the United Kingdom, the Secretary of State, and in relation to any other country the authority responsible under the law of that country for promoting the safety of life at sea and the avoidance of collisions; Merchant Shipping (Distress Signals and Prevention of Collisions) Regulations 1983, reg. 1(2)(a).
10 Ibid., Sch. 1, r. 1(b). Rule 1(b) derives from 1960 Rule 30 in the Collision Regulations (Ships and Seaplanes on the Water) and Signals of Distress (Ships) Order 1965, S.I. 1965, No. 1525 (revoked). For a comparative table of the 1972 Rules and the 1960 Rules, see para. 6.01, *post*. For a case on 1972 Rule 1(b), see *The Maritime Harmony* [1982] 2 Lloyd's Rep. 400; and see *The Stella Antares* [1978] 1 Lloyd's Rep. 41. An inconsistent local custom will not, however, excuse a breach of the collision regulations; *The Sylph* (1854) 2 So. 75; *The Unity* (1856) Sw. 101; *The Hand of Providence* (1856) Sw. 107; *The Araxes* v. *The Black Prince* (1861) 15 Moo. P.C. 122; *The Velocity* (1869) L.R. 3 P.C. 44; *The Tranmere* [1920] P. 454; *H.M.S. Topaze* (1864) 10 L.T. 659; *The Hjortholm* (1935) 52 Ll.L.Rep. 223, 228, but a well-recognized practice may ultimately acquire sufficient respectability to be enforced by the courts in civil actions; *Imperial Royal Privileged Danubian Steam Navigation Co.* v. *Greek and Oriental Steam Navigation Co.*, *The Smyrna* (1864) 2 Moo. P.C. C.N.S. 435; and see *The Humbergate* [1952] 1 Lloyd's Rep. 168. The rules of good seamanship are discussed at para. 1.14, *post*.
11 Merchant Shipping Act 1894, s. 421(1). This is the saving for local harbour by-laws, etc. Where any such rules are not and cannot be made, Her Majesty may make them by Order in Council, on the application from any person having authority over the waters or, if there is no such person, any person interested in their navigation; ibid., s. 421(2). These rules have the same force as regards vessels navigating in those waters as if they were part of the collision regulations; s. 421(2). Offences under rules made under s. 421(2) are triable either way; *Cashen* v. *Fitzsimmons* (1980) 4th February, Q.B.D. (unreported).
12 See the Convention on the Territorial Sea and the Contiguous Zone (Geneva, 29th April 1958; T.S.3 (1965); Cmnd. 2511), art. 17.
13 *The Esso Brussels* [1973] 2 Lloyd's Rep. 73, C.A.

1.08 *Application of the regulations to non-United Kingdom vessels*

The 1972 Rules[1] apply to United Kingdom vessels[2] and hovercraft wherever they may be and to other vessels and hovercraft while they are within the United Kingdom[3] or the territorial waters of the United Kingdom.[4] They apply also (with the exception of the provisions as to distress signals) to foreign registered seaplanes on the surface of those waters.[5]

The power of Her Majesty by Order in Council to extend safety regulations made by the Secretary of State to "relevant" countries and to the ships registered in those countries has already been described.[6] This power has been exercised to extend the Merchant Shipping (Distress Signals and Prevention of Collisions) Regulations 1983 to the Cayman Islands, The Falkland Islands, The Falkland Island Dependencies, Gibraltar, Montserrat, Saint Helena and Dependencies and the Turks and Caicos Islands, and to apply the regulations (and the 1972 Rules which are scheduled to them) to vessels registered in those territories wherever they may be and to other vessels while they are within any of the territories[7] or within the territorial waters of such territories.[8]

No order has been made extending the regulations and the 1972 Rules to non-United Kingdom hovercraft[9] or to non-British seaplanes outside United Kingdom territorial waters.[10]

English courts will not exercise jurisdiction over ships, hovercraft or seaplanes owned by a foreign sovereign or State, unless the sovereign or State submits to the jurisdiction.[11]

Subject to the defence of sovereign immunity just mentioned, therefore, enforcement of the regulations and the 1972 rules[12] against non-United Kingdom vessels, hovercraft and seaplanes depends generally on their being within United Kingdom territorial waters or internal waters; although in the case of the colonial territories mentioned above,[13] the regulations and the 1972 Rules apply even to foreign vessels in the territorial or internal waters of the relevant territories.

This accords with international law which holds that ships outside territorial or internal waters are subject to the exclusive jurisdiction of the State under whose flag the ship sails.[14] No penal proceedings may generally be taken against the personnel of a ship involved in a navigational incident in such waters except before the courts of the flag State or national State of the personnel.[15]

The territorial waters of the United Kingdom,[16] are at present thought to be the waters within three nautical miles[17] seawards from certain baselines.[18] The normal baseline from which the breadth of the territorial sea is measured is the low-water line along the coast.[19] However, the outermost part of permanent harbour works which form an integral part of a harbour system is treated as a baseline.[20] There are special rules applying a straight line baseline across the mouths of bays[21] and between Cape Wrath and the Mull of Kintyre.[22] Islands within a distance of twice the territorial sea from a mainland coast are treated as natural appendages of it.[23] Where such islands are more than twice the breadth of the territorial sea from the coast, they have their own territorial sea.[24] A low tide elevation is a naturally formed area of drying land surrounded by water which is below water at mean high-water spring-tides.[25] Where a low tide elevation lies wholly or partly within the breadth of the territorial sea, it is treated as an island and its low-water line may therefore be used as the baseline.[26]

Internal waters are those waters lying to the landward side of a baseline.[27]

[1] I.e. the International Regulations for Preventing Collisions at Sea 1972 (as amended by IMO Resolution A.464 (XII)) set out in the First Schedule to the Merchant Shipping (Distress Signals and Prevention of Collisions) Regulations 1983, S.I. 1983, No. 708.

[2] "United Kingdom vessel" has the same meaning in S.I. 1983, No. 708 as "United Kingdom ship" in the Merchant Shipping Act 1979, s. 21(2) (see para. 1.05, note 4, *ante*); Merchant Shipping (Distress Signals and Prevention of Collisions) Regulations 1983, reg. 1(2)(a). Thus the meaning of "United Kingdom vessels" has been equated with "United Kingdom ships" and the *ultra vires* problem mentioned at para. 1.04, *ante*, does not arise. The problem may still arise in respect of "other vessels", however; see para. 1.04, *ante*.

[3] I.e. within the internal waters of the United Kingdom; as to which see the text and note 27, *infra*.

[4] See the Merchant Shipping (Distress Signals and Prevention of Collisions) Regulations 1983, reg. 2; Hovercraft (Application of Enactments) Order 1972, S.I. 1972, No. 971, Sch. 1; Hovercraft (Application of Enactments) (Amendment) Order 1983, S.I. 1983, No. 769, art. 3(b). As to territorial waters, see the text and notes 15-26, *infra*.

[5] See the Collision Rules (Seaplanes) Order 1983, S.I. 1983, No. 768, arts. 2, 4(a), (b). As to the power to apply the collision regulations to seaplanes registered outside the United Kingdom, see para. 1.06, note 15, *ante*.

[6] See para. 1.06, text and notes 4-13, *ante*.

[7] I.e. within the internal waters of the territories.

[8] See the Merchant Shipping (Distress Signals and Prevention of Collisions) (Overseas Territories) Order 1983, S.I. 1983, No. 762, art. 2.

[9] I.e. to hovercraft not registered in the United Kingdom. As to foreign hovercraft in United Kingdom waters, see the text and notes 1-4, *supra*.

[10] Her Majesty has power by Order in Council to direct that various provisions of the Civil Aviation Act 1982, including s. 97 are to extend to certain "relevant" overseas territories and to aircraft registered in them; see ibid., s. 108(1), (2).

[11] *The Constitution* (1879) 4 P.D. 39; *The Parlement Belge* (1880) 5 P.D. 197; *The Jassy* [1906] P. 270; *The Jupiter* [1924] P. 236.

[12] I.e. the enforcement of the Merchant Shipping (Distress Signals and Prevention of Collisions) Regulations 1983 and the International Regulations for Preventing Collisions at Sea 1972 (as amended by Resolution A464 (XII)) which are scheduled to them.

[13] See the text to note 7, *supra*.

[14] See the Convention on the High Seas (Geneva, 29th April 1958; T.S.5 (1963): Cmnd. 1929), art. 6, para. 1; see also the United Nations Convention on the Law of the Sea (1982), U.N. Document A/CONF. 62/122 of 7th October 1982, Part VII, s. 1, art. 92. As to this convention see note 17, *infra*.

[15] Convention on the High Seas, art. 11, para. 1. See also the International Convention for the Unification of Certain Rules Relating to Penal Jurisdiction in Matters of Collisions or other Incidents of Navigation (Brussels, 10th May 1952; T.S. (1960) Cmnd. 1128); United Nations Convention on the Law of the Sea (1982), Part VII, s. 1, art. 97.

[16] "The United Kingdom" means Great Britain and Northern Ireland, when used in any Act or public document passed or issued after 12th April 1927; Interpretation Act 1978, ss. 5, 22, 23, Sch. 1, Sch. 2, para. 4. "Great Britain" means England, Wales and Scotland; Union with Scotland Act 1706, art. 1; Wales and Berwick Act 1746, art. 3; Welsh Language Act 1967, s. 4.

[17] The rightful jurisdiction of Her Majesty, her heirs and successors, extends and has always extended over the open seas adjacent to the coasts of the United Kingdom and of all other parts of Her Majesty's dominions to such a distance as is necessary for the defence and security of such dominions; Territorial Waters Jurisdiction Act 1878, preamble; and see *The Fagernes* [1927] P. 311. For authorities on the three-mile limit, see *The Anna* (1805) 5 Ch. Rob. 373 at p. 385, 2 B.I.L.C. 694, *per* Sir William Scott; *The Twee Gerbroeders* (1800) 3 Ch. Rob. 162, 2 B.I.L.C. 638; *Gann* v. *Free Fishers of Whitstable* (1865) 11 H.L. Cas. 192 at p. 218, *per* Lord Chelmsford; *R.* v. *Kent Justices, Ex parte Lye* [1967] 2 Q.B. 153; [1967] 1 All E.R. 560. It should be noted that the Third United Nations Conference on the Law of the Sea has agreed upon the international adoption of a 12 mile limit for the breadth of the territorial sea; and although the United Kingdom and the United States have declined to become signatories to the Convention, 117 other States signed it on 10th December 1982 and there was no dispute over the territorial waters provision; see the United Nations Convention on the Law of the Sea (1982), s. 2, art. 3.

[18] As to the baselines generally, see *infra*; and the Convention on the Territorial Sea and the Contiguous Zone (Geneva, 29th April 1958; T.S.3 (1965); Cmnd. 2511; the Territorial Waters Order in Council 1964; and the United Nations Convention on the Law of the Sea (1982) Part II, s. 2, art. 5. Legislation providing for British jurisdiction over parts of the continental shelf is not dealt with in this work.
[19] I.e. along the coast of the United Kingdom, the Channel Islands and the Isle of Man, including the coast of all islands comprised in those territories; Territorial Waters Order in Council 1964, art. 2(1).
[20] ibid., art. 5(2). See also the United Nations Convention on the Law of the Sea (1982) Part II, s.2, art. 11.
[21] Bays include gulfs and estuaries; see *Post Office* v. *Estuary Radio* [1968] 2 Q.B. 740; [1967] 3 All E.R. 663 at p. 679, 9 B.I.L.C. 187, C.A. (which contains a discussion on bay-closing lines in general and the Thames Estuary in particular); see also the Convention on the Territorial Sea and the Contiguous Zone 1958, art. 13. To establish whether a coastal indentation is a bay, the natural entrance points are found and a line drawn between them; if the area of water enclosed by the line on its landward side is not less than that of a semicircle which has the same line as its diameter, the indentation is a bay; see the Territorial Waters Order in Council 1964, art. 5(1). If the line exceeds 24 nautical miles, the line is moved landwards until it becomes a straight line 24 miles long drawn from low-water line to a low-water line within the bay in such a way as to enclose the maximum area of water that is possible with a line of that length; see ibid., art. 4(c). There are special rules where the presence of islands creates a multiple-mouthed bay; arts. 4(b), 5(l). See also the United Nations Convention on the Law of the Sea (1982) Part II, s. 2, art. 10.
[22] See the Territorial Waters Order in Council 1964, art. 3(1).
[23] See *The Anna* (1805) 5 Ch. Rob. 373, 2 B.I.L.C. 694; the *Bulama Arbitration* (1869) Moore Int. Arb. 1909.
[24] Convention on the Territorial Sea and the Contiguous Zone 1958, art. 10(2).
[25] Territorial Waters Order in Council 1964, art. 5(1); and the United Nations Convention on the Law of the Sea (1982) Part II, s. 2, art. 13.
[26] Territorial Waters Order in Council 1964, art. 2(2).
[27] Convention on the Territorial Sea and the Contiguous Zone 1958, art. 5(1); United Nations Convention on the Law of the Sea (1982) Part II, s. 2, art. 8. Cf. the Administration of Justice Act 1956, Sch. 1, para. 4(1).

1.09 *Interpretation of regulations*

The requirement that the content of regulations or Orders in Council made under statutory powers must be within the powers conferred by the enabling statute has already been mentioned,[1] as has the rule that United Kingdom legislation (including delegated legislation) which implements an international convention is to be construed, where it is ambiguous, so as to accord with the convention.[2] In addition, there is a general rule that where the enabling statute was passed after 1889, any Order in Council, rules or regulations made under that statute have the same respective meanings as in the statute, unless the contrary intention appears.[3] Such a contrary intention will be expressed by a definition in the delegated legislation which differs from that in the enabling statute.[4] The courts have on occasion attempted to lay down guidelines for the interpretation of collision regulations and rules of local navigation. In one case it was suggested that they should be construed literally,[5] and in another that they should be construed according to a reasonable and business interpretation, not "according to the strictest and nicest interpretation of language".[6]

There are many decided cases on the meaning of words used in former collision regulations. These cases may no longer constitute binding authorities as to the meaning of such words, owing to changes in other words or in the context, but there is nevertheless a presumption that Parliament intended, by using the same words or clauses in modern legislation, to use those words or clauses with the same meaning.[7] If the courts have put a clear judicial interpretation on words or clauses used in earlier legislation, and those words or clauses are repeated in identical terms in the current legislation, that construction must be applied.[8] The order of 1977 came into force on 15th July 1977 and the regulations of 1983 containing the most recent amendments to the 1972 Rules came into force on 1st June 1983.[9]

There was a statutory presumption of fault (in cases of collision) during the period from 1873 to 1911, which applied whenever a breach of the collision regulations occurred, regardless of whether the breach caused the collision.[10] Cases on the meaning of the regulations which were decided during this period must be viewed with caution. If the decision was one of fault by the party in breach, it must not be regarded as authoritative. If it was decided that there was no fault, then the case may still be authoritative.

[1] See para. 1.04, text and note 5, *ante*.
[2] See para. 1.02, text and note 11, *ante*.
[3] Interpretation Act 1978, s. 11.
[4] Compare the definition of "vessel" in the Merchant Shipping Act 1894, s. 742 (para. 1.04, text and note 14, *ante*) with that in the Merchant Shipping (Distress Signals and Prevention of Collisions) Regulations 1983, S.I. 1983, No. 708, Sch. 1, r. 3(a) but note how this definition has been restricted by ibid., reg. 1(2)(a), to reconcile the definition of "vessel" in the regulations with that of "ship" in the enabling legislation; see para. 1.04, *ante*.
[5] See *The Libra* (1881) 6 P.D. 139, *per* Jessel, M.R., at p. 143; see also *The London* [1904] P. 355, 357, 358, where Sir F. H. Jeune, P., expressed regret that the rules were not stated in clear and simple language.
[6] See *The Dunelm* (1884) 9 P.D. 164, *per* Brett ,M.R., at p. 171.
[7] *Barlow* v. *Teal* (1885) 15 Q.B.D. 403, 404, 405; *Ex parte Campbell* (1870) 5 Ch. App. 703, at p. 706, *per* Sir W. M. James, L.J.
[8] *Mansell* v. *R.* (1857) 8 E. & B. 54, 73; *Barras* v. *Aberdeen Steam Trawling and Fishing Co.* [1933] A.C. 402, 411.
[9] See the Collision Regulations and Distress Signals Order 1977, S.I. 1977, No. 982, art. 1(1) (revoked); Merchant Shipping (Distress Signals and Prevention of Collisions) Regulations 1983, reg. 1(1). The same dates applied to hovercraft except that in their case the order of 1977 came into force on 27th July 1977; see the Hovercraft (Application of Enactments) (Amendment) Order 1977, S.I. 1977, No. 1257, art. 1 (revoked); Hovercraft (Application of Enactments) (Amendment) Order 1983, S.I. 1983, No. 769, art. 1. There were transitional exemptions from the Collision Regulations, contained in the Collision Regulations and Distress Signals Order 1977, for vessels whose keel was laid before 15th July 1977: see ibid., Sch. 1, Part E, r. 38 (revoked), and paras. 3.01, 3.02, *post*. See now a similar provision in the Merchant Shipping (Distress Signals and Prevention of Collisions) Regulations 1983, reg. 1(2)(a), Sch. 1, r. 38.
[10] See para. 5.24, text and note 7, *post*.

1.10 *Duty to obey regulations*

Vessels to which the Merchant Shipping (Distress Signals and Prevention of Collisions) Regulations 1983[1] apply must comply with the 1972 Rules.[2] Where any of the regulations is contravened, the owner[3] of the vessel,[4] the master[5] and any person for the time being responsible for the conduct of the vessel[6] are each guilty of an offence.[7] The offence is punishable on conviction on indictment by imprisonment for a term not exceeding two years and a fine.[8] Alternatively the offence is punishable on summary conviction by a fine not exceeding the statutory maximum;[9] except that in the case of any intentional infringement[10] of the Rule which requires a vessel to proceed with traffic flow in lanes of traffic schemes,[11] the maximum fine on summary conviction is £50,000.[12] It is a defence for any person charged under the regulations to show that he took all reasonable precautions to avoid the commission of the offence.[13]

In any case where a ship[14] does not comply with the requirements of the regulations, she is liable to be detained.[15] Where the ship is to be or may be detained, certain prescribed officials may detain her.[16] If after detention[17] the ship proceeds to sea before she is released by competent authority, the master, the owner and any person who sends the ship to sea,[18] are liable on conviction on indictment to a fine or on summary conviction to a fine not exceeding the statutory maximum.[19] Where the ship so proceeding to sea takes to sea with the detaining officer on board, the owner and master of the ship are each liable on conviction on indictment to a fine or on summary conviction to a fine not exceeding the statutory maximum.[20]

The Merchant Shipping (Signals of Distress) Rules 1977[21] prescribe the circumstances in which, and the purposes for which, the prescribed signals of distress[22] are to be used and the circumstances in which they are to be revoked.[23] If the master of a ship uses or displays or causes or permits any person under his authority to use or display any prescribed signal[24] except in the circumstances and for the purposes prescribed by the Merchant Shipping (Signals of Distress) Rules 1977, or any private signal, whether registered or not,[25] that is liable to be mistaken for a prescribed signal, he is liable on conviction on indictment to a fine, and on summary conviction to a fine not exceeding the statutory maximum.[26] An act which constitutes an offence under any of the provisions described in this paragraph could in some circumstances constitute also another offence, such as manslaughter,[27] criminal damage,[28] or misconduct endangering the ship or persons on board the ship.[29]

---

[1] S.I. 1983, No. 708. The vessels, hovercraft and seaplanes to which these regulations apply are described in paras. 1.07, text and notes 1-7, 1.08, text and notes 1-8, *ante*.
[2] Merchant Shipping (Distress Signals and Prevention of Collisions) Regulations 1983, reg. 4; see also the application to ships of "relevant" countries mentioned in para. 1.08, text and notes 6-8, *ante*; and the exemptions for the ships of the British Government and foreign sovereigns; paras. 1.07, text and notes 4, 5, 1.08, text and note 11, *ante*. Nothing in the Merchant Shipping (Distress Signals and Prevention of Collisions) Regulations 1983 is to be taken to require compliance by any vessel or class of vessels, which by virtue of 1972 Rule 38 may be exempted from compliance, with any of the regulations specified in r. 38(a)-(h) at any time when the Rule exempts that vessel or class of vessels; ibid., reg. 4, proviso. As to r. 38, see paras. 3.01, 4.01, *post*. The duty to obey the regulations described in the text to this note is applied to the vessels, whereas under the previous law (which still applies to seaplanes) the duty to obey was cast upon owners and masters; see the Merchant

Shipping Act 1894, s. 419(1). Any damage resulting from a breach was deemed to have been occasioned by the wilful default of the person in charge of the deck unless it could be shown that a departure from the regulations was necessary; ibid., s. 419(3). These provisions are now repealed, except as to seaplanes, and the new defence (see the text to note 13, *infra*.) may not have the same effect in civil cases as s. 419(3). The numerous cases on the application of the collision regulations (and on when non-compliance may be excused) now need to be treated with reserve but see, e.g., *The Henry, The St. Cyran* (1864) 12 W.R. 1014; *The Beryl* (1884) 9 P.D. 137, C.A.; *The Test* (1847) 5 Not. of Cas. 276. Where the collision regulations apply, compliance must be prompt; *The Stadacona* (1847) 5 Not. of Cas. 371; and effective; *The Durmitor* [1951] 1 Lloyd's Rep. 22. As to the overriding duty to take seaman-like precautions, see para. 1.14, *post*.

[3] The register is *prima facie* but not conclusive evidence as to the identity of the owner; *Baumwoll* v. *Furness* [1893] A.C. 8; *Hibbs* v. *Ross* (1866) L.R. 1 Q.B. 534.

[4] For the meaning of "vessel" see para. 1.04, text and notes 15-17, *ante*. This provision applies to hovercraft; see paras. 1.07, text and note 6, 1.08, text and notes 1-4, *ante*.

[5] "Master" includes every person (except a pilot) having command or charge of any ship; Merchant Shipping Act 1894, s. 742. References in ibid., s. 419, to the master or the person in charge of the deck are to be construed, in the application of that section to seaplanes on the surface of the water, as references to the pilot or other person on duty in charge of the seaplane: Civil Aviation Act 1982, s. 97(1), exception (ii).

[6] In view of the definition of "master" in note 5, *supra*, the reference to "person for the time being responsible for the conduct of the vessel" might seem superfluous but it was held in *Foreman* v. *MacNeill* (1979) S.C. 17, that a person who was merely in charge of the deck, although temporarily responsible for the ship's navigation, was not "the master", within the Merchant Shipping Act 1894, s. 742, even although he was *in charge* so as to make him criminally liable for breach of the duty to render assistance in case of collision; see para. 1.11, text and notes 1-5, *post*.

[7] Merchant Shipping (Distress Signals and Prevention of Collisions) Regulations 1983, reg. 5(1)(a). This provision appears to make any breach, however unintentional, an offence but the regulations are subject to the statutory defence mentioned in the text and note 13, *infra*. Moreover the 1972 Rules themselves provide that in construing and complying with the Rules due regard is to be had to all dangers of navigation and collision and to any special circumstances, including the limitations of the vessels involved, which may make a departure from the Rules necessary to avoid immediate danger; Merchant Shipping (Distress Signals and Prevention of Collisions) Regulations 1983, Sch. 1, r. 2(b); for recent cases on the meaning of the equivalent 1960 Rule 27 (as to which see para. 6.02, *post*) see *The Savina* [1974] 2 Lloyd's Rep. 317; (C.A.) [1975] 2 Lloyd's Rep. 141; (H.L.) [1976] 2 Lloyd's Rep. 123; *Sagittarius (Owners)* v. *Schwarzburg (Owners)* ("*The Schwarzburg*") [1976] 1 Lloyd's Rep. 26; *Alonso de Ojeda (Owners)* v. *Sestriere (Owners)* ("*The Sestriere*") [1976] 1 Lloyd's Rep. 125; *The Sea Star* [1976] 1 Lloyd's Rep. 115; (C.A.) [1976] 2 Lloyd's Rep. 477; *The Vysotsk* [1981] 1 Lloyd's Rep. 439. See also the use of the word "normally" in the Merchant Shipping (Distress Signals and Prevention of Collisions) Regulations 1983, Sch. 1, r. 10; para. 2.06, *post*; and see *The City of Corinth* (1890) 6 Asp. 602. Nevertheless the duty to obey is now much stricter than the former duty to obey collision regulations, which only created an offence where the infringement of the regulations was caused by the "wilful default" of the master or owner; see the Merchant Shipping Act 1894, s. 419(2). This enabled the master to escape conviction by merely delegating navigation to a subordinate; see *Bradshaw* v. *Ewart-James* [1983] 1 All E.R. 12 The requirement of wilful default still applies where seaplanes are concerned; see note 8, *infra*.

[8] Merchant Shipping (Distress Signals and Prevention of Collisions) Regulations 1983, reg. 5(1)(a). See also, as to hovercraft, the Hovercraft (Application of Enactments) (Amendment) Order 1983, S.I 1983, No. 769, art. 3; and as to the vessels of "relevant" countries, the Merchant Shipping (Distress Signals and Prevention of Collisions) (Overseas Territories) Order 1983, S.I. 1983, No. 762, art. 5(1). As to seaplanes, see the Merchant Shipping Act 1894, s. 419(2); Merchant Shipping Act 1979, s. 43(3), Sch. 6, Part VII; Collision Rules (Seaplanes) Order 1983, S.I. 1983, No. 768, art. 4. It should be noted that although the pilot or owner of a seaplane is liable to the same penalties for a breach of the 1972 Rules as the master or owner of a vessel, conviction still rests upon the prosecution proving wilful default, a concept now repealed except as to seaplanes; see note 7, *supra*.

[9] Merchant Shipping (Distress Signals and Prevention of Collisions) Regulations 1983, reg. 5(1)(a)(ii). As to the statutory maximum, see ibid., reg. 5(1)(b); and para. 1.11, note 13, *post*. As to trial on indictment and summary trial, see para. 5.13, *post*.

[10] It follows that where the infringement is unintentional the maximum fine on summary conviction, assuming an offence has been committed at all, is the statutory maximum.

[11] I.e. Rule 10(b)(i) of the 1972 Rules, as to which see para. 2.06, *post*.

[12] Merchant Shipping (Distress Signals and Prevention of Collisions) Regulations 1983, reg. 5(1)(a)(i). As to hovercraft, vessels of "relevant" countries and seaplanes, see note 8, *supra*.

[13] Ibid., reg. 5(2). In contrast to the former law, where the prosecution had to prove wilful default, it is now for the defendant to prove he took all reasonable precautions, although the standard of proof required of the defence is less high than that required of the prosecution; see para. 5.18, *post*. Presumably an owner will be able to take advantage of this defence more readily than a master, although it is no doubt still the law that owners must at least ensure that masters are properly supervised, adequately informed of the Rules and reminded of the duty to obey; see *Grill* v. *General Iron Screw Collier Co.* (1866) L.R. 1 C.P. 600; on appeal (1868) L.R. 3 C.P. 476; *The Lady Gwendolen, Arthur Guinness, Son & Co. (Dublin) Ltd.* v. *Owners of Motor Vessel Freshfield* [1965] 2 All E.R. 283, C.A.

[14] For the meaning of "ship", see para. 1.04, note 14, *ante*.

[15] Merchant Shipping (Distress Signals and Prevention of Collisions) Regulations 1983, reg. 6.

[16] See ibid., reg. 6, applying the Merchant Shipping Act 1894, s. 692. The officials prescribed by ibid., s. 692, are: any commissioned officer of the Royal Navy or Army, any officer of the Department of Transport, any Customs officer and any British consular officer.

[17] The provisions described in the text to this note and to notes 18, 19, *infra*, also apply if any notice of or order for detention has been served on the master; ibid., s. 692(1).

[18] The owner or person who sends the ship to sea only commit an offence if they are party or privy to the offence; ibid., s. 692(1).

[19] Ibid., s. 692(1); Merchant Shipping Act 1979, s. 43(3), Sch. 6, Part VII, para. 10; Criminal Justice Act 1982, s. 49(1). As to the statutory maximum, see para. 1.11, note 13, *post*.

[20] Merchant Shipping Act 1894, s. 692(2); Merchant Shipping Act 1979, s. 43(3), Sch. 6, Part VII, para. 11; Criminal Justice Act 1982, s. 49(1).

[21] S.I. 1977, No. 1010.

[22] I.e. the signals of distress prescribed by the Merchant Shipping (Distress Signals and Prevention of Collisions) Regulations 1983, reg. 3. As to these signals, see para. 4.05, *post*.

[23] See the Merchant Shipping (Signals of Distress) Rules 1977, S.I. 1977, No. 1010, r. 3. As to the power to prescribe these matters, see now the Merchant Shipping Act 1979, s. 21(1), (3).

[24] I.e. prescribed by the Merchant Shipping (Distress Signals and Prevention of Collisions) Regulations 1983, reg. 3; see note 22, *supra*.

[25] As to private signals and their registration, see the Merchant Shipping Act 1894, s. 733.

[26] Merchant Shipping (Safety Convention) Act 1949, s. 21(3); Merchant Shipping Act 1979, s. 43(2), Sch. 6, Part V; Criminal Justice Act 1982, s. 49(1). See also the Hovercraft (Application of Enactments) Order 1972, S.I. 1972, No. 971, Sch. 1; Hovercraft (Application of Enactments) (Amendment) Order 1983, S.I. 1983, No. 769, art. 3(a)(ii). As to the liability of the master to pay compensation, see para. 5.24, text and notes 4, 5, *post*. The provisions described in the text to this note do not apply to seaplanes.

[27] See *R.* v. *Spence* (1846) 1 Cox C.C. 352.

[28] See the Criminal Damage Act 1971, s. 1.

[29] See the Merchant Shipping Act 1970, s. 27.

1.11 *Duty of vessel to assist in case of collision*

In every case of collision between two vessels, it is the duty of the master[1] or person in charge[2] of each vessel,[3] if and so far as he can do so without danger to his own vessel,[4] crew and passengers (if any), to take certain steps.[5] He must render to the other vessel, her master, crew and passengers (if any) such assistance as may be practicable, and may be necessary to save them from any danger caused by the collision, and must stay by the other vessel until he has ascertained that she has no need of further assistance.[6] He must also give to the master or person in charge of the other vessel the name of his own vessel and of the port[7] to which she belongs, and also the names of the ports from which she comes and to which she is bound.[8] If the master or other person in charge fails without reasonable cause[9] to comply with these requirements, he is guilty of an offence and, in the case of a failure to assist or stay by the other vessel,[10] liable on conviction on indictment to a fine and imprisonment for a term not exceeding two years and on summary conviction to a fine not exceeding £50,000 and imprisonment for a term not exceeding six months.[11] In the case of a failure to give a name,[12] he is liable on indictment to a fine and on summary conviction to a fine not exceeding the statutory maximum.[13] If he is a certificated officer, an inquiry into his conduct may be held, and his certificate cancelled or suspended.[14]

[1] For the meaning of "the master" see para. 1.10, note 5, *ante*.
[2] It is not certain whether "person in charge" includes a compulsory pilot: cf., the Pilotage Act 1983, s. 35); contrast *The Queen* (1869) L.R. 2 A. & E. 354. It does include a mate who is the senior man on watch and in charge; *Foreman* v. *MacNeill* (1979) S.C. 17. See para. 1.10, note 5, *ante*.
[3] The duty to stand by also applies to a tug whose tow alone has been involved in the collision; *The Hannibal, The Queen* (1867) L.R. 2 A. & E. 53; and see *The Harvest Home* [1904] P. 409. For the meaning of "vessel" see para. 1.04, notes 15-17, *ante*. The reference to "vessels" includes a reference to hovercraft; Hovercraft (Application of Enactments) Order 1972, S.I. 1972, No. 971, art. 4, Sch. 1, Part A.
[4] As to cases on the danger to the assisting vessel see *The Thuringia* (1872) 1 Asp. M.L.C. 283; *The San Onofre* [1922] P. 243; [1922] All E.R. Rep. 720, C.A.; *The Adriatic* (1875) 3 Asp. M.L.C. 16; *The Emmy Haase* (1884) 9 P.D. 81.
[5] Merchant Shipping Act 1894, s. 422(1). There is also a general duty to assist persons in danger at sea: see the Maritime Conventions Act 1911, s. 6. The duty does not prevent a vessel giving assistance from claiming salvage; see *The Hannibal, The Queen* (1867) L.R. 2 A. & E. 53; and *Melanie (Owners)* v. *San Onofre (Owners)* [1925] A.C. 246.
[6] Merchant Shipping Act 1894, s. 422(1) (a).
[7] "Port" includes place; ibid., s. 742.
[8] Ibid., s. 422(1) (b).
[9] For the meaning of "reasonable cause" see para. 5.06, note 8, *post*.
[10] I.e. a breach of the Merchant Shipping Act 1894, s. 422(1)(a). See the text and notes 1-6, *supra*.
[11] Ibid., s. 422(3). As to trial on indictment, see para. 5.13, *post*.
[12] I.e. a breach of s. 422(1)(b). See the text and notes 7, 8, *supra*.
[13] Ibid., s. 422(3); Merchant Shipping Act 1979, s. 43(3), Sch. 6, Part VII, para. 6; Criminal Justice Act 1982, s. 49(1). The statutory maximum means the sum prescribed by the Magistrates' Courts Act 1980, s. 32. See the Criminal Justice Act 1982, s. 74(1). The sum at present prescribed by the Magistrates' Courts Act 1980, s. 32, is £1,000. This may be varied by order; ibid., s. 143. No such order has been made at the date at which this edition states the law.
[14] Merchant Shipping Act 1894, s. 422(3). As to inquiries see para. 5.22, text and notes 12-24, *post*. As to the power to cancel or suspend certificates see para. 5.22, text and note 21, *post*.

1.12 *Obligation to assist vessels in distress*

The master[1] of a British ship[2] registered[3] in the United Kingdom,[4] on receiving at sea a signal of distress[5] or information from any source that a vessel[6] or aircraft is in distress, must proceed with all speed to the assistance of the persons in distress (informing them if possible that he is doing so), unless he is unable, or in the special circumstances of the case considers it unreasonable or unnecessary to do so, or unless one of the statutory exemptions[7] applies to him.[8] Where the master of any ship in distress has requisitioned any British ship registered in the United Kingdom that has answered his call, it is the duty of the master of the requisitioned ship to comply with the requisition by continuing to proceed with all speed to the assistance of the persons in distress.[9] However, a master is released from the obligation to proceed on receiving a distress signal, as soon as he is informed of the requisition of one or more ships other than his own and that the requisition is being complied with by the ship or ships requisitioned.[10] He is also released from his obligations[11] if he is informed by the persons in distress, or by the master of any ship that has reached the persons in distress, that assistance is no longer required.[12] If a master fails to comply with his obligations he is guilty of an offence and punishable on indictment with a fine and by imprisonment for a term not exceeding two years, or on summary conviction with a fine not exceeding the statutory maximum or imprisonment for a term not exceeding six months.[13]

[1] For the meaning of "master" see para. 1.10, note 5, *ante*.

[2] For the meaning of "ship" see para. 1.04, text and note 14, *ante*. The meaning of "British ship" is not easy to determine. It probably means a ship wholly owned by British subjects and/or a body or bodies corporate established under and subject to the laws of some part of Her Majesty's dominions, and having their principal place of business in those dominions; Merchant Shipping Act 1894, s. 1. For an example of a ship owned by Australian citizens being held to be a British ship, see *Oteri* v. *The Queen* [1977] 1 Lloyd's Rep. 105, P.C. The expression "ship" in the provision expounded in the text to this note includes hovercraft; see the Hovercraft (Application of Enactments) Order 1972, S.I. 1972, No. 971, art. 4, Sch. 1, Part A.

[3] As to the registry of British ships see the Merchant Shipping Act 1894, ss. 2-23; Merchant Shipping Act 1983.

[4] For the meaning of "the United Kingdom" see para. 1.08, note 16, *ante*.

[5] As to the signals of distress see para. 4.05, *post*.

[6] For the meaning of "vessel" in the Merchant Shipping Acts see para. 1.04, text and notes 15-17, *ante*.

[7] The master is released if the provisions of the Merchant Shipping (Safety Convention) Act 1949, s. 22(3), (4), apply; see the text and notes 10-12, *infra*.

[8] Ibid., s. 22(1).

[9] Ibid., s. 22(2).

[10] Ibid., s. 22(3).

[11] I.e. from his obligations to comply with s. 22(1), (2) of the Act of 1949; see the text and notes 1-9, *supra*.

[12] Ibid., s. 22(4).

[13] Ibid., s. 22(5); Merchant Shipping Act 1894, s. 680(1) (a); Merchant Shipping Act 1979, s. 43(3), Sch. 6, Part VII, para. 9; Criminal Justice Act 1982, s. 49(1). As to the statutory maximum see para. 1.11, note 13, *ante*. Nothing in the Merchant Shipping (Safety Convention) Act 1949, s. 22 affects the provisions of the Maritime Conventions Act 1911, s. 6 (general duty to render assistance to persons in danger at sea); compliance by a master with the obligation to proceed to vessels in distress does not affect his right or the right of any other person to salvage; Merchant Shipping (Safety Convention) Act 1949, s. 22(8).

1.13 *Duty to log and report casualties, etc.*

An official log book must be kept in most ships registered in the United Kingdom.[1] Regulations made by the Secretary of State for Transport[2] provide that entries must be made in the log book, as soon as practicable after the relevant occurrence,[3] recording the following events:— (1) Every signal of distress[4] and every message that a vessel,[5] aircraft or person is in distress at sea observed or received;[6] (2) A statement of the master's[7] reasons for not going to the assistance of persons in distress, where he receives at sea a signal of distress or information from any source that a vessel or aircraft is in distress and is unable, or in the special circumstances of the case considers it unreasonable or unnecessary, to go to their assistance;[8] (3) A description of specified casualties[9] and the place where, or the position of the vessel when, the casualty occurred.[10] These entries must be signed by the master and witnessed by a member of the crew.[11] If an entry is not made, signed and witnessed in accordance with these provisions, the master of the vessel at the time when the entry is or should have been made, signed and witnessed is guilty of an offence and liable on summary conviction to a fine not exceeding level 2 on the standard scale.[12]

Where a casualty[13] occurs in the case of a ship or a ship's boat, and at the time it occurs the ship is registered in the United Kingdom, the owner[14] or master of the ship must report the casualty to the Secretary of State.[15] The report must be made as soon as practicable and in any case not later than 24 hours after the ship's arrival at the next port.[16] The report must give a brief description of the casualty and state the time and place where it occurred, the name and official number of the ship, her position at the time of the report and the next port of call.[17] If the owner or master of a ship fails without reasonable cause[18] to comply with these provisions, he is guilty of an offence and liable on summary conviction to a fine not exceeding level 5 on the standard scale.[19]

[1] See the Merchant Shipping Act 1970, s. 68(1). For the meaning of "ship" see para. 1.04, text and note 14, *ante*. As to the registry of British ships see the Merchant Shipping Act 1894, ss. 2-23 Merchant Shipping Act 1983. As to the power to exempt ships from the requirements as to log books see the Merchant Shipping Act 1970, s. 68(4).
[2] The power to make regulations under this provision was originally vested in the Board of Trade. As to the devolution of functions on the Secretary of State see para. 5.01, *post*. As to the regulations made under this power see the Merchant Shipping (Official Log Books) Regulations 1981, S.I. 1981, No. 569. Merchant Shipping (Official Log Books) (Fishing Vessels) Regulations 1981, S.I. 1981, No. 570.
[3] As to this requirement and the time for making alterations to the log book see the Merchant Shipping (Official Log Books) Regulations 1981, reg. 7(1) (f); Merchant Shipping (Official Log Books) (Fishing Vessels) Regulations 1981, reg. 7(1) (e).
[4] As to the obligation to assist vessels in distress see para. 1.12, *ante*.
[5] For the meaning of "vessel" see para. 1.04, text and notes 15-17, *ante*.
[6] Merchant Shipping (Official Log Books) Regulations 1982, Sch., para. 13; Merchant Shipping (Official Log Books) (Fishing Vessels) Regulations 1981, Sch., para. 10.
[7] For the meaning of "master" see para. 1.10, note 5, *ante*.
[8] Merchant Shipping (Official Log Books) Regulations 1981, Sch., para. 14; Merchant Shipping (Official Log Books) (Fishing Vessels) Regulations 1981, Sch., para. 11.
[9] As to the casualties to which this provision applies see the regulations noted in note 8, *supra*, and para. 5.19, text and notes 1-5, *post*.
[10] Merchant Shipping (Official Log Books) Regulations 1981, Sch., para. 12; Merchant Shipping (Official Log Books) (Fishing Vessels) Regulations 1981, Sch., para. 9.
[11] Merchant Shipping (Official Log Books) Regulations 1981, reg. 4, Sch.; Merchant Shipping (Official Log Books) (Fishing Vessels) Regulations 1981, reg. 4, Sch.

[12] Merchant Shipping (Official Log Books) Regulations 1981, regs. 5, 11; Merchant Shipping (Official Log Books) (Fishing Vessels) Regulations 1981, regs. 5, 11; Criminal Justice Act 1982, ss. 37(2), 46(1), (4). As to the standard scale, see note 19, *infra.*
[13] As to the casualties to which this provision applies, and the power to hold inquiries and investigations into them, see paras. 5.19 et seq., *post.*
[14] As to owners see para. 1.10, note 3, *ante.*
[15] Merchant Shipping Act 1970, s. 73(1).
[16] Ibid., s. 73(1).
[17] Ibid., s. 73(1). For the meaning of "port" see para. 1.11, note 7, *ante.*
[18] As to "reasonable cause", cf. "reasonable excuse" discussed at para. 5.06, note 8, *post.*
[19] Merchant Shipping Act 1970, s. 73(2); Merchant Shipping Act 1979, s. 43(1), Sch. 6, Part IV; Criminal Justice Act 1982, ss. 37(2), 46(1), (4). The provisions of ss. 37, 46 have the effect of converting references in legislation to fines of certain specified amounts for summary offences to references to various levels on the standard scale (which may be increased by order), The standard scale is as follows:

Level	Amount of fine
1	£25
2	£50
3	£200
4	£500
5	£1,000

See ibid., s. 37(2). No order increasing the standard scale had been made at the date at which this edition states the law.

1.14 *Duty to obey the rules of good seamanship*

Nothing in the 1972 Rules exonerates any vessel, or its owner, master or crew, from the consequences of any neglect to comply with the Rules or of the neglect of any precaution which may be required by the ordinary practice of seamen, or by the special circumstances of the case.[1] There is a considerable overlap between these rules of good seamanship, which are said to accord with commonsense,[2] and the 1972 Rules; many of the latter have their origins in historic rules of good seamanship[3] and vessels which are not bound by the collision regulations may nevertheless be expected to treat them as rules of good seamanship.[4] No criminal prosecution can follow from a breach of the rules of good seamanship as such, although an act which constitutes a breach may well also constitute a criminal offence under the Merchant Shipping Acts.[5] Even if no crime is committed, the breach may result in a master losing his certificate following a Department of Transport inquiry.[6] A brief outline of the principal rules is therefore necessary for completeness.

A vessel is required to give reasonable notice of launching[7] and take certain precautions while doing so.[8] She should also take special care and precautions if moving or manoeuvring in bad weather.[9] There are rules as to the dropping of anchor[10] and coming to anchor.[11] While she is at anchor or moored alongside, she should keep watch[12] and may be under a duty to move.[13] Other vessels should keep clear of a vessel at anchor.[14] Vessels should not stand too close to one another.[15] There are various rules governing the behaviour of and towards tug and tow,[16] sailing vessels,[17] dangerous vessels[18] and dumb barges.[19] There are also numerous decisions on duties in confined waters, relating to reactions to the effects of tide and current,[20] waiting at a bend,[21] dredging up stern first,[22] warping,[23] crossing and turning,[24] anchoring,[25] vessels aground,[26] waiting for outgoing vessels[27] and behaviour in docks and harbours.[28]

[1] Merchant Shipping (Distress Signals and Prevention of Collisions) Regulations 1983, S.I. 1983 No. 708, Sch. 1, Part A, r. 2(a).
[2] See *The Roseline* [1981] 2 Lloyd's Rep. 410, at p. 411, *per* Sheen, J.
[3] See, e.g., 1972 r. 5 (look-out), para. 2.01, *post*.
[4] See, e.g., *The Estrella* [1977] 1 Lloyd's Rep. 525 and the other cases noted at para. 2.06, note 4, *post*.
[5] See para. 1.10, text and note 29, *ante*.
[6] See paras. 5.19-5.23, *post*.
[7] See *The Blenheim* (1846) 2 Wm. Rob. 421.
[8] See *The George Roper* (1883) 8 P.D. 119, 5 Asp. M.L.C. 134; *The Gertor* (1894) 7 Asp. M.L.C. 472 (duty to have tug assistance in gale off Dover).
[9] See *The Borussia* (1856) Sw. 94; *The Pladda* (1876) 2 P.D. 34.
[10] *The City of Peking* v. *Compagnie des Messageries Maritimes, The City of Peking* (1888) 14 App. Cas. 40, 6 Asp. M.L.C. 396, C.A.
[11] *The Ceres* (1857) Sw. 250.
[12] *Mary Tug Co.* v. *British India Steam Navigation Co., The Meanatchy* [1897] A.C. 351, P.C.
[13] *The Woburn Abbey* (1869) 3 Mar. L.C. 240.
[14] *The Girolamo* (1834) 3 Hag. Adm. 169 at p. 173.
[15] *The Globe* (1848) 6 Not. of Cas. 275.
[16] See, e.g., *The Jane Bacon* (1878) 27 W.R. 35, C.A.; *Comet (Owners)* v. *The W.H. No. 1 (Owners), The W.H. No. 1 and The Knight Errant* [1911] A.C. 30, 11 Asp. M.L.C. 497, H.L.
[17] See *The Ida* v. *The Wasa Nicolaistadt* (1866) 15 L.T. 103.
[18] *H.M.S. Bellerephon* (1874) 3 Asp. M.L.C. 58.
[19] *The Ralph Creyke* (1866) 6 Asp. M.L.C. 19.
[20] *The City of Peking, supra*.
[21] *The Talabot* (1890) 15 P.D. 194, 6 Asp. M.L.C. 602. See now *The Toluca*, 1st November 1983, C.A.
[22] *The Frankfort* [1910] P. 50, 11 Asp. M.L.C. 326, C.A.
[23] *The Hope* (1843) 2 Wm. Rob. 8.
[24] See, e.g., *The Thetford* (1887) 6 Asp. M.L.C. 179.
[25] *The Aguadallina* (1889) 6 Asp. M.L.C. 390.
[26] *The Industrie* (1871) L.R. 3 A. & E. 303, 1 Asp. M.L.C. 17.
[27] *Taylor* v. *Burger* (1898) 8 Asp. M.L.C. 364, H.L.
[28] *Taylor* v. *Burger, supra*. For a detailed exposition of the rules of good seamanship, see *Halsbury's Laws of England*, 4th edn., SHIPPING, vol. 43, paras. 922-948.

CHAPTER TWO

COLLISION REGULATIONS—STEERING AND SAILING RULES

SECT. (1) Conduct of vessels in any condition of visibility

2.01 *Look-out—Rule 5*

Every vessel[1] must at all times maintain a proper look-out by sight and hearing as well as by all available means appropriate in the prevailing circumstances and conditions, so as to make a full appraisal of the situation of the risk of the collision.[2]

This rule was formerly a rule of good seamanship and was referred to in previous regulations.[3] In cases on the former rule, it has been held that the look-out must be particularly vigilant in the light of any special circumstances.[4] Normally one or more hands should be stationed on the look-out by day and night.[5] The look-out should not be engaged upon any other duty and should usually be in the bows.[6] Special attention is necessary in poor weather and visibility,[7] when the vessel is passing over a fishing ground[8] or when she is towing another vessel.[9] In some cases vessels at anchor should have a look-out.[10] If a vessel has radar, this should be used where it would help in keeping a good look-out[11] and should be used properly.[12] IMO has issued a Recommendation on basic principles and operational guidance relating to navigational watchkeeping[13] which has been incorporated in a Department of Transport "M" Notice.[14]

---

[1] For the meaning of "vessel" in the Merchant Shipping (Distress Signals and Prevention of Collisions) Regulations 1983, S.I. 1983, No. 708, see para. 1.04, text and notes 15-17, *ante*.

[2] Merchant Shipping (Distress Signals and Prevention of Collisions) Regulations 1983, Sch. 1, r. 5. This rule and rr. 6-10 (see paras. 2.02-2.07, *post*) apply in any condition of visibility; r. 4. As to the power to make collision regulations, and their application to United Kingdom and other vessels, see paras. 1.04-1.08, *ante*. For the meaning of "risk of collision" see para. 2.03, note 2, *post*. The rules expounded in this Chapter and in Chapters 3 and 4, *post*, are cited verbatim, except where insignificant changes in style and punctuation are warranted by the narrative method of exposition. The rules are expounded in full, as enacted, in Appendix I, paras. 6.01 *et seq.*, *post*.

[3] See the Collision Regulations (Ships and Seaplanes on the Water) and Signals of Distress (Ships) Order 1965, S.I. 1965, No. 1525, Sch. 1, r. 29 (revoked). The reference to a proper look-out in previous regulations since 1863 was probably no more than a solemn warning that compliance with collision regulations did not terminate the ever present duty of using reasonable skill and care; see *The Queen Mary* (1949) 82 Ll.L.Rep. 303, at p. 341, H.L., *per* Lord MacDermott. For a case where the look-out rule was considered in combination with other rules of good seamanship see *Alonso de Ojeda (Owners)* v. *Sestriere (Owners) (The Sestriere)* [1976] 1 Lloyd's Rep. 125. See also *The Almizar* [1971] 2 Lloyd's Rep. 290, H.L.; *The Elazig* [1972] 1 Lloyd's Rep. 355; *Stein and others* v. *The Kathy K and S.N. No. 1, Egmont Towing and Sorting Ltd., Shields Navigation Ltd., Helsing and Iverson* (Can. Ct.) [1972] 2 Lloyd's Rep. 36; *The Carebeka I* [1973] 1 Lloyd's Rep. 396; *The Hagen* [1973] 1 Lloyd's Rep. 257; *The Savina* [1974] 2 Lloyd's Rep. 317; [1975] 2 Lloyd's Rep. 141, C.A.; [1976] 2 Lloyd's Rep. 123, H.L.; *The Sea Star* [1976] 1 Lloyd's Rep. 115; [1976] 2 Lloyd's Rep. 477, C.A.; *The Ercole* [1977] 1 Lloyd's Rep. 516; [1979] 1 Lloyd's Rep. 539, C.A.; *The Zaglebie Dabrowskie* [1978] 1 Lloyd's Rep. 564; *The Devotion II* (Sc. Ct.) [1979] 1 Lloyd's Rep. 509.

[4] See *The Henry Stanley* (1946) 79 Ll.L.Rep. 579; *The Benrinnes* (1946) 79 Ll.L.Rep. 541; *The Appledore* (1946) 79 Ll.L.Rep. 131; *The Corsea* (1938) 61 Ll.L.Rep. 266. The look-out should also check up on the working of the navigational equipment of his own ship; *The Staffordshire* (1948) 81 Ll.L.Rep. 141. The 1972 Rule expounded in this paragraph expressly states that the look-out should be kept by all available means; see the text and notes 1, 2, *supra*. For recent cases where this rule has been applied to radar observation, see *The Sanshin Victory* [1980] 2 Lloyd's Rep. 359; *The Roseline* [1981] 2 Lloyd's Rep. 410; *The Coral I* [1982] 1 Lloyd's Rep. 441; *The Maritime Harmony* [1982] 2 Lloyd's Rep. 400.

[5] See *Ellerman Lines Ltd.* v. *Trustees of The Harbour of Dundee* (1922) 38 T.L.R. 299; *The Spirality* [1954] 2 Lloyd's Rep. 59, *per* Willmer, J., at p. 63. Even when radar is in operation, a visual look-out should be kept; *The Anneliese* [1970] 1 Lloyd's Rep. 36.

[6] See *The British Confidence* [1951] 2 Lloyd's Rep. 615, *per* Willmer, J., at p. 621 (but see *Anchor Line* (*Henderson Brothers*) *Ltd.* v. *Trustees of The Harbour of Dundee* (1921) 38 T.L.R. *per* Lord Dunedin, at p. 311; and *The Beaverdell* [1952] 1 Lloyd's Rep. 421). See also *The Tynwald* [1953] 1 Lloyd's Rep. 271; *The Saxon Queen* [1954] 2 Lloyd's Rep. 286; *The Dea Mazzella* [1958] 1 Lloyd's Rep. 10; *The Fogo* [1967] 2 Lloyd's Rep. 208; *The Sea Star* [1976] 1 Lloyd's Rep. 115, [1976] 2 Lloyd's Rep. 447.

[7] See *The Mellona* (1847) 3 W. Rob. 7; *The Cabo Santo Tome* (1933) 46 Ll.L.Rep. 123.

[8] See *The Robert and Ann* v. *The Lloyds* (1864) Holt. Ad. Ca. 55. See also *The Devotion II* (Sc. Ct.) [1979] 1 Lloyd's Rep. 509.

[9] See *The Jane Bacon* (1878) 27 W.R. 35, C.A.

[10] See *Lack* v. *Seward* (1829) 4 C. & P. 106; *Vanderplank* v. *Miller* (1828) M. & M. 169; *The Prospector* [1958] 2 Lloyd's Rep. 288; *The Gerda Toft* [1953] 2 Lloyd's Rep. 249, *per* Willmer, J., at p. 257; *The Cedartree* [1957] 1 Lloyd's Rep. 51, *per* Willmer, J., at p. 57.

[11] See *The Chusan* [1955] 2 Lloyd's Rep. 685; *The Esso Plymouth* [1955] 1 Lloyd's Rep. 429; *The Indus* [1957] 1 Lloyd's Rep. 335; *The Greathope* [1957] 2 Lloyd's Rep. 197; cf., *The Verena* [1960] 2 Lloyd's Rep. 286. Information from shore radar stations obtained by VHF radio should also be correctly appreciated; see *The Bovenkerk* [1973] 1 Lloyd's Rep. 62; *The Vechtstroom* [1964] 1 Lloyd's Rep. 118.

[12] See *The Southport* (1949) 82 Ll.L.Rep. 862; *The Anna Salen* [1954] 1 Lloyd's Rep. 475; *The Guildford* [1956] 2 Lloyd's Rep. 74. See also *The Gunnar Knudsen* [1961] 2 Lloyd's Rep. 433; *The Kurt Arlt* [1962] 1 Lloyd's Rep. 31; *The Fina Canada* [1962] 2 Lloyd's Rep. 113, [1962] 2 Lloyd's Rep. 445, C.A.; *The Sitala* [1963] 1 Lloyd's Rep. 205. See further para. 2.03, text and notes 5, 6, *post*.

[13] See IMO Resolution A.285 (VIII), as to which see note 14 *infra* and para. 8.02, *post*. As to watch-keeping on board fishing vessels see Resolution A.484 (XII).

[14] See M.756—"Keeping a Safe Navigational Watch", para. 8.01, *post*. The Department of Transport has also issued a Notice on Bridge Manning, Watchkeeping and the Command of Fishing Vessels (see M.997, para. 8.03 *post*); and a further Notice on Keeping a Safe Navigational Watch on Board Fishing Vessels, which incorporates IMO Resolution A.484 (XII) (noted at note 13, *supra*); see M.1020, para. 8.04, *post*.

2.02 *Safe speed—Rule 6*

Every vessel[1] must at all times proceed at a safe speed so that she can take proper and effective action to avoid collision and be stopped within a distance appropriate to the prevailing circumstances and conditions.[2] The following factors must be taken into account by all vessels in determining a safe speed:— (i) the state of visibility; (ii) the traffic density including concentrations of fishing vessels or any other vessels; (iii) the manoeuvrability of the vessel with special reference to stopping distance and turning ability in the prevailing conditions; (iv) at night the presence of background light such as from shore lights or from back scatter of her own lights; (v) the state of wind, sea and current, and the proximity of navigational hazards; (vi) the draught in relation to the available depth of water.[3] In addition, vessels with operational radar must take into account the following factors:— (i) the characteristics, efficiency and limitations of the radar equipment; (ii) any constraints imposed by the radar range scale in use; (iii) the effect or radar detection of the sea state, weather and other sources of interference; (iv) the possibility that small vessels, ice and other floating objects may not be detected by radar at an adequate range; (v) the number, location and movement of vessels detected by radar; (vi) the more exact assessment of the visibility that may be possible when radar is used to determine the range of vessels or other objects in the vicinity.[4]

[1] For the meaning of "vessel" in the Merchant Shipping (Distress Signals and Prevention of Collisions) Regulations 1983, S.I. 1983, No. 708, see para. 1.04, text and notes 15-17, *ante*.
[2] Merchant Shipping (Distress Signals and Prevention of Collisions) Regulations 1983, Sch. 1, r. 6. This rule is new, although the 1960 rules contained a rule requiring vessels to go at moderate speed in restricted visibility; see the Collision Regulations (Ships and Seaplanes on the Water) and Signals of Distress (Ships) Order 1965, S.I. 1965, No. 1525, r. 16 (revoked); and para. 2.13, text and note 4, *post*. For cases on the 1972 "safe speed" r. 6, see *The Sanshin Victory* [1980] 2 Lloyd's Rep. 359; *The Roseline* [1981] 2 Lloyd's Rep. 410; *The Maritime Harmony* [1982] 2 Lloyd's Rep. 400; *The Coral I* [1982] 1 Lloyd's Rep. 441. As to the power to make collision regulations, and their application to United Kingdom and other vessels, see paras. 1.04-1.08, *ante*. For a comparative table of the 1972 and 1960 Rules, see para. 6.06, *post*.
[3] Merchant Shipping (Distress Signals and Prevention of Collisions) Regulations 1983, Sch. 1, r. 6(a) (i)-(vi). These factors were considered in *The Maritime Harmony* [1982] 2 Lloyd's Rep. 400; *The Coral I* [1982] 1 Lloyd's Rep. 441.
[4] Merchant Shipping (Distress Signals and Prevention of Collisions) Regulations 1983, Sch. 1, r. 6(b) (i)-(vi). See also *The Fina Canada* [1962] 2 Lloyd's Rep. 113; *The Niceto de Larrinaga* [1963] 1 Lloyd's Rep. 205. As to the necessity to extend the radar range from time to time see *The Nassau* [1964] 2 Lloyd's Rep. 509. See further *The Marimar* [1968] 2 Lloyd's Rep. 165; *The Gannet* [1967] 1 Lloyd's Rep. 97; *The Bonifaz* [1967] 1 Lloyd's Rep. 321. See also para. 2.04, text and note 6, *post*.

2.03 *Risk of collision—Rule 7*

Every vessel[1] must use all available means appropriate to the prevailing circumstances and conditions to determine if risk of collision[2] exists.[3] If there is any doubt, such risk is deemed to exist.[4] Proper use must be made of radar equipment if fitted and operational,[5] including long-range scanning to obtain early warning of risk of collision and radar plotting or equivalent systematic observation of detected objects.[6] Assumptions must not be made on the basis of scanty information, especially scanty radar information.[7] In determining if risk of collision exists the following considerations must be among those taken into account: (i) the risk is to be deemed to exist if the compass bearing of an approaching vessel does not appreciably change; (ii) the risk may sometimes exist even when an appreciable bearing change is evident, particularly when approaching a very large vessel or a tow or when approaching a vessel at close range.[8]

[1] For the meaning of "vessel" in the Merchant Shipping (Distress Signals and Prevention of Collisions) Regulations 1983, S.I. 1983, No. 708, see para. 1.04, text and notes 15-17, *ante*.
[2] The courts have declined to lay down hard and fast rules for determining when risk of collision exists. "That must always be decided, according to the circumstances of each case, by men of nautical experience"; see *The Mangerton* (1856) Sw. 120, *per* Dr Lushington. "Risk of collision" means, it seems, a "chance", a "probability", a "strong" or "reasonable" probability of collision; see *The Cleopatra* (1856) Sw. 135; *The Ericsson* (1856) Sw. 38; *The Duke of Sussex* (1841) 1 W. Rob.

274; *The Dumfries* (1856) Sw. 63. Cf. a "possibility" of collision; see *The Ericsson, supra*, cf., *The Voorwaarts and The Khedive* (1880) 5 App. Cas. 876, *per* Lord Hatherley at p. 905; *General Steam Navigation Co.* v. *Mann* (1853) 14 C.B. 127, *per* Pollock, C.B., at p. 132. If the bearing of the other vessel remains constant for an appreciable period, the risk of collision amounts to a mathematical certainty if neither vessel alters her course or speed; *The City of Berlin* [1908] P. 110, C.A. The foregoing cases were decided on a provision which was worded differently; and see the text to notes 4, 8, *infra*.
[3] Merchant Shipping (Distress Signals and Prevention of Collisions) Regulations 1983, Sch. 1, r. 7(a). 1972 Rule 7 applies in any condition of visibility; ibid. r. 4. As to the power to make collision regulations, and their application to United Kingdom and other vessels, see paras. 1.04-1.08, *ante*.
[4] Ibid., Sch. 1, r. 7(a).
[5] As to the use of radar in keeping a look-out, see para 2.01, text and notes 11, 12, *ante*.
[6] Merchant Shipping (Distress Signals and Prevention of Collisions) Regulations 1983, Sch. 1, r. 7(b). 1972 Rule 7(b) was discussed in *The Roseline* [1981] 2 Lloyd's Rep. 410, at pp. 414-416. For a comparative table of the 1972 and the 1960 Rules, see para. 6.07, *post*.
[7] Merchant Shipping (Distress Signals and Prevention of Collisions) Regulations 1983, Sch. 1, r. 7(c). This provision is derived from Recommendation (1) of the Annex to the 1960 Rules contained in the First Schedule to the Collision Regulations (Ship and Seaplanes on the Water) and Signals of Distress (Ships) Order 1965, S.I. 1965, No. 1525 (revoked). See *The Evje* [1960] 2 Lloyd's Rep. 221; *The Toni* [1973] 1 Lloyd's Rep. 79.
[8] Merchant Shipping (Distress Signals and Prevention of Collisions) Regulations 1983, Sch. 1, r. 7(d). The first part of this Rule is derived from paragraph 2 of the Preliminary to Part D of the 1960 Rules.

2.04 *Action to avoid collision—Rule 8*

Any action taken to avoid collision must, if the circumstances of the case admit, be positive, made in ample time and with due regard to the observance of good seamanship.[1] Any alteration of course and/or speed to avoid collision must, if the circumstances of the case admit, be large enough to be readily apparent to another vessel[2] observing visually or by radar; a succession of small alterations of course and/or speed should be avoided.[3] If there is sufficient sea room, alteration of course alone may be the most effective action to avoid a close-quarters situation provided that it is made in good time, is substantial and does not result in another close-quarters situation.[4] Action taken to avoid collision with another vessel must be such as to result in passing at a safe distance.[5] The effectiveness of the action must be carefully checked until the other vessel is finally past and clear.[6] If necessary to avoid collision or allow more time to assess the situation, a vessel must slacken her speed or take all way off by stopping or reversing her means of propulsion.[7]

[1]Merchant Shipping (Distress Signals and Prevention of Collisions) Regulations 1983, S.I. 1983, No. 708, Sch. 1, r. 8(a). Rule 8 applies in any condition of visibility; r. 4. As to the power to make collision regulations, and their application to United Kingdom and other vessels, see paras. 1.04-1.08, *ante*. Rule 8(a) is derived from paragraph 1 of the Preliminary to the 1960 Steering and Sailing Rules (Part D) contained in the First Schedule to the Collision Regulations (Ships and Seaplanes on the Water) and Signals of Distress (Ships) Order 1965, S.I. 1965, No. 1525, (revoked) (which, however, applied only to vessels in sight of one another). For a comparative table of 1972 and 1960 Rules, see para. 6.08, *post*. For a recent case on the old rule, see *The Estrella* [1977] 1 Lloyd's Rep. 525. See also *The Toluca* [1981] 2 Lloyd's Rep. 548.
[2] For the meaning of "vessel" in the Merchant Shipping (Distress Signals and Prevention of Collisions) Regulations 1983, see para. 1.04, text and notes 15-17, *ante*. Alterations of course should leave no doubt as to the give-way vessel's intentions; see *The Billings Victory* (1949) 82 Ll.L.Rep. 877.

[3] Merchant Shipping (Distress Signals and Prevention of Collisions) Regulations 1983, Sch. 1, r. 8(b). See *The Sanshin Victory* [1980] 2 Lloyd's Rep. 359. Rule 8(b) is derived from Recommendations (5)(c) and (7) of the Annex to the 1960 Rules.
[4] Merchant Shipping (Distress Signals and Prevention of Collisions) Regulations 1983, Sch. 1, r. 8(c). This provision is derived from Recommendation (5)(a)-(d) of the Annex to the 1960 Rules. For the meaning of "close-quarters situation" see para. 2.13, note 9, *post*. The provisions of Rule 8(c), (d), (e) were referred to in *The Roseline* [1981] 2 Lloyd's Rep. 410.
[5] Ibid., Sch. 1, r. 8(d).
[6] Ibid., Sch. 1, r. 8(d). This provision is derived from Recommendation (4) of the Annex to the 1960 Rules. See further para. 2.02, note 4, *ante*.
[7] Merchant Shipping (Distress Signals and Prevention of Collisions) Regulations 1983, Sch. 1, r. 8(e). This provision is partly derived from Rule 23 and Recommendation (8) of the Annex to the 1960 Rules. 1972 Rule 8(e) must be read with rr. 6 (see para. 2.02, *ante*), 19(b) and (e) (see para. 2.13, *post*). For cases on the 1960 Rule 23, see *Stein and Others* v. *The Kathy K and S.N. No. 1, Egmont Towing and Sorting Ltd., Shields Navigation Ltd., Helsing and Iverson* (Can. Ct.) [1972] 2 Lloyd's Rep. 36; *The Frosta* [1973] 2 Lloyd's Rep. 348; *Alonso de Ojeda* (Owners) v. *Sestriere* (Owners) (*The Sestriere*) [1976] 1 Lloyd's Rep. 125; *The Estrella* [1977] 1 Lloyd's Rep. 325; *The Zaglebie Dabrowskie* (No. 1) [1978] 1 Lloyd's Rep. 564. See also *The Roseline* (*supra*).

2.05 *Narrow channels—Rule 9*

A vessel[1] proceeding along the course of a narrow channel or fairway[2] must keep as near to the outer limit of the channel or fairway which lies on her starboard side as is safe and practicable.[3] A vessel of less than 20 metres in length or a sailing vessel must not impede the passage of a vessel which can safely navigate only within a narrow channel or fairway.[4] A vessel engaged in fishing[5] must not impede the passage of any other vessel navigating within a narrow channel or fairway.[6] A vessel must not cross[7] a narrow channel or fairway if such crossing impedes the passage of a vessel which can safely navigate only within such channel or fairway.[8] The latter vessel may use the prescribed sound signal[9] if in doubt as to the intention of the crossing vessel.[10] In a narrow channel or fairway when overtaking can take place only if the vessel to be overtaken has to take action to permit safe passing, the vessel intending to overtake must indicate her intention by sounding the appropriate prescribed signal.[11] The vessel to be overtaken must, if in agreement, sound the appropriate prescribed signal[12] and take steps to permit safe passing.[13] This rule does not relieve the overtaking vessel of her obligation under the overtaking rule.[14] A vessel nearing a bend or an area of a narrow channel or fairway where other vessels may be obscured by an intervening obstruction must navigate with particular alertness and caution and must sound the appropriate prescribed signal.[15] Any vessel must, if the circumstances of the case admit, avoid anchoring in a narrow channel.[16] No specific provision is made as to vessels entering a narrow channel.[17]

[1] For the meaning of "vessel" in the Merchant Shipping (Distress Signals and Prevention of Collisions) Regulations 1983, S.I. 1983, No. 708, see para. 1.04, text and notes 15-17, *ante*. As to the power to make collision regulations, and their application to United Kingdom and other vessels, see paras. 1.04-1.08, *ante*.
[2] The meaning of "narrow channel" has been discussed in numerous cases concerning former regulations. Its length is immaterial and it may consist of the entrance between the piers of a harbour

or two lines of mooring buoys; see *The Kaiser Wilhelm der Grosse* [1907] P. 259, C.A., at pp. 263, 264, *per* Alverstone, C.J.: *The Wheatear* (1920) 3 Ll.L.Rep. 229; but see *The Treherbert* [1934] P. 31, C.A. (stretch of water open to an indefinite distance at one end not a narrow channel); *The Contractor* (1941) 69 Ll.L.Rep. 170 at p. 175, *per* Langton, J.; *The Kirsten Skou* (1950) 83 Ll.L.Rep. 279. A list of waters which have been held to be narrow channels is set out in *Halsbury's Laws of England*, 4th edn., vol. 43, para. 890. See, as to the Bosporus, *The Elazig* [1972] 1 Lloyd's Rep. 355; as to the River Maas, *The Adolf Leonhardt* [1973] 2 Lloyd's Rep. 318; and *The Oldekerk* [1974] 1 Lloyd's Rep. 95; as to the River Parana, *The Martin Fierro* [1974] 2 Lloyd's Rep. 203; (C.A.) [1975] 2 Lloyd's Rep. 130; as to the Irako Channel, *The Glenfalloch* [1979] 1 Lloyd's Rep. 247; as to the Eastham Channel, *The City of Leeds* [1978] 2 Lloyd's Rep. 346; as to the Mae Nam Chao Phraya, *The Toluca* [1981] 2 Lloyd's Rep. 548. A channel four miles wide has been held not to be a narrow channel; *The Anna Salen* [1954] 1 Lloyd's Rep. 475. "The fairway" has been defined (in relation to a local rule for the Thames) as "an open navigable passage used by vessels proceeding up and down a river or channel"; *The Blue Bell* [1895] P. 242 at p. 264, *per* Bruce, J. See also *The Clutha Boat* 147 [1909] P. 36; *The Zillah* [1929] P. 266; *The Crackshot* (1949) 82 Ll.L.Rep. 594; *The Lake Farragut* [1921] P. 305.

[3] Merchant Shipping (Distress Signals and Prevention of Collisions) Regulations 1983, Sch. 1, r. 9(a). This provision, which applies in any condition of visibility (r. 4), is derived from 1960 Rule 25(a) in the First Schedule to the Collision Regulations (Ships and Seaplanes on the Water) and Signals of Distress (Ships) Order 1965, S.I. 1965, No. 1525 (revoked). For a comparative table of the 1972 Rules and the 1960 Rules, see para. 6.09, *post*. Rule 25(a) of the 1960 Rules has been applied to harbours by local by-laws; see *The Koningin Juliana* [1973] 2 Lloyd's Rep. 308; (C.A.) [1974] 2 Lloyd's Rep. 353; (H.L.) [1975] 2 Lloyd's Rep. 111. See also *The Stella Antares* [1978] 1 Lloyd's Rep. 41. As to the meaning of "keep" in the former rule, see *The Mersey No. 30*, [1952] 2 Lloyd's Rep. 183, *per* Willmer, J. at p. 190; and *The Osprey* [1967] 1 Lloyd's Rep. 76; *The British Patrol* [1967] 2 Lloyd's Rep. 16, [1968] 1 Lloyd's Rep. 117, C.A. As to the qualifying words "safe and practicable", see *The Try Again* (1908) "Shipping Gazette", 2nd June. *The Unity* (1856) Sw. 101; *The Hand of Providence* (1856) Sw. 107; *The Nimrod* (1851) 15 Jur. 1201; *The Panther* (1853) 1 Sp. 31; *The Salford City* [1952] 1 Lloyd's Rep. 273. Full use of navigational equipment should be made to ensure that the vessel keeps to as near to the outer limit as is practicable; *The British Tenacity* [1963] 2 Lloyd's Rep. 1. For a case on the 1972 Rule 9(b), see *The Maritime Harmony* [1982] 2 Lloyd's Rep. 400.

[4] Merchant Shipping (Distress Signals and Prevention of Collisions) Regulations 1983, Sch. 1, r. 9(b). This provision is derived from rr. 20(b) and 25(c) of the 1960 Rules. As to the length of vessels see para. 2.06, note 19, *post*.

[5] "A vessel engaged in fishing" means any vessel fishing with nets, lines, trawls or other fishing apparatus which restrict manoeuvrability, but does not include a vessel fishing with trolling lines or other fishing apparatus which do not restrict manoeuvrability: Merchant Shipping (Distress Signals and Prevention of Collisions) Regulations 1983, Sch. 1, r. 3(d).

[6] Merchant Shipping (Distress Signals and Prevention of Collisions) Regulations 1983, Sch. 1, r. 9(c). This provision is derived from r. 26 of the 1960 Rules.

[7] Further rules as to crossing in traffic lanes are expounded in para. 2.06, text and note 10, *post*.

[8] Merchant Shipping (Distress Signals and Prevention of Collisions) Regulations 1983, Sch. 1, r. 9(d).

[9] I.e. the sound signal prescribed in ibid., r. 34(d); see para. 4.02, text and note 20, *post*.

[10] Ibid., Sch. 1, r. 9(d). This Rule is similar to numerous river by-laws and the rules of good seamanship.

[11] Ibid., Sch. 1, r. 9(e) (i). The appropriate signal is prescribed in r. 34(c) (i); see para. 4.02, text and note 18, *post*.

[12] I.e. the signal prescribed in ibid., r. 34(c)(ii); see para. 4.02, text and note 19, *post*.

[13] Ibid., Sch. 1, r. 9(e) (i). If in doubt she may sound the signal prescribed in r. 34(d) (see para. 4.02, text and note 20, *post*): Sch. 1, r. 9(e) (i).

[14] Ibid., Sch. 1, r. 9(e) (ii). As to the overtaking rule see r. 13, and para. 2.09, *post*.

[15] Ibid., Sch. 1, r. 9(f). The appropriate signal is prescribed in r. 34(e); see para. 4.02, text and notes 22, 23, *post*. Rule 9(f) is derived from r. 25(b) contained in the 1960 Rules. As to the precautions required by the rules of good seamanship when two vessels approach a bend from opposite directions see *The Trevethick* (1890) 6 Asp. M.L.C. 602.

[16] Merchant Shipping (Distress Signals and Prevention of Collisions) Regulations 1983, Sch. 1, r. 9(g). There are rules of good seamanship relating to anchoring in a fairway; see para. 1.14, *ante*.

[17] As to the rules of good seamanship which would be applied in such a situation see *The Canberra Star* [1962] 1 Lloyd's Rep. 24; *The Burton* (1908) 11 Asp. M.L.C. 203.

2.06 *Traffic Separation Schemes—Rules 1(d), 10*

Traffic separation schemes[1] may be adopted by IMO[2] for the purpose of the Rules.[3] Such schemes require implementation in English municipal law before they are binding upon Her Majesty's subjects.[4] The provisions described below apply to traffic separation schemes adopted by IMO. A vessel[5] using a traffic separation scheme must proceed in the appropriate traffic lane[6] in the general direction of traffic flow for that lane.[7] She must so far as practicable keep clear of a traffic separation line or separation zone;[8] and she must normally join or leave a traffic lane at the termination of the lane, but when joining or leaving from the side she must do so at as small an angle to the general direction of traffic flow as practicable.[9] A vessel must so far as practicable avoid crossing traffic lanes, but if obliged to do so must cross as nearly as practicable at right angles to the general direction of traffic flow.[10] Inshore traffic zones[11] must not normally be used by through traffic which can safely use the appropriate traffic lane within the adjacent traffic separation scheme, although vessels of less than 20 metres in length and sailing vessels may under all circumstances use inshore traffic zones.[12] A vessel, other than a crossing vessel or a vessel joining or leaving a lane must not normally enter a separation zone or cross a separation line except (i) in cases of emergency to avoid immediate danger; and (ii) to engage in fishing[13] within a separation zone.[14] A vessel navigating in areas near the terminations of traffic separation schemes must do so with particular caution.[15] A vessel must so far as practicable avoid anchoring in a traffic separation scheme or in areas near its terminations.[16] A vessel not using a traffic separation scheme must avoid it by as wide a margin as is practicable.[17] A vessel engaged in fishing must not impede the passage of any vessel following a traffic lane.[18] A vessel of less than 20 metres in length[19] or a sailing vessel[20] must not impede the passage of a power-driven vessel[21] following a traffic lane.[22] A vessel restricted in her ability to manoeuvre[23] when engaged in an operation for the maintenance of safety of navigation in a traffic separation scheme is exempted from Rule 10 to the extent necessary to carry out the operation;[24] it is also exempt, and to the same extent, when engaged in an operation for the laying, servicing or picking up of a submarine cable, within a traffic separation scheme.[25]

[1] The expression "traffic separation scheme" is not defined in the Merchant Shipping (Distress Signals and Prevention of Collisions) Regulations 1983, S.I. 1983, No. 708, but is explained by IMO as meaning a scheme which separates traffic proceeding in opposite or nearly opposite directions by the use of a separation zone or line, traffic lanes or by other means; IMO Resolution A.284 (viii). The use of the word "normally" in this paragraph implies that there may be overriding circumstances which justify non-observance, such as the need to obey another Rule.
[2] As to IMO see para. 1.03, *ante.*
[3] Merchant Shipping (Distress Signals and Prevention of Collisions) Regulations 1983, Sch. 1, r. 1(d). The reference to "the Rules" means the International Regulations for Preventing Collisions at Sea 1972 which are set out in Schedule 1 to the 1983 regulations.
[4] See para. 1.02, *ante.* The traffic separation scheme Rule (r. 10) applies in all conditions of visibility (r. 4) and, it is thought, applies whether or not any other ship is in the vicinity. A substantial number of prosecutions have been brought for breaches of the schemes set out in the Collision Regulations

(Traffic Separation Schemes) Order 1972, S.I. 1972, No. 809 (revoked) and those within the scope of 1972 Rule 10. As to the schemes which are binding in English law as part of the collision regulations, see para. 2.07, *infra*. As to the application of traffic separation schemes which have merely the force of recommendations, see *The Estrella* [1977] 1 Lloyd's Rep. 525; *The Genimar* [1977] 2 Lloyd's Rep. 17; *The Zaglebie Dabrowskie* (No. 1) [1978] 1 Lloyd's Rep. 564. As to the power to make collision regulations, and their application to United Kingdom and other vessels, see paras. 1.04-1.08, *ante*.

[5] For the meaning of "vessel" in the Merchant Shipping (Distress Signals and Prevention of Collisions) Regulations 1983, see para. 1.04, text and notes 15-17, *ante*.

[6] "Traffic lane" is explained by IMO as meaning an area within definite limits inside which one-way traffic is established; see IMO Resolution A.284 (VIII).

[7] Merchant Shipping (Distress Signals and Prevention of Collisions) Regulations 1983, Sch. 1, r. 10(b) (i). In some cases the outer limits of lanes are not parallel to each other and the general direction of flow may legitimately vary through a substantial arc. Compare the Collision Regulations (Traffic Separation Schemes) Order 1972, Sch., reg. 3 (revoked). For a comparative table of the old and new separation rules, see para. 6.10, *post*.

[8] Merchant Shipping (Distress Signals and Prevention of Collisions) Regulations 1983, Sch. 1, r. 10(b) (ii). IMO has explained a "separation zone or line" as meaning a zone or line separating traffic proceeding in one direction from traffic proceeding in another direction; IMO Resolution A.284 (VIII). A separation zone may also be used to separate a traffic lane from the adjacent inshore traffic zone; ibid., A.284 (VIII).

[9] Merchant Shipping (Distress Signals and Prevention of Collisions) Regulations, Sch. 1, r. 10(b) (iii).

[10] Ibid., r. 10(c). This provision is derived from the Collision Regulations (Traffic Separation Schemes) Order 1972, Sch., reg. 5 (revoked). See para. 6.10, *post*. It is thought that this provision requires that the course made good, rather than the course laid off, must be as nearly as possible at right angles to the general direction of traffic flow. There may be circumstances in which a right angle course cannot be made good or in which departure from it is justified by the need to observe some other Rule. As to vessels crossing narrow channels or fairways see para. 2.05, text and notes 7, 8, *ante*.

[11] "Inshore traffic zones" are explained by IMO as meaning designated areas between the landward boundary of a traffic separation scheme and the adjacent coast intended for coastal traffic; see IMO Resolution A.284 (VIII).

[12] Merchant Shipping (Distress Signals and Prevention of Collisions) Regulations 1983, Sch. 1, r. 10(d). There is considerable doubt as to the meaning of "through traffic", particularly where one traffic separation scheme adjoins another. The Department of Transport has issued guidance on this point; see M.1029, para. 8.06, *post*.

[13] For the meaning of "vessel engaged in fishing" see para. 2.05, note 5, *ante*.

[14] Merchant Shipping (Distress Signals and Prevention of Collisions) Regulations 1983, Sch. 1, r. 10(e). This provision is derived from the Collision Regulations (Traffic Separation Schemes) Order 1972, Sch., reg. 4 (revoked); see para. 6.10, *post*.

[15] Ibid., Sch. 1, r. 10(f).

[16] Ibid., Sch. 1, r. 10(g).

[17] Ibid., Sch. 1, r. 10(h).

[18] Ibid., Sch. 1, r. 10(i). It would appear from the wording of this rule that there is no absolute prohibition on fishing in a traffic lane, but that a vessel engaged in fishing must not impede the passage of vessels using the lane. This rule overrides r. 18; see para. 2.12, *post*.

[19] The "length" of a vessel means her length overall; ibid., Sch. 1, r. 3(j).

[20] A "sailing vessel" means any vessel under sail provided that propelling machinery, if fitted, is not being used; ibid., Sch. 1, r. 3(c).

[21] A "power-driven vessel" means any vessel propelled by machinery; ibid., Sch. 1, r. 3(b).

[22] Ibid., Sch. 1, r. 10(j). The Department of Transport has issued guidance on the observance of Traffic Separation Schemes; see Merchant Shipping Notice No. M.834; see para. 8.05, *post*; see also "Ships' Routeing," published by IMO. For an unsuccessful attempt to claim damages from the Crown on the ground that the Canadian Department of Transport was negligent in implementing a traffic separation scheme see *The Irish Stardust* [1977] 1 Lloyd's Rep. 195.

[23] For the meaning of "vessel restricted in her ability to manoeuvre", see para. 2.12, note 9, *post*.

[24] Merchant Shipping (Distress Signals and Prevention of Collisions) Regulations 1983, Sch. 1, r. 10(k).

[25] Ibid., Sch. 1, r. 10(l). This provision and r. 10(k) are new to the 1983 regulations, implementing IMO Resolution A.464 (XII).

2.07 *Separation schemes currently in force*

As has been explained, the traffic separation schemes which are binding upon United Kingdom vessels[1] as part of the collision regulations are those which have been both adopted by IMO and implemented in English law.[2] The Merchant Shipping (Distress Signals and Prevention of Collisions) Regulations 1983[3] provide that the schemes in question are those specified as adopted by IMO in Admiralty Notices to Mariners Number 17 of 1983 and documents amending the schemes.[4] Notice Number 17 is reprinted in Appendix II to this work. The details of IMO schemes are set out in detail in the IMO resolutions adopting them[5] and printed on the Admiralty charts.[6] Schemes which are not adopted by IMO or which are not specified in Notice Number 17 may nevertheless be enforceable in civil cases as representing rules of good seamanship.[7] Where the schemes lie within the territorial waters of foreign States, United Kingdom vessels may be subject to them as part of the municipal law of those States.[8]

Admiralty Notice No. 17 specifies numerous schemes, both IMO and national. The IMO schemes are marked with an asterisk in Notice No. 17 and affect parts of the British Isles, including the English Channel and western part of the southern North Sea;[9] the USSR, north coast, Norway, Faeroe Islands and Iceland;[10] the Baltic Sea;[11] the North Sea and north and west coasts of Denmark, Germany, Netherlands and Belgium;[12] France and Spain, north and west coasts, and Portugal;[13] the Mediterranean and Black Seas;[14] the Red Sea, Arabia, Iraq and Iran;[15] the Indian Ocean, Pakistan, India, Sri Lanka, Bangladesh and Burma;[16] Malacca Strait, Singapore Strait and Sumatera;[17] Korea and the Pacific Coasts of USSR;[18] Australia and Papua New Guinea;[19] the Aleutian Islands, Alaska and west coast of North America, including Mexico;[20] west coasts of Central and South America;[21] east coast of North America and Greenland.[22]

[1]For the meaning of "United Kingdom vessel" see para. 1.07, text and note 2, *ante*. The collision regulations may also be enforceable in English courts against other vessels; see para. 1.08, *ante*.
[2] See paras. 1.02, 2.06, text and note 4, *ante*.
[3] S.I. 1983, No 708.
[4] Ibid., art. 1(2) (b). Any reference in the Merchant Shipping (Distress Signals and Prevention of Collisions) Regulations 1983, to the traffic separation schemes adopted by IMO is to be treated as a reference to the schemes specified in Notice to Mariners No. 17 of 1983 having been so adopted and includes a reference to any document amending those schemes which is considered by the Secretary of State to be relevant from time to time and specified in a Notice to Mariners; ibid., reg. 1(2)(b). The schemes and the law relating to them are thus in a constant state of flux. As to the power of the Secretary of State to alter the law in this way, see para. 1.04, text and notes 6-11, *ante*. As to the Secretary of State, see para. 5.01, *post*.
[5] Such resolutions, being obligations of the United Kingdom, can presumably be admitted in evidence if certified by a Secretary of State; cf., *Post Office* v. *Estuary Radio* [1967] 3 All E.R. 663; *The Fagernes* [1927] P. 311, C.A. See the IMO Guide to Ships Routeing which is revised from time to time and contains full details of IMO adopted schemes.
[6] As to the Admiralty chart, see para. 5.17, *post*.
[7] See para. 2.06, note 4, *ante*.
[8] See para. 1.07, text and note 12, *ante*.

[9] See Admiralty Notice to Mariners No. 17 of 1983, List of Traffic Separation Schemes, paras. 7.07-7.15, 7.18-7.21, 7.23, *post.* As to the schemes relating to the British Isles, see para. 7.07, *post.*
[10] See para. 7.08, *post.*
[11] See para. 7.09, *post.*
[12] See para. 7.10, *post.*
[13] See para. 7.11, *post.*
[14] See para. 7.12, *post.*
[15] See para. 7.13, *post.*
[16] See para. 7.14, *post.*
[17] See para. 7.15, *post.*
[18] See para. 7.18, *post.*
[19] See para. 7.19, *post.*
[20] See para. 7.20, *post.*
[21] See para. 7.21, *post.*
[22] See para. 7.23, *post.* The Department of Transport has issued "M" Notices on the Observance of Traffic Separation Schemes (M.834) and on Safe Navigation in the Dover Strait (M.1029). See paras. 8.05, 8.06, *post.*

SECT. (2) Conduct of vessels in sight of one another

2.08 Sailing vessels—Rule 12

When two sailing vessels[1] are approaching one another, so as to involve risk of collision,[2] one of them must keep out of the way of the other as follows: when each has the wind on a different side, the vessel which has the wind on the port side must keep out of the way of the other;[3] when both have the wind on the same side, the vessel which is to windward must keep out of the way of the vessel which is to leeward;[4] if a vessel with the wind on the port side sees a vessel to windward and cannot determine with certainty whether the other vessel has the wind on the port or on the starboard side, she must keep out of the way of the other.[5] For the purpose of the Rule the windward side is deemed to be the side opposite to that on which the mainsail is carried or, in the case of a square-rigged vessel, the side opposite to that on which the largest fore-and-aft sail is carried.[6] This Rule and the Rules described in the remaining paragraphs of this Section apply to vessels in sight of one another.[7] Vessels are deemed to be in sight on one another only when one can be observed visually from the other.[8]

[1] For the meaning of "sailing vessel" see para. 2.06, note 20, *ante.* For the meaning of "vessel" see para. 1.04, text and notes 15-17, *ante.*
[2] For the meaning of "risk of collision" see para. 2.03, note 2, *ante.*
[3] Merchant Shipping (Distress Signals and Prevention of Collisions) Regulations 1983, S.I. 1983, No. 708, Sch. 1, r. 12(a) (i). This provision is derived from 1960 Rule 17(a) (i) contained in the First Schedule to the Collision Regulations (Ships and Seaplanes on the Water) and Signals of Distress (Ships) Order 1965, S.I. 1965, No. 1525 (revoked); for a comparative table of the 1972 and the 1960 Rules, see para. 6.12, *post.* As to the power to make collision regulations, and their application to United Kingdom and other vessels, see paras. 1.04-1.08, *ante.*
[4] Ibid., Sch. 1, r. 12(a) (ii). This provision is derived from 1960 Rule 17(a) (ii) (revoked); see para. 6.12, *post.*
[5] Ibid., Sch. 1, r. 12(a) (iii). This provision is not derived from any previous Rule. Rule 12 must be read subject to Rules 13 and 17 in the First Schedule to the Merchant Shipping (Distress Signals and Prevention of Collisions) Regulations 1983; as to those Rules see paras. 2.09, 2.11, *post.* See also *The Annie* [1909] P. 176.

[6] Merchant Shipping (Distress Signals and Prevention of Collisions) Regulations 1983, Sch. 1, r. 12(b). This provision is derived from 1960 Rule 17(b); see para. 6.12, *post*.
[7] Ibid., Sch. 1, r. 11. See further Rules 13-18, paras. 2.09-2.12, *post*.
[8] Ibid., Sch. 1, r. 3(k).

2.09 *Overtaking—Rule 13*

Any vessel[1] overtaking any other must keep out of the way of the vessel being overtaken.[2] A vessel is deemed to be overtaking when coming up with another vessel from a direction more than 22.5 degrees abaft her beam, i.e. in such a position with reference to the vessel she is overtaking that at night she would be able to see only the sternlight of that vessel but neither of her sidelights.[3] When a vessel is in any doubt as to whether she is overtaking another, she must assume that this is the case and act accordingly.[4] Any subsequent alteration of the bearing between the two vessels must not make the overtaking vessel a crossing vessel,[5] or relieve her of the duty of keeping clear of the overtaken vessel until she is finally past and clear.[6]

[1] For the meaning of "vessel" see para. 1.04, text and notes 15-17, *ante*.
[2] Merchant Shipping (Distress Signals and Prevention of Collisions) Regulations 1983, S.I. 1983, No. 708, Sch. 1, r. 13(a). As to the power to make collision regulations, and their application to United Kingdom and other vessels, see paras. 1.04-1.08, *ante*. Rule 13(a) is derived from 1960 Rule 24(a) in the First Schedule to the Collision Regulations (Ships and Seaplanes on the Water) and Signals of Distress (Ships) Order 1965, S.I. 1965, No. 1525, r. 24 (revoked). For a comparative table of the 1972 and the 1960 Rules, see para. 6.13, *post*. Rule 13 of the 1972 Rules applies to vessels in sight of one another (see para. 2.08, text and notes 7-8, *ante*) and applies notwithstanding anything contained in the 1972 Rules, Part B, sections I, II (i.e. rr. 4-18); r. 13(a). As to such Rules see paras. 2.01-2.08, *ante*, 2.10-2.12, *post*. When Rule 13 applies, the ships should not be allowed to approach so closely as to bring the forces of interaction into existence; see *The Queen Mary* (1949) 82 Ll.L.Rep. 303, *per* Lord Porter at p. 315.
[3] Merchant Shipping (Distress Signals and Prevention of Collisions) Regulations 1983, Sch. 1, r. 13(b). This provision is derived from 1960 Rule 24(b) (revoked); see para. 6.13, *post*. It seems that for a ship to be "overtaking", she must be "coming up with," i.e., going faster, than the ship ahead; see *The Franconia* (1876) 2 P.D. 8, C.A., *per* Lord Herschell at p. 12; *The Main* (1886) 11 P.D. 132, at p. 139.
[4] Merchant Shipping (Distress Signals and Prevention of Collisions) Regulations 1983, Sch. 1, r. 13(c). This provision is derived from 1960 Rule 24(c) (revoked); see para. 6.13, *post*. It was formerly held that the overtaking rule did not apply until the moment at which there would be danger of collision if either ship does something contrary to the rules; see *The Manchester Regiment* [1938] P. 17; but it has now been held that the rule may apply before the risk of collision arises, provided that there is an element of proximity; *The Nowy Sacz* [1976] 2 Lloyd's Rep. 682; (C.A.) [1977] 2 Lloyd's Rep. 91; [1979] Q.B. 236. For other cases on the 1960 overtaking rule, see *The Frosta* [1973] 2 Lloyd's Rep. 348; *The Auriga* [1977] 1 Lloyd's Rep. 384; *The Kylix and Rustringen* [1979] 1 Lloyd's Rep. 123. For a case on 1972 Rule 13, see *The Telendos* (Can. Ct. of Appeal) 28th April 1982.
[5] I.e. a crossing vessel within the meaning of the 1972 Rules. As to the crossing situation see para. 2.10, *post*.
[6] Merchant Shipping (Distress Signals and Prevention of Collisions) Regulations 1983, Sch. 1, r. 13(d). This provision is derived from 1960 Rule 24(b) (revoked); see para. 6.13, *post*.

2.10 *Head-on situation—Rule 14. Crossing situation—Rule 15*

When two power-driven vessels[1] are meeting on reciprocal or nearly reciprocal courses[2] so as to involve risk of collision[3] each must alter her course to starboard so that each must pass on the port side of the other.[4] Such a situation is deemed to exist when a vessel sees the other ahead or nearly ahead and by night she could see the mast-head lights of the other in a line or nearly in line and/or both sidelights and by day she observes the corresponding aspect of the other vessel.[5] When a vessel is in any doubt as to whether such a situation exists, she must assume that it does exist and act accordingly.[6]

When two power-driven vessels are crossing[7] so as to involve risk of collision, the vessel which has the other on her own starboard side must keep out of the way and must, if the circumstances of the case admit, avoid crossing ahead of the other vessel.[8]

[1] For the meaning of "power-driven vessel" see para. 2.06, note 21, *ante*. For the meaning of "vessel" see para. 1.04, text and notes 15-17, *ante*.
[2] The reference to "reciprocal courses" is new to the 1972 Rules. Rule 18 of the 1960 Rules in the First Schedule to the Collision Regulations (Ships and Seaplanes on the Water) and Signals of Distress (Ships) Order 1965, S.I. 1965, No. 1525 (revoked) referred to vessel meeting "end-on", as did earlier collision regulations. Cases on the meaning of "end-on" may not now be authoritative as to the meaning of "on reciprocal course", especially in view of the new guidelines expounded in the text to notes 5, 6, *infra*. However, the old principle that it is the aspect of the vessel, rather than the course made good which is relevant, may still apply. It seems that when a vessel is not on any definite course, she is not "crossing"; see *The Savina* [1975] 2 Lloyd's Rep. 141, [1976] 2 Lloyd's Rep. 123, H.L.; and see *Alonso de Ojeda (Owners)* v. *Sestriere (Owners) (The Sestriere)* [1976] 1 Lloyd's Rep. 125.
[3] For the meaning of "risk of collision" see para. 2.03, note 2, *ante*.
[4] Merchant Shipping (Distress Signals and Prevention of Collisions) Regulations 1983, S.I. 1983, No. 708, Sch. 1, r. 14(a). This rule which applies to vessels in sight of one another (see para. 2.08, text and notes 7, 8, *ante*), is derived from the first part of 1960 Rule 18(a) (revoked); for a comparative table of the 1972 Rules and the 1960 Rule, see para. 6.14, *post*. As to the power to make collision regulations, and their application to United Kingdom and other vessels, see paras. 1.04-1.08, *ante*.
[5] Ibid., Sch. 1, r. 14(b). This provision is derived from the second part of 1960 Rule 18(a) (revoked).
[6] Ibid., Sch. 1, r. 14(c).
[7] It can sometimes be difficult to determine whether ships are overtaking, crossing or head-on; see *The Franconia* (1876) 2 P.D. 6 C.A.; *The Peckforton Castle* (1878) 3 P.D. 11, C.A.; *The Breadalbane* (1881) 7 P.D. 186; *The Seaton* (1883) 9 P.D. 1. See also *The Nassau* [1964] 2 Lloyd's Rep. 509; *The Statue of Liberty* [1971] 2 Lloyd's Rep. 277, H.L.; *The Homer* [1972] 1 Lloyd's Rep. 429; *The Nowy Sacz* [1976] 2 Lloyd's Rep. 682; *The Auriga* [1977] 1 Lloyd's Rep. 384; *The Estrella* [1977] 1 Lloyd's Rep. 525; *The Genimar* [1977] 2 Lloyd's Rep. 17; *The Diego Silang (Owners)* v. *The Vysotsk (Owners) (The Vysotsk)* [1981] 1 Lloyd's Rep. 439. Where there is a conflict between the overtaking rule and the crossing rule, the former prevails; see para. 2.09, note 2, *ante*.
[8] Merchant Shipping (Distress Signals and Prevention of Collisions) Regulations 1983, Sch. 1, r. 15. This rule applies to vessels in sight of one another; see para. 2.08, text and notes 7, 8, *ante*. Rule 15 comes into operation when two vessels, which are not on reciprocal courses, are likely to reach the same point simultaneously if each continues as expected; see *The Pekin* [1897] A.C. 532, P.C., at p. 536; *The Albano* [1907] A.C. 193, P.C.; *The Fancy* [1917] P. 13; *The Tojo Maru* [1968] 1 Lloyd's Rep. 365. See also *Owners S.S. Haugland* v. *Owners S.S. Karamea* [1922] 1 A.C. 68, H.L.; *The Leverington* (1886) 11 P.D. 117, C.A.; *The Chittagong* [1901] A.C. 597, P.C. Cf., *The Red Cross* (1906) 10 Asp. M.C. 521; *The Ashton* [1905] P. 21; *The Ada, The Sappho* (1873) 2 Asp. M.C. 4; *The Roanoke* [1908] P. 231, C.A.; *The Treherbert* [1934] P. 31, C.A.; *The Kirsten Skou* (1950) 83 Ll.L.Rep. 279. A vessel lying stationary at sea is not under an obligation to keep out of the way under this rule; *The Devotion II* (Sc. Ct.) [1979] 1 Lloyd's Rep. 509; but a vessel wrongly carrying "not under command" lights and making way must abide by the rule; *The Djerada* [1976] 1 Lloyd's Rep. 50; (C.A.) [1976] 2 Lloyd's Rep. 40. Rule 15 is derived from 1960 Rules 19 and 22 (revoked); for the comparative table, see para. 6.15, *post*. There are special rules for crossing narrow channels and traffic lanes; see paras. 2.05, text and notes 7-10, 2.06, text and note 10, *ante*.

2.11 *Action by give-way vessel—Rule 16. Action by stand-on vessel—Rule 17*

Every vessel[1] which is directed to keep out of the way of another vessel[2] must, so far as possible, take early and substantial action to keep well clear.[3]

Where one of two vessels is to keep out of the way, the other must keep her course and speed.[4] However, the latter vessel may take action to avoid collision by her manoeuvre alone, as soon as it becomes apparent to her that the vessel required to keep out of the way is not taking appropriate action in compliance with the Rules.[5] When, from any cause, the vessel required to keep her course and speed finds herself so close that collision cannot be avoided by the action of the give-way vessel alone, she must take such action as will best aid to avoid the collision.[6] A power-driven vessel[7] which takes action in a crossing situation as mentioned above[8] to avoid collision with another power-driven vessel must, if the circumstances of the case admit, not alter course to port for a vessel on her own port side.[9] This Rule does not relieve the give-way vessel of her obligation to keep out of the way.[10]

---

[1] For the meaning of "vessel" see para. 1.04, text and notes 15-17, *ante*.
[2] I.e. required to keep out of the way of another vessel by the Merchant Shipping (Distress Signals and Prevention of Collisions) Regulations 1983, S.I. 1983, No. 708, Sch. 1, rr. 12, 13, 15, 18; as to which see paras. 2.08, 2.09, 2.10, text and notes 7, 8, *ante*, 2.12, *post*.
[3] Merchant Shipping (Distress Signals and Prevention of Collisions) Regulations 1983, Sch. 1, r. 16. This Rule, which applies to vessels in sight of one another (see para. 2.08, text and notes 7, 8, *ante*), is derived from part of 1960 Rule 22 contained in the First Schedule to the Collision Regulations (Ships and Seaplanes on the Water) and Signals of Distress (Ships) Order 1965, S.I. 1965, No. 1525 (revoked); see para. 6.13, *post*. As to the power to make collision regulations, and their application to United Kingdom and other vessels, see paras. 1.04-1.08, *ante*. As to responsibilities between vessels see para. 2.12, *post*. For cases on 1960 Rule 22, see *The Statue of Liberty* [1971] 2 Lloyd's Rep. 277 (H.L.); *The Homer* [1972] 1 Lloyd's Rep. 429; (C.A.) [1973] 1 Lloyd's Rep. 501; *Stein and Others* v. *The Kathy K and S.N. No. 1, Egmont Towing and Sorting Ltd., Shields Navigation Ltd., Kelsing and Iverson* (Can. Ct.) [1972] 2 Lloyd's Rep. 36; *The Toni* [1973] 1 Lloyd's Rep. 79; (C.A.) [1974] 1 Lloyd's Rep. 489; *The Savina* [1974] 2 Lloyd's Rep. 317; (C.A.) [1975] 2 Lloyd's Rep. 141; (H.L.) [1976] 2 Lloyd's Rep. 123; *The Estrella* [1977] 1 Lloyd's Rep. 525; see also *The Vysotsk* [1981] 1 Lloyd's Rep. 439. For a comparative table of 1972 Rule 16 and 1960 Rule 22, see para. 6.16, *post*. For Department of Transport guidance on keeping out of the way of dynamically positioned vessels, see M.895, para. 8.07, *post*.
[4] Merchant Shipping (Distress Signals and Prevention of Collisions) Regulations 1983, Sch. 1, r. 17(a) (i). This provision, and that in r. 17(b) (see *infra*.), are derived from Rule 21 of the 1960 Rules. For a comparative table of 1972 Rule 17 and 1960 Rule 16, see para. 6.17, *post*. Rule 17 applies to vessels in sight of one another; see para. 2.08, text and notes 7, 8, *ante*. "Course and speed" means the course and speed in following the nautical manoeuvre in which, to the knowledge of the other vessel, the vessel is at the time engaged; see *The Roanoke* [1908] P. 231, C.A., *per* Alverstone, C.J., at p. 239; *The Echo* [1971] P. 132; *S.S. Whitburn* v. *S.S. Hugo Toelle* (1931) S.L.T. 394; *The Taunton* (1929) 31 Ll.L.Rep. 119; *The Statue of Liberty* [1971] 2 Lloyd's Rep. 277. Cf., *The Manchester Regiment* [1938] P. 117. For further cases on 1960 Rule 17 see *The Homer* [1972] 1 Lloyd's Rep. 429; (C.A.) [1973] 1 Lloyd's Rep. 501; *The Carebeka I* [1973] 1 Lloyd's Rep. 396; *The Toni* [1973] 1 Lloyd's Rep. 79; (C.A.) [1974] 1 Lloyd's Rep. 489; *The Savina* [1974] 2 Lloyd's Rep. 317; (C.A.) [1975] 2 Lloyd's Rep. 141; (H.L.) [1976] 2 Lloyd's Rep. 123; *The Nowy Sacz* [1976] 2 Lloyd's Rep. 682; (C.A.) [1977] 2 Lloyd's Rep. 91; [1979] Q.B. 236; *The Estrella* [1977] 1 Lloyd's Rep. 525; *The Genimar* [1977] 2 Lloyd's Rep. 17; *The Auriga* [1977] 1 Lloyd's Rep. 384; *The Kylix and Rustringen* [1979] 1 Lloyd's Rep. 133; *The Devotion II* (Sc. Ct.) [1979] 1 Lloyd's Rep. 509; *The Vysotsk* [1981] 1 Lloyd's Rep. 439.

[5] Merchant Shipping (Distress Signals and Prevention of Collisions) Regulations 1983, Sch. 1, r. 17(a)(ii). This provision was not found in previous collision regulations. It enables the stand-on vessel to take avoiding action before the danger becomes so acute as to bring into operation r. 17(b), described *infra*.
[6] Ibid., Sch. 1, r. 17(b). In view of the qualification in r. 17(a) (ii), discussed *supra*, the many cases decided under former regulations, whereby it was held that the stand-on vessel must continue to keep her course and speed until a collision can no longer be avoided by the give-way vessel alone, are probably no longer of authority. If the stand-on vessel does have to alter course under r. 17(b), she must generally alter course by the minimum amount necessary; *The Saragossa* (1892) 7 Asp. M.C. 289. Cf., *The Wooda* (1915) 31 T.L.R. 222; *The Inkula* (1921) 9 Ll.L.Rep. 264 ;*The Valonia* (1938) 60 Ll.L.Rep. 314.
[7] For the meaning of "power-driven vessel" see para. 2.06, note 21, *ante*.
[8] I.e. under the Merchant Shipping (Distress Signals and Prevention of Collisions) Regulations 1983, Sch. 1, r. 17(a) (ii); see the text and note 5, *supra*.
[9] Ibid., Sch. 1, r. 17(c). This provision was new to the 1972 Rules and was not found in previous regulations.
[10] Ibid., Sch. 1, r. 17(d).

2.12 *Responsibilities between vessels—Rule 18*

The provisions described in this paragraph have effect except where the narrow channel rule,[1] traffic separation schemes[2] or the overtaking rule[3] otherwise require.[4] A power-driven vessel[5] underway[6] must keep out of the way[7] of a vessel not under command,[8] a vessel restricted in her ability to manoeuvie,[9] a vessel engaged in fishing[10] and a sailing vessel.[11] A sailing vessel underway must keep out of the way of a vessel not under command, a vessel restricted in her ability to manoeuvre and a vessel engaged in fishing.[12] A vessel engaged in fishing when underway must, so far as possible, keep out of the way of a vessel not under command and a vessel restricted in her ability to manoeuvre.[13] Any vessel other than a vessel not under command or a vessel restricted in her ability to manoeuvre must, if the circumstances of the case admit, avoid impeding the safe passage of a vessel constrained by her draught,[14] exhibiting the prescribed signals.[15] A vessel constrained by her draught must navigate with particular caution having full regard to her special condition.[16]

A seaplane[17] on the water must, in general, keep well clear of all vessels and avoid impeding their navigation.[18] However, in circumstances where risk of collision exists,[19] she must comply with the rules for vessels in sight of one another.[20]

[1] As to the narrow channel rule (Rule 9) see para. 2.05, *ante*.
[2] As to traffic separation schemes (Rule 10) see paras. 2.06, 2.07, *ante*.
[3] As to the overtaking rule (Rule 13) see para. 2.09, *ante*.
[4] See the Merchant Shipping (Distress Signals and Prevention of Collisions) Regulations 1983, S.I. 1983, No. 708, Sch. 1, r. 18. This rule applies to vessels in sight of one another; see para. 2.08, text and notes 7-8, *ante*. As to the power to make collision regulations, and their application to United Kingdom and other vessels, see paras. 1.04-1.08, *ante*.
[5] For the meaning of "power-driven vessel" see para. 2.06, note 21, *ante*. For the meaning of "vessel" see para. 1.04, text and notes 15-17, *ante*.
[6] When a vessel is "underway", it is meant that the vessel is not at anchor, or made fast to the shore, or aground: see the Merchant Shipping (Distress Signals and Prevention of Collisions) Regulations 1983, Sch. 1, r. 3(i). For the meaning of "at anchor" and "aground" see para. 3.09, notes 1, 9, *post*.

There are numerous authorities on the meaning of "underway" in former regulations; see, e.g., *The Deutschland* (1920) 3 Ll.L.Rep. 96; *The Esk and The Gitana* (1869) L.R. 2 A. & E. 350; *The Romance* [1901] P. 15; *The Devonian* [1901] P. 221, C.A.

[7] As to the danger of interaction see para. 2.09, note 2, *ante*.

[8] "Vessel not under command" means a vessel which through some exceptional circumstance is unable to manoeuvre as required by the rules and is therefore unable to keep out of the way of another vessel: Merchant Shipping (Distress Signals and Prevention of Collisions) Regulations 1983, Sch. 1, r. 3(f); see also *The P. Capland* [1893] A.C. 207 H.L.; *S.S. Mendip Range* v. *Radcliffe* [1921] 1 A.C. 556, H.L.; *The Albion* [1952] 1 Lloyd's Rep. 38; [1953] 1 Lloyd's Rep. 239, C.A.

[9] "Vessel restricted in her ability to manoeuvre" means a vessel which from the nature of her work is restricted in her ability to manoeuvre as required by the rules and is therefore unable to keep out of the way of another vessel: Merchant Shipping (Distress Signals and Prevention of Collisions) Regulations 1983, Sch. 1, r. 3(g). The following vessels are to be regarded as vessels restricted in their ability to manoeuvre: a vessel engaged in laying, servicing or picking up a navigation mark, submarine cable or pipeline; a vessel engaged in dredging, surveying or underwater operations; a vessel engaged in replenishment or transferring persons, provisions or cargo while underway; a vessel engaged in the launching or recovery of aircraft; a vessel engaged in minesweeping operations; a vessel engaged in a towing operation such as severely restricts the towing vessel and her tow in their ability to deviate from their course: ibid., Sch. 1, r. 3(g) (i)-(vi). For Department of Transport guidance on the application of the collision regulations to dynamically positioned vessels and the dangers to divers operating from such vessels, see M.895, para. 8.07, *post*.

[10] For the meaning of "vessel engaged in fishing" see para. 2.05, note 5, *ante*.

[11] Merchant Shipping (Distress Signals and Prevention of Collisions) Regulations 1983, Sch. 1, r. 18(a) (i)-(iv). For the meaning of "sailing vessel" see para. 2.06, note 20, *ante*.

[12] Ibid., Sch. 1, r. 18(b) (i)-(iii).

[13] Ibid., Sch. 1, r. 18(c) (i), (ii).

[14] "Vessel constrained by her draught" means a power-driven vessel which because of her draught in relation to the available depth of water is severely restricted in her ability to deviate from the course she is following: ibid., Sch. 1, r. 3(h).

[15] Ibid., Sch. 1, r. 18(d) (i). The prescribed signals are those specified in Rule 28, as to which see para. 3.08, *post*.

[16] Ibid., Sch. 1, r. 18(d) (ii).

[17] "Seaplane" includes any aircraft designed to manoeuvre on the water: ibid., Sch. 1, r. 3(e). As to the application of the 1972 Rules to seaplanes, see paras. 1.07, text and note 7, 1.08, text and note 5, *ante*.

[18] Ibid., Sch. 1, r. 18(e).

[19] For the meaning of "risk of collision" see para. 2.03, note 2, *ante*.

[20] Merchant Shipping (Distress Signals and Prevention of Collisions) Regulations 1983, Sch. 1, r. 18(e). The rules for vessels in sight of one another are those described in this paragraph and paras. 2.08-2.11, *ante*. Rule 18 is derived from 1960 rr. 20, 26 contained in the First Schedule to the Collision Regulations (Ships and Seaplanes on the Water) and Signals of Distress (Ships) Order 1965, S.I. 1965, No. 1525 (revoked). As to the power to make collision regulations in respect of seaplanes on the water see paras. 1.05 text and notes 30-31, 1.06 text and note 15, *ante*. For a comparative table of the 1972 Rule 18 and 1960 Rule 20, see para. 6.18, *post*. For cases on 1960 Rules 18(a)(iii), (iv), see respectively, *The Carebeka* 1 [1973] 1 Lloyd's Rep. 396; *Stein and Others* v. *The Kathy K and S.N. No. 1, Egmont Towing and Sorting Ltd., Shields Navigation Ltd., Helsing and Iverson* (Can. Ct.) [1972] 2 Lloyd's Rep. 36.

SECT. (3) Conduct of vessels in restricted visibility

2.13 *Conduct of vessels in restricted visibility—Rule 19*

This rule applies to vessels[1] not in sight of one another[2] when navigating in or near an area of restricted visibility.[3] Every vessel must proceed at a safe speed[4] adapted to the prevailing circumstances and conditions of restricted visibility.[5] A power-driven vessel[6] must have her engines ready for immediate manoeuvre.[7] Every vessel must have due regard to the prevailing circumstances and conditions of restricted visibility when complying with the rules applicable to the conduct of vessels in any condition of visibility.[8] A vessel which detects by radar alone the presence of another vessel must determine if a close-quarters situation[9] is developing and/or risk of collision[10] exists.[11] If so she must take avoiding action in ample time.[12] However, when such action consists of an alteration of course, so far as possible there shall be avoided (i) an alteration of course to port for a vessel forward of the beam, other than for a vessel being overtaken;[13] and (ii) an alteration of course towards a vessel abeam or abaft of the beam.[14] Except where it has been determined that a risk of collision does not exist, every vessel which hears apparently forward of her beam the fog signal[15] of another vessel, or which cannot avoid a close-quarters situation with another vessel forward of her beam, must reduce her speed to the minimum at which she can be kept on her course.[16] She must if necessary take all her way off and in any event she must navigate with extreme caution until danger of collision is over.[17]

[1] For the meaning of "vessel" see para. 1.04, text and notes 15-17, *ante*.
[2] As to when vessels are deemed to be in sight of one another see para. 2.08, text and note 8, *ante*.
[3] Merchant Shipping (Distress Signals and Prevention of Collisions) Regulations 1983, S.I. 1983, No. 708, Sch. 1, r. 19(a). "Restricted visibility" means any condition in which visibility is restricted by fog, falling snow, heavy rainstorms, sandstorms or any other similar causes; ibid., Sch. 1, r. 3(1). Rule 19 is derived from 1960 Rule 16 contained in the First Schedule to the Collision Regulations (Ships and Seaplanes on the Water) and Signals of Distress (Ships) Order 1965, S.I. 1965, No. 1525 (revoked). As to the power to make collision regulations, and their application to United Kingdom and other vessels, see paras. 1.04-1.08, *ante*. For a comparative table of the 1972 Rules and the 1960 Rules, see para, 6.19, *post*.
[4] The term "safe speed" is not defined but decisions on the meaning of "moderate speed" in former regulations may be of assistance; see, e.g., *The City of Brooklyn* (1876) 1 P.D. 276 C.A.; *The Smyrna* (1864) 2 Moo. P.C. (N.S.) 435; *The Zadok* (1883) 9 P.D. 114; *The Attila* (1879) 5 Quebec L.R. 340; *H.M.S. Glorious* (1933) 44 Ll.L.Rep. 321, C.A. See also *The Gunnar Knudsen* [1961] 2 Lloyd's Rep. 433; *The Kurt Arlt* [1962] 1 Lloyd's Rep. 31; *The Almizar* [1971] 2 Lloyd's Rep. 290 (H.L.); *The Elazig* [1972] 1 Lloyd's Rep. 355; *The Zaglebie Dabrowskie (No. 1)* [1978] 1 Lloyd's Rep. 564.
[5] Merchant Shipping (Distress Signals and Prevention of Collisions) Regulations 1983, Sch. 1, r. 19(b). Cf. 1960 Rule 16(a). For cases on the 1972 Rule 19(b), see *The Sanshin Victory* [1980] 2 Lloyd's Rep. 359; *The Roseline* [1981] 2 Lloyd's Rep. 410. For cases on 1972 Rule 6 (safe speed in any condition of visibility), see para. 2.02, *ante*.
[6] For the meaning of "power-driven" vessel see para. 2.06, note 21, *ante*.
[7] Merchant Shipping (Distress Signals and Prevention of Collisions) Regulations 1983, Sch. 1, r. 19(b).
[8] Ibid., Sch. 1, r. 19(c). As to the rules for the conduct of vessels in any condition of visibility see paras. 2.01-2.07, *ante*.
[9] With large ships, a "close-quarters situation" means a distance measurable in miles rather than yards; *The Verena* [1961] 2 Lloyd's Rep. 127, C.A., *per* Willmer, L.J., at p. 133.
[10] For the meaning of "risk of collision" see para. 2.03, note 2, *ante*.
[11] Merchant Shipping (Distress Signals and Prevention of Collisions) Regulations 1983, Sch. 1, r. 19(d).
[12] Ibid., Sch. 1, r. 19(d).
[13] As to the overtaking rule see para. 2.09, *ante*.
[14] Ibid., Sch. 1, r. 19(d).
[15] As to fog signals see paras. 4.02, 4.03, *post*.
[16] Merchant Shipping (Distress Signals and Prevention of Collisions) Regulations 1983, Sch. 1, r. 19(e).
[17] Ibid., Sch. 1, r. 19(e). Cf. 1960 Rule 16(b). (c).

CHAPTER THREE

COLLISION REGULATIONS—LIGHTS AND SHAPES

3.01 *Application of rules and exemptions—Rules 20, 38(a)-(f),(h)*

The rules as to lights and shapes[1] must be complied with in all weathers.[2] The rules concerning lights must be complied with from sunset to sunrise[3]. During such times no other lights may be exhibited, except such lights as cannot be mistaken for the lights specified in the rules or do not impair their visibility or distinctive character, or interfere with the keeping of a proper look-out.[4] The lights prescribed by the rules must, if carried, also be exhibited from sunrise to sunset in restricted visibility[5] and may be exhibited in all other circumstances when it is deemed necessary.[6] The rules concerning shapes must be complied with by day.[7] The lights and shapes specified in the rules must comply with the detailed provisions set out in the first annex to the 1972 Rules.[8] These provisions prescribe rules for the vertical positioning and spacing of lights,[9] horizontal positioning and spacing of lights,[10] location of direction-indicating lights for fishing vessels, dredgers and vessels engaged in underwater operations,[11] screens for sidelights,[12] specifications for shapes,[13] colour specification[14] and intensity of lights,[15] the horizontal[16] and vertical sectors of lights,[17] intensity of non-electric lights,[18] and manoeuvring lights;[19] and require the approval of construction of lanterns and shapes and installation of lanterns by the appropriate authority of the flag State.[20]

Any vessel (or class of vessel), the keel of which was laid or which was at a corresponding stage of construction before the entry into force of the 1972 Rules,[21] and which complies with the old rules,[22] is entitled to certain exemptions with regard to lights.[23] There are permanent exemptions for such vessels from the requirement to re-position lights as a result of conversion from Imperial to metric units and rounding off measurement figures,[24] and from the requirement to re-position masthead lights[25] on vessels of less than 150 metres in length[26] resulting from the prescriptions for horizontal positioning and spacing.[27] In respect of qualifying vessels[28] of 150 metres or more in length, there is an exemption from such re-positioning of masthead lights until nine years after the date of entry into force of the 1972 Rules.[29] There are also nine-year exemptions from the re-positioning of masthead lights in accordance with the rule for vertical separation of masthead lights for power-driven vessels,[30] and from the re-positioning of sidelights on power-driven vessels to the required height above the hull,[31] and from the re-positioning of sidelights on vessels of 20 metres or more in length to comply with the 1972 Rule for horizontal positioning and spacing, as well as a permanent exemption from the requirement to reposition all-round lights.[32] There are four-year exemptions from the rules requiring the installation of lights with the prescribed ranges[33] and colour specifications.[34]

Whenever the Government concerned has determined that a vessel of special construction or purpose cannot comply fully with the provisions of any of the rules with respect to the number, position, range or arc of visibility of lights or shapes, as well as to the disposition and characteristics of sound-signalling appliances, without interfering with the special function of the vessel, the vessel must comply with such other provisions in regard to the number, position, range or arc of visibility of lights or shapes, as well as to the disposition and characteristics of sound-signalling appliances, as her Government has determined to be the closest possible compliance with the rules in respect of that vessel.[35]

Nothing in the rules is to interfere with the operation of any special rules made by the Government of any State with respect to additional station or signal lights, shapes or whistle signals for ships[36] of war and vessels proceeding under convoy, or with respect to additional station or signal lights or shapes for fishing vessels engaged in fishing as a fleet.[37] These additional station or signal lights, shapes or whistle signals must, so far as possible, be such that they cannot be mistaken for any light, shape or signal authorized elsewhere under the rules.[38]

[1] I.e. the rules prescribed in Part C (rr. 20-31) of the First Schedule to the Merchant Shipping (Distress Signals and Prevention of Collisions) Regulations 1983, S.I. 1983, No. 708. As to these rules see paras. 3.02-3.10, *post*. As to the power to make collision regulations and their application to United Kingdom and other vessels, see paras. 1.04-1.08, *ante*.
[2] Merchant Shipping (Distress Signals and Prevention of Collisions) Regulations 1983, Sch. 1, r. 20(a). A ship which has lost her lights through bad weather ought to replace them as soon as possible; *The Saxonia and The Eclipse* (1862) Lush. 410, P.C.; *The Aurora and The Robert Ingram* (1861) Lush. 327. It seems that a breach of the rule will not be excused even where lights are being repaired or became extinguished accidentally; see *The C.M. Palmer and The Larnax* (1874) 2 Asp. M.C. 94, P.C.; *The Victoria* (1848) 3 W. Rob. 49; *The Sylph* (1854) 2 Sp. 75. A surveyor of ships may inspect any ship to see that she is properly provided with lights; see para. 5.05, *post*.
[3] Merchant Shipping (Distress Signals and Prevention of Collisions) Regulations 1983, Sch. 1, r. 20(b). By "sunset" and "sunrise" is probably meant the actual moment at which the sun sets or rises at the place in question; see *Gordon* v. *Cann* (1899) 68 L.J.Q.B. 434, D.C.; *Curtis* v. *March* (1858) 3 H. & N. 866; *MacKinnon* v. *Nicolson* (1916) S.C. (J.) 6.
[4] Merchant Shipping (Distress Signals and Prevention of Collisions) Regulations 1983, Sch. 1, r. 20(b). As to wrong and misleading lights see *The Hassel* [1919] P. 355, C.A.; *H.M.S. Truculent* [1951] 2 Lloyd's Rep. 308; *The Tojo Maru* [1968] 1 Lloyd's Rep. 365. Rule 20(a), (b), (c) is derived from 1960 Rule 1(b) in the First Schedule to the Collision Regulations (Ships and Seaplanes on the Water) and Signals of Distress (Ships) Order 1965, S.I. 1965, No. 1525 (revoked). For a comparative table of the 1972 Rules and the 1960 Rules, see para. 6.20, *post*. For a case on 1960 Rule 1(b), see *The Djerada* [1976] 1 Lloyd's Rep.50; (C.A.) (1976) 2 Lloyd's Rep. 40. For a case on 1972 Rule 20(b), see *The Coral I* [1982] 1 Lloyd's Rep. 441.
[5] As to the conduct of vessels in restricted visibility see para. 2.13, *ante*. As to sound signals in restricted visibility see para. 4.03, *post*.
[6] Merchant Shipping (Distress Signals and Prevention of Collisions) Regulations 1983, Sch. 1, r. 20(c). See *The Roseline* [1981] 2 Lloyd's Rep. 410.
[7] Ibid., Sch. 1, r. 20(d).
[8] Ibid., Sch. 1, r. 20(e). As to Annex 1 see the text and notes 9-20, *infra*; and para. 6.39, *post*.
[9] Ibid., Sch. 1, Annex 1, s. 2.
[10] Ibid., Sch. 1, Annex 1, s. 3.
[11] Ibid., Sch. 1, Annex 1, s. 4. For the meaning of "vessel" see para. 1.04, text and notes 15-17, *ante*.
[12] Ibid., Sch. 1, Annex 1, s. 5. For the meaning of "sidelights" see para. 3.02, note 7, *post*.
[13] Ibid., Sch. 1, Annex 1, s. 6.

[14] Ibid., Sch. 1, Annex 1, s. 7. For each colour, the diagram specified by the International Commission on Illumination must be complied with: Sch. 1, Annex 1, s. 7 and note (3).
[15] Ibid., Sch. 1, Annex 1, s. 8. The chromaticity of navigational lights must conform to the diagram specified in the Chromaticity Chart (1975) published by the International Commission on Illumination: see art. 1(2) (c), Sch. 1, Annex 1, s. 7.
[16] Ibid., Sch. 1, Annex 1, s. 9.
[17] Ibid., Sch. 1, Annex 1, s. 10.
[18] Ibid., Sch. 1, Annex 1, s. 11.
[19] Ibid., Sch. 1, Annex 1, s. 12.
[20] Ibid., Sch. 1, Annex 1, s. 13. As to inspections by surveyors see para. 5.05, *post*. For the meaning of "appropriate authority" see para. 1.07, note 9, *ante*.
[21] I.e. 15th July 1977.
[22] I.e. the 1960 rules set out the First Schedule to the Collision Regulations (Ships and Seaplanes on the Water) and Signals of Distress (Ships) Order 1965 (revoked).
[23] See the Merchant Shipping (Distress Signals and Prevention of Collisions) Regulations 1983, Sch. 1, r. 38(a)-(f).
[24] Ibid., Sch. 1, r. 38(c).
[25] For the meaning of "masthead light" see para. 3.02, note 5, *ante*.
[26] For the meaning of "length" see para. 2.06, note 19, *ante*.
[27] Merchant Shipping (Distress Signals and Prevention of Collisions) Regulations 1983, Sch. 1, r. 38(d) (i), and Annex 1, s. 3(a).
[28] I.e. the vessels described in the text and notes 21-23, *supra*.
[29] Merchant Shipping (Distress Signals and Prevention of Collisions) Regulations 1983, Sch. 1, r. 38(d) (ii), and Annex 1, s. 3(a).
[30] Ibid., Sch. 1, r. 38(e), and Annex 1, s. 2(b). For the meaning of "power-driven vessel" see para. 2.06, note 21, *ante*.
[31] Ibid., Sch. 1, r. 38(f), and Annex 1, s. 2(g). For the meaning of "sidelights" see para. 3.02, note 7, *ante*. "Height above the hull" means height above the uppermost continuous deck: Sch. 1, Annex 1, s. 1.
[32] Ibid., Sch. 1, r. 38(f), and Annex 1, s. 3(b), r. 38(h), and Annex 1, s. 9(b). For the meaning of "all-round light" see para. 3.02, note 10, *post*.
[33] Ibid., Sch. 1, rr. 22, 38(a). As to the prescribed ranges see para. 3.02, *post*.
[34] Ibid., Sch. 1, r. 38(b), and Annex 1, s. 7.
[34] Ibid., Sch. 1, r. 38(b), and Annex 1, s. 7.
[35] Ibid., Sch. 1, r. 1(e). This provision is derived from Rule 13(b) of the 1960 Rules. For the comparative table, see para. 6.01, *post*.
[36] For the meaning of "ship" see para. 1.04, text and note 14, *ante*.
[37] Merchant Shipping (Distress Signals and Prevention of Collisions) Regulations 1983, Sch. 1, r. 1(c). See further para. 3.06, *post*.
[38] Ibid., Sch. 1, r. 1(c). This provision is derived from 1960 Rules 13(a), 28 (revoked). For the comparative table, see para. 6.01, *post*.

3.02 *Visibility of lights—Rule 22*

The lights prescribed in the rules[1] must have the specified intensity[2] so as to be visible at the following minimum ranges. In the case of vessels[3] of 50 metres or more in length,[4] a masthead light[5] must be visible at a minimum distance of six miles,[6] a sidelight,[7] a sternlight[8] and a towing light[9] at three miles and a white, red, green or yellow all-round light[10] at three miles.[11] In the case of vessels of 12 metres or more in length but less than 50 metres in length a masthead light must be visible at a minimum distance of five miles (or where the length of the vessel is less than 20 metres, three miles), a sidelight, a sternlight and a towing light at two miles and a white, red, green or yellow all-round light at two miles.[12] In the case of vessels of less than 12 metres in length, a masthead light must be visible at a minimum distance of two miles, a sidelight at one mile, a sternlight and a towing light at two miles and a white, red, green or yellow all-round light at two miles.[13] In inconspicuous, partly submerged vessels or objects, there must be an all-round light visible at a minimum distance of three miles.[14]

[1] I.e. the rules in the First Schedule to the Merchant Shipping (Distress Signals and Prevention of Collisions) Regulations 1983, S.I. 1983, No. 708. See further paras. 3.03-3.10, *post*. As to the application of these rules see para. 3.01, *ante*.
[2] I.e. the intensity specified in Annex 1, s. 8, of the First Schedule to the Merchant Shipping (Distress Signals and Prevention of Collisions) Regulations 1983; as to which see para 6.39, *post*. Certain vessels are exempted from the installation of lights with the ranges specified in Rule 22 (described in this paragraph): see ibid., Sch. 1, r. 38(a); and para. 3.01, text and note 33, *ante*.
[3] For the meaning of "vessel" see para. 1.04, text and notes 15-17, *ante*.
[4] For the meaning of "length" see para. 2.06, note 19, *ante*.
[5] A "masthead light" means a white light placed over the fore and aft centre line of the vessel showing an unbroken light over an arc of the horizon of 225 degrees and so fixed as to show the light from right ahead to 22.5 degrees abaft the beam on either side of the vessel: Merchant Shipping (Distress Signals and Prevention of Collisions) Regulations 1983, Sch. 1, r. 21(a).
[6] It is assumed that "mile" means an international nautical mile of 1,852 metres.
[7] "Sidelights" means a green light on the starboard side and a red light on the port side each showing an unbroken light over an arc of the horizon of 112.5 degrees and so fixed as to show the light from right ahead to 22.5 degrees abaft the beam on its respective side. In a vessel of less than 20 metres in length the sidelights may be combined in one lantern carried on the fore and aft centre line of the vessel: Merchant Shipping (Distress Signals and Prevention of Collisions) Regulations 1983, Sch. 1, r. 21(b).
[8] A "sternlight" means a white light placed as nearly as practicable at the stern showing an unbroken light over an arc of the horizon of 135 degrees and so fixed as to show the light 67.5 degrees from right aft on each side of the vessel: ibid., Sch. 1, r. 21(c).
[9] A "towing light" means a yellow light having the same characteristics as the sternlight defined *supra*: ibid., Sch. 1, r. 21(d).
[10] An "all-round light" means a light showing an unbroken light over an arc of the horizon of 360 degrees: ibid., Sch. 1, r. 21(e).
[11] Ibid., Sch. 1, r. 22(a).
[12] Ibid., Sch. 1, r. 22(b).
[13] Ibid., Sch. 1, r. 22(c). The requirements as to masthead lights, sidelights and sternlights are derived from those in 1960 rr. 2, 10, of the First Schedule to the Collision Regulations (Ships and Seaplanes on the Water) and Signals of Distress (Ships) Order 1965, S.I. 1965, No. 1525 (revoked). For the 1972 Rule, see para. 6.22, and for the 1960 Rules, see para. 6.23, *post*.
[14] Ibid., Sch. 1, r. 22(d). This is a new provision, implementing part of IMO Resolution A.464(XII).

3.03 *Lights for power-driven vessels under way—Rule 23*

A power-driven vessel[1] underway[2] must exhibit a masthead light[3] forward, a second masthead light abaft of and higher than the forward one, sidelights[4] and a sternlight.[5] A vessel of less than 50 metres in length[6] is not obliged to exhibit the second masthead light but may do so.[7] A power-driven vessel of less than seven metres in length whose maximum speed does not exceed seven knots may, in lieu of the lights prescribed above, exhibit an all-round white light.[8] Such vessel must, if practicable, also exhibit sidelights.[9] A power-driven vessel of less than 12 metres in length may in lieu of the prescribed lights exhibit an all-round white light and sidelights.[10] An air-cushion vessel[11] when operating in the non-displacement mode must, in addition to the prescribed lights for power-driven vessels underway,[12] exhibit an all-round flashing yellow light.[13]

[1] For the meaning of "power-driven vessel" see para. 2.06, note 21, *ante*. For the meaning of "vessel" see para. 1.04, text and notes 15-17, *ante*.
[2] For the meaning of "underway" see para. 2.12, note 12, *ante*.
[3] For the meaning of "masthead light" see para. 3.02, note 5, *ante*.
[4] For the meaning of "sidelights" see para. 3.02, note 7, *ante*.
[5] Merchant Shipping (Distress Signals and Prevention of Collisions) Regulations 1983, S.I. 1983, No. 708, Sch. 1, r. 23(a). For the meaning of "sternlight" see para. 3.02, note 8, *ante*. As to the power to make collision regulations, and their application to United Kingdom and other vessels, see paras. 1.04-1.08, *ante*. As to the application of the rules as to lights and the exemptions see para. 3.01, *ante*. Rule 23(a) is derived from 1960 rr. 2(a), 10(a) of the First Schedule to the Collision Regulations (Ships and Seaplanes on the Water) and Signals of Distress (Ships) Order 1965, S.I. 1965, No. 1525 (revoked). For a comparative table of the 1972 Rules and the 1960 Rules, see para. 6.23, *post*.
[6] For the meaning of "length" see para. 2.06, note 19, *ante*.
[7] Merchant Shipping (Distress Signals and Prevention of Collisions) Regulations 1983, Sch. 1, r. 23(a) (ii), proviso.
[8] Ibid., Sch. 1, r. 23(c) (ii). For the meaning of "all-round light" see para. 3.02, note 10, *ante*.
[9] Ibid., Sch. 1, r. 23(c) (ii). 1972 Rule 23(c) is derived from 1960 Rule 7 (revoked). For the comparative table, see para. 6.23, *post*.
[10] Merchant Shipping (Distress Signals and Prevention of Collisions) Regulations 1983, Sch. 1, r. 23(c) (i). The masthead light or all-round white light on a power-driven vessel of less than 12 metres in length may be displaced from the fore and aft centreline of the vessel if centreline fitting is not practicable but the sidelights must be combined in one lantern carried on the fore and aft centreline of the vessel or located as nearly as practicable in the same fore and aft line as the masthead light or the all-round white light; ibid., Sch. 1, r. 23(c) (iii). Rule 23(c) (i) and (iii) are new provisions implementing IMO Resolution A.464 (XII).
[11] As to the application of collision regulations to hovercraft see paras. 1.07, text and note 6, 1.08, text and notes 3, 4, *ante*.
[12] I.e. the lights prescribed by the Merchant Shipping (Distress Signals and Prevention of Collisions) Regulations 1983, Sch. 1, r. 23(a); see the text and notes 1-5, *supra*.
[13] Ibid., Sch. 1, r. 23(b). A "flashing light" means a light flashing at regular intervals at a frequency of 120 flashes or more per minute: ibid., Sch. 1, r. 21(f). Rule 23(b) is new to the 1972 Rules and was not found in previous collision regulations.

3.04 *Towing and pushing—Rule 24*

A power-driven vessel when towing must generally exhibit,[1] instead of a masthead light forward or a second masthead light abaft of the forward one,[2] two masthead lights forward in a vertical line.[3] When the length of the tow, measuring from the stern of the towing vessel to the after end of the tow exceeds 200 metres, the vessel must exhibit three such lights in a vertical line.[4] A power-driven vessel when towing must also exhibit sidelights,[5] a sternlight,[6] a towing light[7] in a vertical line above the sternlight and, when the length of the tow exceeds 200 metres, a diamond shape where it can best be seen.[8] When a pushing vessel and a vessel being pushed are rigidly connected in a composite unit they are to be regarded as a power-driven vessel and exhibit the lights prescribed in the Rule for power-driven vessels underway.[9] A power-driven vessel when pushing ahead or towing alongside, except in the case of a composite unit, must exhibit, instead of a masthead light forward or a second masthead light abaft of the forward one, two masthead lights forward in a vertical line.[10] She must also exhibit sidelights and a sternlight.[11]

A vessel or object (other than an inconspicuous, partly submerged vessel or object)[12] being towed must exhibit sidelights, a sternlight and, when the length of the tow exceeds 200 metres, a diamond shape where it can best be seen.[13] Subject to the proviso that any number of vessels being towed alongside or pushed in a group must be lighted as one vessel, a vessel being pushed ahead, not being part of a composite unit, must exhibit sidelights at the forward end, and a vessel being towed alongside must exhibit a sternlight and, at the forward end, sidelights.[14] An inconspicuous, partly submerged vessel or object, or combination of such vessels or objects being towed must exhibit: if it is less than 25 metres in breadth, one all-round white light[15] at or near the forward end and one at or near the after end, except that dracones need not exhibit a light at or near the forward end;[16] if it is 25 metres or more in breadth, two additional all-round white lights at or near the extremities of its breadth;[17] if it exceeds 100 metres in length, additional all-round white lights between the all-round lights[18] so that the distance between the lights does not exceed 100 metres;[19] and a diamond shape at or near the aftermost extremity of the last vessel or object being towed.[20] If the length of the tow exceeds 200 metres it must exhibit an additional diamond shape where it can best be seen and located as far forward as practicable.[21] Where from any sufficient cause it is impracticable for a vessel or object being towed to exhibit the prescribed lights,[22] all possible measures must be taken to light the vessel or object towed or at least to indicate the presence of the non-lighted vessel or object.[23]

[1] For the meaning of "power-driven vessel" see para. 2.06, note 21, *ante*. For the meaning of "vessel" see para. 1.04, text and notes 15-17, *ante*. Where from any sufficient cause it is impracticable for a vessel not normally engaged in towing operations to display the lights described in 1972 Rule 24(a) or (c) (see the text to this note and text and notes 2-8, 10, 11, *infra*) the vessel is not required to exhibit those lights when engaged in towing another vessel in distress or otherwise in need of assistance; Merchant Shipping (Distress Signals and Prevention of Collisions) Regulations 1983, S.I. 1983, No. 708, Sch. 1, r. 24(i). All possible measures must be taken to indicate the nature of the relationship between the towing vessel and the vessel being towed as authorized by Rule 36 (see para. 4.04, *post*); ibid., Sch. 1, r. 24(i). Rule 24(i) is a new provision implementing IMO Resolution A.464 (XII).
[2] I.e. instead of the masthead light forward or the second masthead light prescribed in the Merchant Shipping (Distress Signals and Prevention of Collisions) Regulations 1983, Sch. 1, r. 23(a) (i), (ii). As to Rule 23, see para. 3.03, *ante*.
[3] Ibid., Sch. 1, r. 24(a)(i). As to the power to make collision regulations, and their application to United Kingdom and other vessels, see paras. 1.04-1.08, *ante*. As to the application of the rules as to lights and the exemptions see para. 3.01, *ante*. Rule 24(a) is derived from 1960 Rule 3(a), (b) of the First Schedule to the Collision Regulations (Ships and Seaplanes on the Water) and Signals of Distress (Ships) Order 1965, S.I. 1965, No. 1525 (revoked). For a comparative table of the 1972 Rules and the 1960 Rules, see para. 6.24, *post*.
[4] Merchant Shipping (Distress Signals and Prevention of Collisions) Regulations 1983, Sch. 1, r. 24(a) (i).
[5] For the meaning of "sidelights" see para. 3.02, note 7, *ante*.
[6] For the meaning of "sternlight" see para. 3.02, note 8, *ante*.
[7] For the meaning of "towing light" see para. 3.02, note 9, *ante*.
[8] Merchant Shipping (Distress Signals and Prevention of Collisions) Regulations 1983, Sch. 1, r. 24(a) (ii)-(v). 1972 Rule 24(a) (v) is derived from 1960 Rule 3(c). For the comparative table, see para. 6.24, *post*.
[9] Ibid., Sch. 1, r. 24(b). As to the lights prescribed (by r. 23) for power-driven vessels underway see para. 3.03, *ante*.
[10] Ibid., Sch. 1, r. 24(c) (i). This Rule is relaxed for vessels not normally engaged in towing operations; see note 1, *supra*.

[11] Ibid., Sch. 1, r. 24(c) (ii), (iii). A power-driven vessel to which paragraphs (a) or (c) of Rule 24 apply must also comply with Rule 23(a) (ii) (second masthead light abaft of and higher than the forward one—see para. 3.03, *ante*): Sch. 1, r. 24(d).

[12] For an "object" to be subject to the collision regulations in English law, it must probably fall within the definition of "ship"; see para. 1.04, text and note 14, *ante*.

[13] Merchant Shipping (Distress Signals and Prevention of Collisions) Regulations 1983, Sch. 1, r. 24(e). This Rule does not apply to the vessels or objects being towed to which Rule 24(g) applies; see ibid., Sch. 1, r. 24(e); and text and notes 15-21, *infra*. 1972 Rule 24(e), which has been slightly amended in the 1983 Regulations, is derived from 1960 Rule 5(a), (b). For the comparative table see para. 6.24, *post*.

[14] Ibid., Sch. 1, r. 24(f). 1972 Rule 24(f) is derived from 1960 Rule 5(c). For the comparative table see para. 6.24, *post*.

[15] For the meaning of "all-round light" see para. 3.02, note 10, *ante*.

[16] Merchant Shipping (Distress Signals and Prevention of Collisions) Regulations 1983, Sch. 1, r. 24(g) (i). Rule 24(g) is a new rule, implementing IMO Resolution A.464 (xii).

[17] Merchant Shipping (Distress Signals and Prevention of Collisions) Regulations 1983, Sch. 1, r. 24(g) (ii).

[18] I.e. the all-round lights prescribed in ibid., r. 24(g) (i), (ii), *supra*.

[19] Ibid., Sch. 1, r. 24(g) (iii).

[20] Ibid., Sch. 1, r. 24(g) (iv).

[21] Ibid., Sch. 1, r. 24(g) (iv).

[22] I.e. the lights prescribed in ibid., Sch. 1, r. 24(e), (g); see the text and notes 12, 13, *supra*.

[23] Ibid., Sch. 1, r. 24(h).

3.05 *Sailing vessels underway and vessels under oars—Rule 25*

A sailing vessel[1] underway[2] must exhibit sidelights[3] and a sternlight.[4] In a sailing vessel of less than 20 metres in length[5] the sidelights and sternlight may be combined in one lantern carried at or near the top of the mast where it can best be seen.[6] A sailing vessel underway may, in addition to sidelights and a sternlight, exhibit at or near the top of the mast, where they can best be seen, two all-round lights[7] in a vertical line, the upper being red and the lower green, but these lights must not be exhibited in conjunction with a combined pattern lantern permitted for sailing vessels of less than 12 metres in length.[8] A sailing vessel of less than seven metres in length must, if practicable, exhibit sidelights and a sternlight or a combined pattern lantern, but if she does not, she must have ready at hand an electric torch or lighted lantern showing a white light which must be exhibited in sufficient time to prevent collision.[9] A vessel proceeding under sail when also being propelled by machinery must exhibit forward where it can best be seen a conical shape, apex downwards.[10]

A vessel under oars[11] may exhibit the lights prescribed above for sailing vessels, but if she does not, she must have ready at hand an electric torch or lighted lantern showing a white light which must be exhibited in sufficient time to prevent collision.[12]

[1] For the meaning of "sailing vessel" see para 2.06, note 20, *ante*. For the meaning of "vessel" see para. 1.04, text and notes 15-17, *ante*.
1.04, text and notes 15-17, *ante*.

[2] For the meaning of "underway" see para. 2.12, note 6, *ante*.

[3] For the meaning of "sidelights" see para. 3.02, note 7, *ante*.

[4] Merchant Shipping (Distress Signals and Prevention of Collisions) Regulations 1983, S.I. 1983 No. 708, Sch. 1, r. 25(a). For the meaning of "sternlight" see para. 3.02, note 8, *ante*. As to the power

to make collision regulations, and their application to United Kingdom and other vessels, see paras. 1.04-1.08, *ante*. For the application of the rules as to lights, and the exemptions, see para. 3.01, *ante*. 1972 Rule 25(a), (b), (c), is derived from 1960 Rule 5(a), (d), (b), of the First Schedule to the Collision Regulations (Ships and Seaplanes on the Water) and Signals of Distress (Ships) Order 1965, S.I.1965, No. 1525 (revoked). For a comparative table of the 1972 Rules and the 1960 Rules, see para. 6.25, *post*.
[5] For the meaning of "length" see para. 2.06, note 19, *ante*.
[6] Merchant Shipping (Distress Signals and Prevention of Collisions) Regulations 1983, Sch. 1, r. 25(b).
[7] For the meaning of "all-round light" see para. 3.02, note 10, *ante*.
[8] Merchant Shipping (Distress Signals and Prevention of Collisions) Regulations 1983, Sch. 1, r. 25(c).
[9] Ibid., Sch. 1, r. 25(d) (i).
[10] Ibid., Sch. 1, r. 25(e). This provision is derived from r. 14 of the 1960 Rules. For the comparative table, see para. 6.25, *post*.
[11] As to the application of collision regulations to vessels propelled by oars see para. 1.04, text and note 18, *ante*.
[12] Merchant Shipping (Distress Signals and Prevention of Collisions) Regulations 1983, Sch. 1, r. 25(d) (ii). This provision is derived from 1960 Rule 7(f). For the comparative table, see para.6.25, *post*.

3.06 *Fishing vessels—Rule 26*

A vessel engaged in fishing,[1] whether underway[2] or at anchor, must exhibit only the lights and shapes prescribed in the Rule expounded in this paragraph.[3] A vessel when engaged in trawling[4] must exhibit two all-round lights[5] in a vertical line, the upper being green and the lower white.[6] Alternatively, she may exhibit a shape consisting of two cones with their apexes together in a vertical line one above the other; a vessel of less than 20 metres in length[7] may instead of this shape exhibit a basket.[8] Additionally, a vessel when engaged in trawling must exhibit a masthead light abaft of and higher than the all-round green light; a vessel of less than 50 metres in length is not obliged to exhibit such a light but may do so.[9] A vessel engaged in trawling, when making way through the water, must in addition exhibit sidelights,[10] and a sternlight.[11]

A vessel engaged in fishing other than trawling must exhibit two all-round lights in a vertical line, the upper being red and the lower white, or a shape consisting of two cones with apexes together in a vertical line one above the other; a vessel of less than 20 metres in length may instead of this shape exhibit a basket.[12] When there is outlying gear extending more than 150 metres horizontally from the vessel, a vessel engaged in fishing other than trawling must also exhibit an all-round white light or a cone apex upwards in the direction of the gear.[13] Additionally, a vessel engaged in fishing, when making way through the water, must exhibit sidelights and a sternlight.[14]

A vessel engaged in fishing in close proximity to other vessels engaged in fishing may exhibit certain additional signals.[15]

A vessel when not engaged in fishing must not exhibit the lights or shapes prescribed in the Rule for vessels engaged in fishing, but only those prescribed for a vessel of her length.[16]

[1] For the meaning of "vessel engaged in fishing" see para. 2.05, note 5, *ante*. For the meaning of "vessel" see para. 1.04, notes 15-17, *ante*.
[2] For the meaning of "underway" see para. 2.12, note 6, *ante*.
[3] Merchant Shipping (Distress Signals and Prevention of Collisions) Regulations 1983, S.I. 1983, No. 708, Sch. 1, r. 26(a). As to the power to make collision regulations, and their application to United Kingdom and other vessels, see paras. 1.04-1.08, *ante*. As to the application of the rules as to lights and the exemptions see para. 3.01, *ante*. 1972 Rule 26 is derived from 1960 Rule 9 of the First Schedule to the Collision Regulations (Ships and Seaplanes on the Water) and Signals of Distress (Ships) Order 1965, S.I. 1965, No. 1525 (revoked). For a comparative table of the 1972 Rules and the 1960 Rules, see para. 6.26, *post*.
[4] "Trawling" means the dragging through the water of a dredge net or other apparatus used as a fishing appliance: Merchant Shipping (Distress Signals and Prevention of Collisions) Regulations 1983, Sch. 1, r. 26(b).
[5] For the meaning of "all-round light" see para. 3.02, note 10, *ante*.
[6] Merchant Shipping (Distress Signals and Prevention of Collisions) Regulations 1983, Sch. 1, r. 26(b) (i).
[7] For the meaning of "length" see para. 2.06, note 19, *ante*.
[8] Merchant Shipping (Distress Signals and Prevention of Collisions) Regulations 1983, Sch. 1, r. 26(b) (i).
[9] Ibid., Sch. 1, r. 26(b) (ii). For the meaning of "masthead light" see para. 3.02, note 5, *ante*.
[10] For the meaning of "sidelights" see para. 3.02, note 7, *ante*.
[11] Merchant Shipping (Distress Signals and Prevention of Collisions) Regulations 1983, Sch. 1, r. 26(b) (iii). For the meaning of "sternlight" see para. 3.02, note 8, *ante*.
[12] Ibid., Sch. 1, r. 26(c) (i).
[13] Ibid., Sch. 1, r. 26(c) (ii).
[14] Ibid., Sch. 1, r. 26(c) (iii). "Making way through the water" is to be distinguished from "underway"; cf., para. 2.12, note 6, *ante*.
[15] Ibid., Sch. 1, r. 26(d). The optional additional signals are for trawlers and purse seiners and if exhibited must comply with certain requirements. The appropriate signals and the requirements are described in Annex II to the regulations; see para. 6.40, *post*.
[16] Ibid., Sch. 1, r. 26(e).

3.07 *Vessels not under command or restricted in their ability to manoeuvre—Rule 27*

A vessel not under command[1] must exhibit two all-round red lights[2] in a vertical line where they can best be seen, two balls or similar shapes in a vertical line where they can best be seen, and in addition, when making way through the water, sidelights[3] and a sternlight.[4] A vessel restricted in her ability to manoeuvre,[5] except a vessel engaged in mineclearance operations, must exhibit three all-round lights in a vertical line where they can best be seen (the highest and lowest to be red and the middle light white) and three shapes in a vertical line where they can best be seen (the highest and lowest to be balls and the middle shape a diamond); additionally, when the vessel is making way through the water, she must exhibit a masthead light or lights,[6] sidelights and a sternlight and, when at anchor, she must exhibit the lights of shape prescribed for anchored vessels.[7]

A power-driven vessel engaged in a towing operation such as severely restricts the towing vessel and her tow in their ability to deviate from her course must, in addition to the lights or shapes prescribed for power-driven vessels when towing,[8] exhibit the lights or shapes prescribed for vessels restricted in their ability to manoeuvre.[9]

A vessel engaged in dredging or underwater operations, when restricted in her ability to manoeuvre, must exhibit the lights and shapes prescribed for vessels restricted in their ability to manoeuvre.[10] In addition, when an obstruction exists, she must exhibit two all-round red lights or two balls in a vertical line to indicate the side on which the obstruction exists and two all-round green lights or two diamonds in a vertical line to indicate the side on which another vessel may pass.[11] When at anchor, she must exhibit the lights or shapes mentioned above instead of those prescribed for vessels at anchor.[12] Whenever the size of a vessel engaged in diving operations makes it impracticable to exhibit all lights and shapes mentioned above, a rigid replica of the International Code flag "A" not less than one metre in height must be exhibited.[13] Measures must be taken to ensure all-round visibility.[14] There must also be exhibited three all-round lights in a vertical line where they can best be seen, the highest and lowest being red and the middle light being white.[15]

A vessel engaged in mineclearance operations must, in addition to the lights prescribed for power-driven vessels underway[16] or to the lights or shape prescribed for a vessel at anchor, as appropriate, exhibit three all-round green lights or three balls.[17] One of these lights or shapes must be exhibited at or near the foremast head and one at each end of the fore yard.[18] These lights or shapes indicate that it is dangerous for another vessel to approach closer than within 1,000 metres of the mineclearance vessel.[19]

Vessels of less than 12 metres in length,[20] except those engaged in diving operations are not required to exhibit the lights and shapes prescribed in this Rule.[21] The signals prescribed in the Rule are not signals of vessels in distress and requiring assistance, which are contained in Annex IV to the Regulations.[22]

---

[1] For the meaning of "vessel not under command" see para. 2.12, note 8, *ante*. For the meaning of "vessel" see para. 1.04, text and notes 15-17, *ante*. For an example of the confusion caused by the unjustified use of "not under command lights" see *The Djerada* [1976] 1 Lloyd's Rep. 50; (C.A.) [1976] 2 Lloyd's Rep. 40.
[2] For the meaning of "all-round light" see para. 3.02, note 10, *ante*.
[3] For the meaning of "sidelights" see para. 3.02, note 7, *ante*.
[4] Merchant Shipping (Distress Signals and Prevention of Collisions) Regulations 1983, Sch. 1, r. 27(a). For the meaning of "sternlight" see para. 3.02, note 8, *ante*. As to the power to make collision regulations, and their application to United Kingdom and other vessels, see paras. 1.04-1.08, *ante*. As to the application of the rules as to lights and the exemptions see para. 3.01, *ante*. 1972 Rule 27 is derived from 1960 Rules 4(a)-(e), (g), 7(g),11 (d) of the First Schedule to the Collision Regulations (Ships and Seaplanes on the Water) and Signals of Distress (Ships) Order 1965, S.I. 1965, No. 1525 (revoked). For a case involving 1960 Rule 4(c), (e) see *The Jin Ping* [1983] 1 Lloyd's Rep. 641. For a comparative table of the 1972 Rules and the 1960 Rules, see para. 6.27, *post*. 1972 Rule 27 has been substantially modified to conform with IMO Resolution A.464 (XII).
[5] For the meaning of "vessel restricted in her ability to manoeuvre" see para. 2.12, note 9, *ante*.
[6] For the meaning of "masthead light" see para. 3.02, note 5, *ante*.
[7] Merchant Shipping (Distress Signals and Prevention of Collisions) Regulations 1983, Sch. 1, r. 27(b). As to the lights and shapes prescribed for vessels at anchor (r. 30) see para. 3.09, *post*.
[8] I.e. the lights or shapes prescribed in ibid., Sch. 1, r. 24(a), Sch. 1, r. 27(c).
[9] Ibid., Sch. 1, r. 27(c). The lights or shapes in question are those prescribed in r. 27(b) (i), (ii).

[10] Ibid., Sch. 1, r. 27(d). The lights or shapes in question are those prescribed in ibid., Sch. 1, r. 27(b) (i), (ii). The Department of Transport has issued guidance on the duties of other vessels in relation to those displaying the signals required by Rule 27(b) and (d); see M.895, para. 8.07, *post*.
[11] Ibid., Sch. 1, r. 27(d) (i), (ii).
[12] Ibid., Sch. 1, r. 27(d) (iii). The lights mentioned above referred to in the text are those prescribed in r. 27(d) and must be exhibited in lieu of those prescribed in r. 30 (see para. 3.09, *post*).
[13] Ibid., Sch. 1, r. 27(e).
[14] Ibid., Sch. 1, r. 27(e)(ii).
[15] Ibid., Sch. 1, r. 27(e)(i).
[16] For the meaning of "underway" see para. 2.12, note 6, *ante*.
[17] Merchant Shipping (Distress Signals and Prevention of Collisions) Regulations 1983, Sch. 1, r. 27(f).
[18] Ibid., Sch. 1, r. 27(f).
[19] Ibid., Sch. 1, r. 27(f).
[20] For the meaning of "length" see para. 2.06, note 19, *ante*.
[21] Merchant Shipping (Distress Signals and Prevention of Collisions) Regulations 1983, Sch. 1, r. 27(g).
[22] Ibid., Sch. 1, r. 27(h). As to the signals of vessels in distress and requiring assistance see para. 4.05, *post*.

3.08 *Vessels constrained by their draught—Rule 28. Pilot vessels—Rule 29*

A vessel constrained by her draught[1] may, in addition to the lights prescribed for power-driven vessels underway,[2] exhibit where they can best be seen three all-round red lights[3] in a vertical line, or a cylinder.[4]

A vessel engaged on pilotage duty must exhibit at or near the masthead two all-round lights in a vertical line, the upper being white and the lower red.[5] When under-way[6] she must in addition exhibit sidelights[7] and a sternlight.[8] When at anchor she must exhibit, in addition to the two all-round lights mentioned above, the light, lights, or shapes prescribed for vessels at anchor.[9] A pilot vessel when not engaged on pilotage duty must exhibit the lights or shapes prescribed for a similar vessel of her length.[10]

[1] For the meaning of "vessel constrained by her draught" see para. 2.12, note 14, *ante*. For the meaning of "vessel" see para. 1.04, text and notes 15-17, *ante*.
[2] As to the lights prescribed for power-driven vessels underway see para. 3.03, *ante*.
[3] For the meaning of "all-round light" see para. 3.02, note 10, *ante*.
[4] Merchant Shipping (Distress Signals and Prevention of Collisions) Regulations 1983, S.I. 1983, No. 708, Sch. 1, r. 28. As to the power to make collision regulations, and their application to United Kingdom and other vessels, see paras. 1.04-1.08, *ante*. As to the application of the rules as to lights and the exemptions see para. 3.01, *ante*. Rule 28 is a rule which was new to the 1972 Rules and was not found in previous regulations.
[5] Merchant Shipping (Distress Signals and Prevention of Collisions) Regulations 1983, Sch. 1, r. 29(a) (i). 1972 Rule 29 is derived from 1960 Rule 8 of the First Schedule to the Collision Regulations (Ships and Seaplanes on the Water) and Signals of Distress (Ships) Order 1965, S.I. 1965, No. 1525 (revoked). For a comparative table of the 1972 Rules and the 1960 Rules see para. 6.29, *post*.
[6] For the meaning of "underway" see para. 2.12, note 6, *ante*.
[7] For the meaning of "sidelights" see para. 3.02, note 7, *ante*.
[8] Merchant Shipping (Distress Signals and Prevention of Collisions) Regulations 1983, Sch. 1, r. 29(a) (ii). For the meaning of " sternlight"see para. 3.02, note 8, *ante*.
[9] Merchant Shipping (Distress Signals and Prevention of Collisions) Regulations 1983, Sch. 1, r. 29(a) (iii). As to the lights and shapes for anchored vessels see para. 3.09, *post*.
[10] Merchant Shipping (Distress Signals and Prevention of Collisions) Regulations 1983, Sch. 1, r. 29(b).

3.09 *Anchored vessels and vessels aground—Rule 30*

A vessel at anchor[1] must exhibit where it can best be seen, in the fore part, an all-round white light[2] or one ball, and, at or near the stern and at a lower level,[3] an all-round white light.[4] A vessel of less than 50 metres in length[5] may exhibit an all-round white light where it can best be seen instead of the lights mentioned above.[6] A vessel at anchor may, and a vessel of 100 metres and more in length must, also use the available working or equivalent lights to illuminate her decks.[7] A vessel aground must exhibit the prescribed lights[8] and in addition, where they can best be seen, two all-round red lights in a vertical line and three balls in a vertical line.[9] A vessel of less than seven metres in length, when at anchor or aground, not in or near a narrow channel,[10] fairway[11] or anchorage, or where other vessels normally navigate, is not required to exhibit the prescribed lights or shapes.[12] A vessel of less than 12 metres in length, when aground, is not required to exhibit the lights or shapes prescribed for vessels aground.[13]

[1] For the meaning of "vessel" see para. 1.04, text and notes 15-17, *ante*. It seems that a vessel is at anchor if actually held to an anchor or fast to moorings which are attached to the ground by an anchor or its equivalent; see *The Esk and The Gitana* (1869) L.R. 2 A. & E. 350; *The Curlew* [1937] P. 30; *The Dunelm* (1884) 9 P.D. 164 C.A., at p. 171. For cases where a vessel has been held not to be at anchor see *The Romance* [1901] P. 15; *The Devonian* [1901] P. 221; *The Esk and The Gitana* (*supra*); *The Faedrelandet* [1895] P. 205, C.A.; *The Titan, The Rambler* (1906) 10 Asp. M.C. 350.
[2] For the meaning of "all-round light" see para. 3.02, note 10, *ante*.
[3] I.e. at a lower level than the all-round white light required to be exhibited in the fore part.
[4] Merchant Shipping (Distress Signals and Prevention of Collisions) Regulations 1983, S.I. 1983, No. 708, Sch. 1, r. 30(a). For a case where a ship has been held partly liable for a collision which occurred when she wrongly failed to exhibit anchor lights, see *The Coral I* [1982] 1 Lloyd's Rep. 441. As to the power to make collision regulations, and their application to United Kingdom and other vessels, see paras. 1.04-1.08, *ante*. As to the application of the rules as to lights and the exemptions see para. 3.02, *ante*. 1972 Rule 30(a)-(d) is derived from 1960 Rule 11 of the First Schedule of the Collision Regulations (Ships and Seaplanes on the Water) and Signals of Distress (Ships) Order 1965, S.I. 1965, No. 1525 (revoked). 1972 Rule 30(e) is derived from 1960 Rule 7(g). For a comparative table of the 1972 Rules and the 1960 Rules see para. 6.30, *post*. A light amidships is not in the "fore part"; see *H.M.S. Truculent* [1951] 2 Lloyd's Rep. 308. As to "at or near the stern" see *The Gannet* [1900] A.C. 234, H.L.
[5] For the meaning of "length" see para. 2.06, note 19, *ante*.
[6] I.e. instead of the lights prescribed in the Merchant Shipping (Distress Signals and Prevention of Collisions) Regulations 1983, Sch. 1, r. 30(a): Sch. 1, r. 30(b).
[7] Ibid., Sch. 1, r. 30(c). This Rule was referred to in *The Coral I*; see note 4, *supra*.
[8] I.e. in addition to the lights prescribed in ibid., Sch. 1, r. 30(a) or (b).
[9] Ibid., Sch. 1, r. 30(d). A vessel dragging through mud is not "aground"; *The Bellanoch* [1907] P. 170, C.A., at p. 174; and see *The Turquoise* [1908] P. 148.
[10] For the meaning of "narrow channel" see para. 2.05, note 2, *ante*.
[11] For the meaning of "fairway" see para. 2.05, note 2, *ante*.
[12] Merchant Shipping (Distress Signals and Prevention of Collisions) Regulations 1983, Sch. 1, r. 30(e). The prescribed lights are those referred to in Sch. 1, r. 30(a), (b), or (d); see *supra*. 1972 Rule 30(e) is derived from 1960 Rule 7(g). See the comparative table, para. 6.30, *post*.
[13] Ibid., Sch. 1, r. 30(f). This is a new provision, implementing IMO Resolution A.464 (XII).

3.10 *Seaplanes—Rule 31*

The application of collision regulations to seaplanes on the water has already been discussed.[1] Where it is impracticable for a seaplane to exhibit lights and shapes of the characteristics or in the positions prescribed in the rules for lights and shapes,[2] she must exhibit lights and shapes as closely similar in characteristics and position as is possible.[3]

[1] See paras. 1.05, text and notes 30, 31; 1.06, text and note 15; 1.07, text and note 7; 1.08, text and note 5; 2.12, text and notes 17-20, *ante*.

[2] I.e. in the Merchant Shipping (Distress Signals and Prevention of Collisions) Regulations 1983, S.I. 1983, No. 708, Sch. 1, rr. 20-30; as to which, see paras. 3.01-3.09, *ante*. As to the power to make collision regulations generally, see paras. 1.04-1.08, *ante*.

[3] Merchant Shipping (Distress Signals and Prevention of Collisions) Regulations 1983, S.I. 1983, No. 708, Sch. 1, r. 31. 1972 Rule 31 is derived from 1960 Rule 1(a) contained in the First Schedule of the Collision Regulations (Ships and Seaplanes on the Water) and Signals of Distress (Ships) Order 1965, S.I. 1965, No. 1525 (revoked). For a comparative table of the 1972 Rules and the 1960 Rules, see para. 6.31, *post*.

EXAMPLES OF LIGHTS

PLATE 1. Examples of Lights

i. Rule 23(a).
   A power-driven vessel underway.

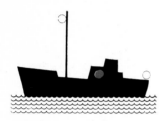

ii. Rule 23(a)(ii).
   A power-driven vessel of less than
   50 metres in length, underway.

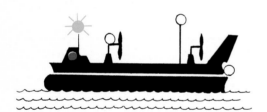

iii. Rule 23(b).
   An air-cushion vessel operating
   in the non-displacement mode,
   length of vessel exceeding 50
   metres.

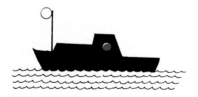

iv. Rule 23(c)(i).
   A power-driven vessel of less than
   12 metres in length, underway.

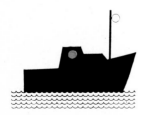

v. Rule 23(c)(ii).
   A power-driven vessel of less than
   7 metres in length whose speed
   does not exceed 7 knots,
   underway.

PLATE 2. EXAMPLES OF LIGHTS

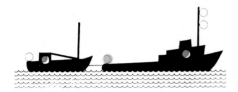

vi. Rule 24(a), (e).
   A power-driven vessel towing another vessel, length of tow not exceeding 200 metres.

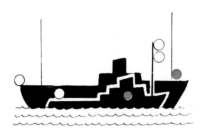

vii. Rule 24(c), (f)(ii).
   A power-driven vessel towing alongside, with a vessel being towed alongside. Towing vessel less than 50 metres in length.

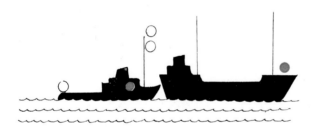

viii. Rule 24(f)(i).
   A vessel being pushed ahead, not being part of a composite unit. Pushing vessel less than 50 metres in length.

ix. Rule 24(g)(i).
   A vessel towing a partly submerged vessel or object of less than 25 metres in breadth.

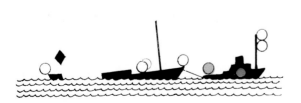

x. Rule 24(g)(ii).
   A vessel towing a partly submerged vessel or object of 25 metres or more in breadth but less than 100 metres in length.

PLATE 3. EXAMPLES OF LIGHTS

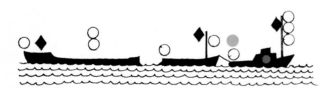

xi. Rule 24(g)(iii).
A vessel towing a partly submerged vessel or object exceeding 100 metres in length and 25 metres in breadth. Length of tow exceeding 200 metres.

xii. Rule 25(a), (c).
A sailing vessel underway.

xiii. Rule 25(b).
A sailing vessel of less than 20 metres in length, underway.

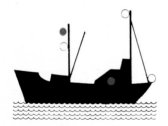

xiv. Rule 26(b).
A vessel engaged in trawling, making way through the water.

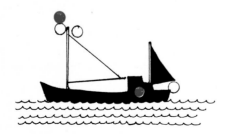

xv. Rule 26(c).
A vessel engaged in fishing other than trawling; making way through the water, with outlying gear extending more than 150 metres horizontally from the vessel.

PLATE 4. EXAMPLES OF LIGHTS

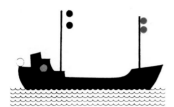

xvi. Rule 27(a).
A vessel not under command, making way through the water.

xvii. Rule 27(b).
A vessel restricted in her ability to manoeuvre, not engaged in mineclearance operations, making way through the water.

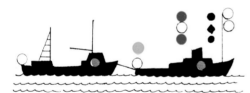

xviii. Rule 27(c).
A vessel engaged in a towing operation such as severely restricts the towing vessel and her tow in their ability to deviate from their course.

xix. Rule 27(d).
A vessel engaged in dredging, when restricted in her ability to manoeuvre and making way through the water.

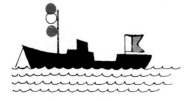

xx. Rule 27(e).
A vessel engaged in diving operations and unable to exhibit the lights and shapes prescribed by Rule 27(d).

PLATE 5. EXAMPLES OF LIGHTS

xxi. Rule 27(f).
A vessel of less than 50 metres in length engaged in mineclearance operations, underway.

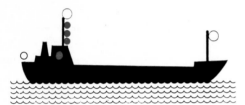

xxii. Rule 28.
A vessel constrained by her draught, underway.

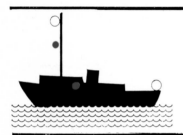

xxiii. Rule 29(a).
A vessel engaged on pilotage duty, underway.

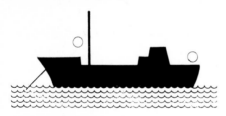

xxiv. Rule 30(a).
A vessel at anchor.

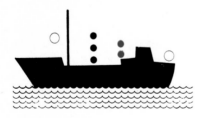

xxv. Rule 30(d).
A vessel aground.

xxvi. Rule 31.
A seaplane at anchor.

CHAPTER FOUR

COLLISION REGULATIONS—SOUND AND LIGHT SIGNALS. DISTRESS SIGNALS

4.01 *Equipment for sound signals—Rule 33*

A vessel[1] of 12 metres or more in length[2] must be provided with a whistle[3] and a bell and a vessel of 100 metres or more in length must, in addition, be provided with a gong, the tone and sound of which cannot be confused with that of the bell.[4] The whistle, bell and gong must comply with the specifications set out in the third annex to the 1972 Rules.[5] The bell or gong, or both, may be replaced by other equipment having the same respective sound characteristics, provided that manual sounding of the prescribed signals must always be possible.[6] A vessel of less than 12 metres in length is not obliged to carry the sound signalling appliances mentioned above but, if she does not, she must be provided with some other means of making an efficient sound signal.[7]

A "whistle" is defined as meaning any sound signalling appliance capable of producing the prescribed blasts and which complies with the third annex specifications.[8] The third annex prescribes details as to the frequency and range of audibility of whistles,[9] the limits of their fundamental frequencies,[10] sound signal intensity and range of audibility,[11] directional properties[12] and positioning of whistles,[13] and lays down rules as to the fitting of more than one whistle[14] and combined whistle systems.[15] The third annex also provides that a bell or gong, or other device having similar sound characteristics, must produce a sound pressure level of not less than 110 dB at a distance of one metre from it.[16] There are also laid down detailed requirements for the construction of bells and gongs including minimum diameters for bell-mouths.[17] The construction of sound signal appliances, their performance and their installation on board the vessel, must be to the satisfaction of the appropriate authority of the State whose flag the vessel is entitled to fly.[18]

The special provision as to additional whistle signals for ships of war and vessels proceeding under convoy has already been mentioned,[19] as has the exemption from the rules for the disposition and characteristics of sound-signalling appliances in cases where full compliance with the rules is impossible.[20] In addition there is an exemption, until nine years after the date of entry into force of the 1972 Rules,[21] from the requirements for sound signal appliances prescribed in the third annex.[22] The exemption applies to any vessel (or class of vessels), provided that she complies with the requirements of the 1960 Rules,[23] the keel of which was laid or which was at a corresponding stage of construction before the entry into force of the 1972 Rules.[24]

[1] For the meaning of "vessel" see para. 1.04, text and notes 15-17, *ante.*
[2] For the meaning of "length" see para. 2.06, note 9, *ante.*
[3] For the meaning of "whistle" see the text to note 8, *infra.*
[4] Merchant Shipping (Distress Signals and Prevention of Collisions) Regulations 1983, S.I. 1983, No. 708, Sch. 1, r. 33(a). 1972 Rule 33(a) is derived from 1960 Rule 15(a) of the First Schedule to the Collision Regulations (Ships and Seaplanes on the Water) and Signals of Distress (Ships) Order 1965, S.I. 1965, No. 1525 (revoked). As to the power to make collision regulations, and their application to United Kingdom and other vessels, see paras. 1.04-1.08, *ante.* For a comparative table of the 1972 Rules and the 1960 Rules, see para. 6.33, *post.* As to exemptions see the text and notes 20-24, *infra.* It should be noted that there was formerly no express power to prescribe sound signals other than fog signals; but see *The Aristocrat* [1908] P. 9, C.A. There are now ample powers to prescribe any signals; see the Merchant Shipping Act 1979, s. 21; and para. 1.05, *ante.*
[5] Merchant Shipping (Distress Signals and Prevention of Collisions) Regulations 1983, Sch. 1, r. 33(a). As to Annex III see para. 6.41, *post,* and the text and notes 9-17, *infra.*
[6] Ibid., Sch. 1, r. 33(a).
[7] Ibid., Sch. 1, r. 33(b).
[8] Ibid., Sch. 1, r. 32(a).
[9] Ibid., Sch. 1, Annex III, s. 1(a).
[10] Ibid., Sch. 1, Annex III, s. 1(b).
[11] Ibid., Sch. 1, Annex III, s. 1(c).
[12] Ibid., Sch. 1, Annex III, s. 1(d).
[13] Ibid., Sch. 1, Annex III, s. 1(e).
[14] Ibid., Sch. 1, Annex III, s. 1(f).
[15] Ibid., Sch. 1, Annex III, s. 1(g).
[16] Ibid., Sch. 1, Annex III, s. 2(a).
[17] Ibid., Sch. 1, Annex III, s. 2(b).
[18] Ibid., Sch. 1, Annex III, s. 3. As to the powers of surveyors, see para. 5.05, *post.* For the meaning of "the appropriate authority" see para. 1.07, note 9, *ante.*
[19] See para. 3.01, text and notes 36, 37, *ante.*
[20] See para. 3.01, text and note 35, *ante.*
[21] I.e. nine years after 15th July 1977.
[22] Merchant Shipping (Distress Signals and Prevention of Collisions) Regulations 1983, Sch. 1, r. 38(g).
[23] I.e. with the requirements of the 1960 Rules set out in the First Schedule to the Order of 1965 (revoked).
[24] See the Merchant Shipping (Distress Signals and Prevention of Collisions) Regulations 1983, Sch. 1, r. 38.

4.02 *Manoeuvring and warning signals—Rule 34*

When vessels[1] are in sight of one another,[2] a power-driven vessel[3] underway,[4] when manoeuvring[5] as authorized or required by the rules,[6] must indicate that manoeuvre by the following signals on her whistle:[7]—one short blast to mean "I am altering my course[8] to starboard;"—two short blasts[9] to mean "I am altering my course to port;"—three short blasts to mean "I am operating astern propulsion."[10] Any vessel may supplement these whistle signals by light signals, repeated as appropriate, while the manoeuvre is being carried out.[11] These light signals have the following significance:—one flash[12] to mean "I am altering my course to starboard;"—two flashes to mean "I am altering my course to port;"—three flashes to mean "I am operating astern propulsion."[13]

When vessels are in sight of one another in a narrow channel[14] or fairway[15] a vessel intending to overtake another must, in compliance with the rule for overtaking in

narrow channels,[16] indicate her intention by the following signals on her whistle:—
two prolonged blasts[17] followed by one short blast to mean "I intend to overtake you
on your starboard side;"—two prolonged blasts followed by two short blasts to mean
"I intend to overtake you on your port side."[18] The vessel about to be overtaken, when
acting in accordance with the rule for overtaking in narrow channels, must indicate her
agreement by the following signal on her whistle:— one prolonged, one short, one
prolonged and one short blast, in that order.[19]

When vessels in sight of one another are approaching each other and from any
cause either vessel fails to understand the intentions or actions of the other, or is in
doubt whether sufficient action is being taken by the other to avoid collision, the
vessel in doubt must immediately indicate such doubt by giving at least five short and
rapid blasts on the whistle.[20] This signal may be supplemented by a light signal of at
least five short and rapid flashes.[21]

A vessel nearing a bend or an area of a channel or fairway where other vessels may
be obscured by an intervening obstruction must sound one prolonged blast.[22] This
signal must be answered with a prolonged blast by any approaching vessel which may
be within hearing around the bend or behind the intervening obstruction.[23]

If whistles are fitted on board a vessel at a distance apart of more than 100 metres,
one whistle only must be used for giving manoeuvring and warning signals.[24]

[1] For the meaning of "vessel" see para. 1.04, text and notes 15-17, *ante*.
[2] "In sight of one another" means "in sight with reference to the manoeuvres which a vessel is
authorized or required to take, having regard to the other vessel approaching, for the purposes of
avoiding collision . . ."; *The Bellanoch* [1907] P. 170, C.A., at p. 181, per Alverstone, C.J.; [1907]
A.C. 269, H.L. See also *The Lucile Bloomfield* [1966] 2 Lloyd's Rep. 239 at p. 245, *per* Karminski, J.
[3] For the meaning of "power-driven vessel" see para. 2.06, note 21, *ante*.
[4] For the meaning of "underway" see para. 2.12, note 6, *ante*.
[5] It seems that manoeuvring involves some alteration of course or a reversal of direction, although
only a small alteration may cause the rule to come into operation; see *The Aristocrat* [1908] P. 9,
C.A.; *The Varundo* (1939) 65 Ll.L.Rep. 20; but cf., *The Royalgate* [1967] 1 Lloyd's Rep. 352. These
cases were decided on the words "taking a course" in previous regulations.
[6] I.e. as authorized or required by the steering and sailing rules; as to which see Chapter 2, *ante*.
"Authorized" includes any course which, for the safety of vessels, good seamanship requires to be
taken with reference to the other vessel then in sight: see *The Uskmoor* [1902] P. 250 at p. 254, *per*
Sir Francis Jeune, P.; and *The Anselm* [1907] P. 151, C.A.; *The Aristocrat* [1908] P. 9, C.A.; *The
Hero* [1911] P. 128; *The Bellanoch* [1907] P. 170; *The Castor* (1937) 58 Ll.L.Rep. 127 at p. 134,
H.L.
[7] For the meaning of "whistle" see para. 4.01, text and note 8, *ante*. The whistle signals must not be
used to indicate a mere future intention; see *The Shell Spirit 2* [1962] 2 Lloyd's Rep. 252; *The Friston*
[1963] 1 Lloyd's Rep. 74; *The Century* [1963] 1 Lloyd's Rep. 99. Local rules may, however,
allow for whistle signals to be used to indicate an intention to manoeuvre; *The Carl Julius* [1963] 1
Lloyd's Rep. 104.
[8] It seems that "course" does not mean course by the compass, but the action of the vessel; see
The Hochelaga (1931) 41 Ll.L.Rep. 133, P.C.
[9] A "short blast" means a blast of about one second's duration: Merchant Shipping (Distress Signals
and Prevention of Collisions) Regulations 1983, S.I. 1983, No. 708, Sch. 1, r. 32(b).
[10] Ibid., Sch. 1, r. 34(a). 1972 Rule 34(a) is derived from 1960 Rule 28(a) of the First Schedule to the
Collision Regulations (Ships and Seaplanes on the Water) and Signals of Distress (Ships) Order
1965, S.I. 1965, No. 1525 (revoked). As to the power to make collision regulations, and their

application to United Kingdom and other vessels, see paras 1.04-1.08, *ante*. For a comparative table of the 1972 Rules and the 1960 Rules, see para. 6.34, *post*. The provisions of Rule 34(a) are mandatory and apply whether or not the signal will be heard and whether or not it is superfluous; see *Owners S.S. Haugland* v. *Owners S.S. Karamea* [1922] 1 A.C. 68, H.L.; *The Kashmir* (1920) 3 Ll.L.Rep. 240; cf., *The Testbank* (1941) 70 Ll.L.Rep. 270: 72 Ll.L. Rep. 6, C.A. Failure to sound a manoeuvring signal may amount to contributory negligence; see *The Dayspring* [1965] 1 W.L.R. 311; [1965] 1 Lloyd's Rep. 103. See also *The Statue of Liberty* [1971] 2 Lloyd's Rep. 277 (H.L.); *The Homer* [1972] 1 Lloyds Rep. 429; (C.A.) [1973] 1 Lloyd's Rep. 501; *The Adolf Leonhardt* [1973] 2 Lloyd's Rep. 318; *The Sea Star* [1976] 1 Lloyd's Rep. 115; (C.A.) [1976] 2 Lloyd's Rep. 477; *The Kylix and The Rustringen* [1979] 1 Lloyd's Rep. 133.

[11] Merchant Shipping (Distress Signals and Prevention of Collisions) Regulations 1983, Sch. 1, r. 34(b). The light used for such signals must, if fitted, be an all-round white light, visible at a range of five miles and must comply with the provisions of Annex 1: Sch. 1, r. 34(b) (iii). As to Annex 1, see paras. 3.01, text and notes 9-20, *ante*, 6.39, *post*. For the meaning of "all-round light" see para. 3.02, note 10, *ante*. For the meaning of "mile" see para. 3.02, note 6, *ante*.

[12] The duration of each flash must be about one second, the interval between flashes must be about one second, and the interval between successive signals must be not less than 10 seconds: Merchant Shipping (Distress Signals and Prevention of Collisions) Regulations 1983, Sch. 1, r. 34(b) (ii).

[13] Ibid., r. 34(b) (i). 1972 Rule 34(b) is derived from 1960 Rule 28(c) of the 1960 Rules (revoked). For the comparative table, see para. 6.34, *post*.

[14] For the meaning of "narrow channel" see para. 2.05, note 2, *ante*.

[15] For the meaning of "fairway" see para. 2.05, note 2, *ante*.

[16] I.e. in compliance with Rule 9(e) (i) of the Schedule to the Merchant Shipping (Distress Signals and Prevention of Collisions) Regulations 1983, see para. 2.05, text and notes 11-14, *ante*.

[17] A "prolonged blast" means a blast of from four to six seconds duration: Merchant Shipping (Distress Signals and Prevention of Collisions) Regulations 1983, Sch. 1, r. 32(c).

[18] Ibid., Sch. 1, r. 34(c) (i).

[19] Ibid., Sch. 1, r. 34(c) (ii). Rule 34(c) is a new rule, not found in previous regulations. As to the appropriate action for a vessel being overtaken in a narrow channel or fairway, see para. 2.05,text and notes 12,13, *ante*.

[20] Merchant Shipping (Distress Signals and Prevention of Collisions) Regulations 1983, Sch. 1, r. 34(d). 1972 Rule 34(d) is derived from 1960 Rule 28(b) (revoked); for an application of the old rule, see *The Jaladhir* [1961] 2 Lloyd's Rep. 13. For the comparative table, see para 6.34, *post*.

[21] Merchant Shipping (Distress Signals and Prevention of Collisions) Regulations 1983, Sch. 1, r. 34(d).

[22] Ibid., Sch. 1, r. 34(e). 1972 Rule 34(e) is derived from 1960 Rule 25(b) (revoked). For the comparative table, see para. 6.34, *post*.

[23] Ibid., Sch. 1, r. 34(e).

[24] Ibid., Sch. 1, r. 34(f). Rule 34(f) was new to the 1972 Rules and was not found in previous regulations.

4.03 *Sound signals in restricted visibility—Rule 35*

In or near an area of restricted visibility,[1] whether by day or night the following signals are prescribed and must be used as follows.[2] A power-driven vessel[3] making way through the water must sound at intervals of not more than two minutes one prolonged blast.[4] A power-driven vessel underway[5] but stopped and making no way through the water must sound at intervals of not more than two minutes two prolonged blasts in succession with an interval of about two seconds between them.[6] A vessel not under command,[7] a vessel restricted in her ability to manoeuvre,[8] a vessel constrained by her draught,[9] a sailing vessel,[10] a vessel engaged in fishing[11] and a vessel engaged in towing or pushing another vessel must, instead of the signals described above,[12] sound at intervals of not more than two minutes three blasts in succession, namely one prolonged followed by two short blasts.[13] A vessel engaged in fishing, when at anchor, and a vessel restricted in her ability to manoeuvre when carrying out her work at anchor, must instead of the signals prescribed for a vessel at anchor[14] sound the signal prescribed above for a vessel not under command.[15] A vessel towed or if more than one vessel is towed the last vessel of the tow, if manned, must at intervals of not more than two minutes sound four blasts in succession, namely one prolonged blast folllowed by three short blasts.[16] When practicable, this signal must be made immediately after the signal made by the towing vessel.[17] When a pushing vessel and a vessel being pushed are rigidly connected in a composite unit, they are to be regarded as a power-driven vessel and must give the appropriate signals.[18]

A vessel at anchor[19] must at intervals of not more than one minute ring the bell[20] rapidly for about five seconds. In a vessel of 100 metres or more in length the bell must be sounded in the forepart[21] of the vessel and immediately after the ringing of the bell the gong[22] must be sounded rapidly for about five seconds in the after part of the vessel.[23] A vessel at anchor may in addition sound three blasts in succession, namely one short, one prolonged and one short blast, to give warning of her position and of the possibility of collision to an approaching vessel.[24] A vessel aground[25] must give the bell signal (and if required the gong signal) prescribed for vessels at anchor;[26] and must in addition give three separate and distinct strokes on the bell immediately before and after the rapid ringing of the bell.[27] A vessel aground may in addition sound an appropriate whistle signal.[28]

A vessel of less than 12 metres in length[29] is not obliged to give the signals mentioned above but, if she does not, she must make some other efficient sound signal at intervals of not more than two minutes.[30] A pilot vessel when engaged on pilotage duty may, in addition to the signals prescribed for vessels underway or at anchor, sound an identity signal consisting of four short blasts.[31]

---

[1] For the meaning of "restricted visibility" see para. 2.13, note 3, *ante*.

[2] Merchant Shipping (Distress Signals and Prevention of Collisions) Regulations 1983, S. I. 1983, No. 708, Sch.1, r. 35. 1972 Rule 35 (apart from r. 35(d)) is derived from 1960 Rule 15(c) of the First Schedule to the Collision Regulations (Ships and Seaplanes on the Water) and Signals of Distress (Ships) Order 1965, S.I. 1965, No. 1525 (revoked). As to the power to make collision regulations, and their application to United Kingdom and other vessels, see paras. 1.04-1.08, *ante*. For a comparative table of the 1972 Rules and the 1960 Rules, see para. 6.35, *post*. English courts have not defined the degree of restriction on visibility which is necessary to make the use of these signals obligatory but it has been held that a vessel should give the signals, even though she is not in an area of restricted visibility, if she is near such an area. It seems that failure to do so might be a failure to act in a seamanlike manner; see *The Milanese* (1881) 4 Asp. M.C. 318. Cf., *The Bernard Hall* (1902) 71 L.J. Ad. 72. See also *The N. Strong* [1892] P. 105; *The St. Paul* [1909] P. 43, C.A. The fact that another ship hears no signal, when it is proved that signals were properly sounded by a ship, does not raise any presumption that a proper look-out was not kept, nor will proof that a proper look-out has been kept on board a ship which hears no signal raise a presumption that no signal was given by the first ship; *The Zadok* (1883) 9 P.D. 114, C.A.; *The Rosetta* (1888) 6 Asp. M.C. 310; *The Merthyr* (1898) 8 Asp. M.C. 475; *The Campania* [1901] P. 289, C.A.; *The Chiankiang* [1908] A.C. 251, P.C.; *The Nador* [1909] P. 300; *The Curran* [1910] P. 184; *The Emlyn* [1918] P. 67; cf., *The Plover* [1956] 2 Lloyd's Rep. 261. As to the duty to keep a look-out see para 2.01, *ante*.

³ For the meaning of "power-driven vessel" see para. 2.06, note 21, *ante*. For the meaning of "vessel" see para. 1.04, text and notes 15-17, *ante*.
⁴ Merchant Shipping (Distress Signals and Prevention of Collisions) Regulations 1983, Sch. 1, r. 35(a). For the meaning of "prolonged blast" see para. 4.02, note 17, *ante*.
⁵ For the meaning of "underway" see para. 2.12, note 6, *ante*.
⁶ Merchant Shipping (Distress Signals and Prevention of Collisions) Regulations 1983, Sch. 1, r. 35(b). This signal should be given only when the vessel is completely stopped; see *The Lifland* (1934) 49 Ll.L.Rep. 285; cf., *The Haliotis* (1932) 44 Ll.L.Rep. 288, C.A.; *The British Confidence* [1951] 1 Lloyd's Rep. 447, H.L.; *The Almizar* [1971] 2 Lloyd's Rep. 290, (H.L.) Other vessels are entitled to assume that the two-blast signal will only be given when the signalling vessel is stopped; *The Matiana* (1908) 25 T.L.R. 51; *The Kaiser Wilhelm II* (1915) 85 L.J.P. 26, C.A.; *The Marcel* (1920) 2 Ll.L.Rep. 52. However, if the other vessel is not misled, the vessel giving a two-blast signal while not completely stopped will be excused if the error did not cause or contribute to the collision; *The Yewvalley* (1932) 44 Ll.L.Rep. 252, 262; *The Burma* (1932) 43 Ll.L.Rep. 245. When a vessel re-starts she should change her signal to one prolonged blast; *The Dimitrios Chandris* (1944) 72 Ll.L.Rep. 489; cf., *The Canada* (1939) 63 Ll.L.Rep. 112.
⁷ For the meaning of "vessel not under command" see para. 2.12, note 8, *ante*.
⁸ For the meaning of "vessel restricted in her ability to manoeuvre" see para. 2.12, note 9, *ante*.
⁹ For the meaning of "vessel constrained by her draught" see para. 2.12, note 14, *ante*.
¹⁰ For the meaning of "sailing vessel" see para. 2.06, note 20, *ante*.
¹¹ For the meaning of "vessel engaged in fishing" see para. 2.05, note 5, *ante*.
¹² I.e. the signals prescribed in the Merchant Shipping (Distress Signals and Prevention of Collisions) Regulations 1983, Sch. 1, r. 35(a) or (b); see the text and notes 3-6, *supra*.
¹³ Ibid., Sch. 1, r. 35(c). For the meaning of "short blast" see para. 4.02, note 9, *ante*. When a tug is fast to a vessel but not towing, and the vessel about to be towed is giving proper signals, the tug should not give signals until she starts to move; *The Sargasso* [1912] P. 192.
¹⁴ I.e. the signals prescribed by the Merchant Shipping (Distress Signals and Prevention of Collisions) Regulations 1983, Sch 1, r. 35(g); see the text and notes 23-26, *infra*.
¹⁵ Ibid., Sch. 1, r. 35(d). This is a new provision implementing IMO Resolution A.464 (XII).
¹⁶ Merchant Shipping (Distress Signals and Prevention of Collisions) Regulations 1983, Sch. 1, r. 35(e).
¹⁷ Ibid., Sch. 1, r. 35(e).
¹⁸ Ibid., Sch. 1, r. 35(f).
¹⁹ For the meaning of "at anchor" see para. 3.09, note 1, *ante*.
²⁰ As to the bell see para. 4.01, text and notes 16-18, *ante*.
²¹ As to the "the forepart" see para. 3.09, note 4, *ante*.
²² As to the gong see para. 4.01, text and notes 16-18, *ante*.
²³ Merchant Shipping (Distress Signals and Prevention of Collisions) Regulations 1983, Sch. 1, r. 35(g).
²⁴ Ibid., Sch. 1, r. 35(g).
²⁵ For the meaning of "aground" see para. 3.09, note 9, *ante*.
²⁶ I.e. the signals in ibid., Sch. 1, r. 35(g); see the text and notes 17-22, *supra*.
²⁷ Ibid., Sch. 1, r. 35(h).
²⁸ Ibid., Sch. 1, r. 35(h).
²⁹ For the meaning of "length" see para. 2.06, note 19, *ante*.
³⁰ Merchant Shipping (Distress Signals and Prevention of Collisions) Regulations 1983, Sch. 1, r. 34(i).
³¹ Ibid., Sch. 1, r. 35(j). As to the prescribed signals for vessels underway and at anchor see the text to notes 3-6, 19-24, *supra*. As to the signals for fishing vessels and vessels restricted in their ability to manoeuvre when carrying out their work at anchor, see the text and notes 14, 15, *supra*. The Department of Transport has issued guidance on the use of this signal for pilotage and harbour authorities; see M.870, para. 8.08, *post*.

4.04 *Signals to attract attention—Rule 36*

Any vessel¹ may, if necessary to attract the attention of another vessel, make light or sound signals that cannot be mistaken for any signal authorized elsewhere in the rules, or may direct the beam of her searchlight in the direction of the danger, in such a way as not to embarrass any vessel.[2] Any light to attract the attention of another vessel must be such that it cannot be mistaken for any aid to navigation.[3] For the purpose of this Rule the use of high intensity intermittent or revolving lights, such as strobe lights, is to be avoided.[4]

[1] For the meaning of "vessel" see para. 1.04, text and notes 15-17, *ante*
[2] Merchant Shipping (Distress Signals and Prevention of Collisions) Regulations 1983, S.I. 1983, No. 708, Sch. 1, r. 36. The first part of 1972 Rule 36 is derived from 1960 Rule 12 of the First Schedule to the Collision Regulations (Ships and Seaplanes on the Water) and Signals of Distress (Ships) Order 1965, S.I. 1965, No. 1525 (revoked). As to the power to make collision regulations, and their application to United Kingdom and other vessels, see paras. 1.04-1.08, *ante*. For a comparative table of the 1972 Rules and the 1960 Rules, see para. 6.36, *post*. For a case on 1960 Rule 12 see *Stein and Others* v. *The Kathy K and S.N. No. 1, Egmont Towing & Sorting Ltd., Shields Navigation Ltd., Helsing and Iverson* (Can. Ct.) [1972] 2 Lloyd's Rep. 36; (Can. Sup. Ct.) [1976] 1 Lloyd's Rep. 153.
[3] Merchant Shipping (Distress Signals and Prevention of Collisions) Regulations 1983, Sch. 1, r. 36.
[4] Ibid., Sch. 1, r. 36. The provisions expounded in the text to this note and note 3, *supra*, are new, implementing IMO Resolution A.464 (XII).

4.05 *Distress Signals—Rule 37*

When a vessel[1] is in distress and requires assistance, she must use or exhibit the following prescribed signals which, used or exhibited either together or separately, indicate distress and need of assistance: a gun or other explosive signal fired at intervals of about a minute;[2] a continuous sounding with any fog-signalling apparatus;[3] rockets or shells, throwing red stars fired one at a time at short intervals;[4] a signal made by radiotelegraphy or by any other signalling method consisting of the group . . . - - - . . .(SOS) in the Morse Code;[5] a signal sent by radiotelephony consisting of the spoken word "Mayday";[6] the International Code Signal of distress indicated by N.C.;[7] a signal consisting of a square flag having above or below it a ball or anything resembling a ball;[8] flames on board the vessel (as from a burning tar barrel, oil barrel, etc.);[9] a rocket parachute flare or a hand flare showing a red light;[10] a smoke signal giving off orange-coloured smoke;[11] slowly and repeatedly raising and lowering arms outstretched to each side;[12] the radiotelegraph alarm signal;[13] the radiotelephone alarm signal; [14] signals transmitted by emergency position-indicating radio beacons.[15] The use or exhibition of any of the foregoing signals except for the purpose of indicating distress and need of assistance and the use of other signals which may be confused with any of the above signals is prohibited.[16]

Attention is drawn to the relevant sections of the International Code of Signals,[17] the Merchant Ship Search and Rescue Manual[18] and the following signals: a piece of orange-coloured canvas with either a black square and circle or other appropriate symbol (for identification from the air);[19] a dye-marker.[20]

[1] For the meaning of "vessel" see para. 1.04, text and notes 15-17, *ante*.
[2] Merchant Shipping (Distress Signals and Prevention of Collisions) Regulations 1983, S.I. 1983, No. 708, Sch. 1, r. 37, Annex IV, s. 1(a). 1972 Rule 37 and Annex IV are derived from 1960 Rule 31 of the

First Schedule to the Collision Regulations (Ships and Seaplanes on the Water) and Signals of Distress (Ships) Order 1965, S.I. 1965, No. 1525 (revoked). For a comparative table of the 1972 Rules and the 1960 Rules, see para. 6.42, *post*. As to the power to prescribe signals of distress see para 1.05, text and note 10, *ante*. As to the power to apply such signals to foreign vessels, see para. 1.06, *ante*. See also paras. 1.07, 1.08, *ante*. As to the rules which have been made prescribing the circumstances in which signals of distress are to be used or revoked see para. 4.06, *post*.
[3] Merchant Shipping (Distress Signals and Prevention of Collisions) Regulations 1983, Sch. 1, Annex IV, s. 1(b).
[4] Ibid., Sch. 1, Annex IV, s. 1(c).
[5] Ibid., Sch. 1, Annex IV, s. 1(d).
[6] Ibid., Sch. 1, Annex IV, s. 1(e).
[7] Ibid., Sch. 1, Annex IV, s. 1(f).
[8] Ibid., Sch. 1, Annex IV, s. 1(g).
[9] Ibid., Sch. 1, Annex IV, s. 1(h).
[10] Ibid., Sch. 1, Annex IV, s. 1(i).
[11] Ibid., Sch. 1, Annex IV, s. 1(j).
[12] Ibid., Sch. 1, Annex IV, s. 1(k).
[13] Ibid., Sch. 1, Annex IV, s. 1(l).
[14] Ibid., Sch. 1, Annex IV, s. 1(m).
[15] Ibid., Sch. 1, Annex IV s. 1(n). As to the obligation to assist vessels in distress see para. 1.12, *ante*.
[16] Merchant Shipping (Distress Signals and Prevention of Collisions) Regulations 1983, Sch. 1, Annex IV, s. 2. 1972 Annex IV, s. 2, is derived from 1960 Rule 31(b). For the comparative table, see para. 6.42, *post*. Using or displaying the signals described, *supra*, otherwise than as prescribed, is an offence; see para. 1.10, text and notes 24-26, *ante*.
[17] I.e. the International Code of Signals (1969) published by Her Majesty's Stationery Office; Merchant Shipping (Distress Signals and Prevention of Collisions) Regulations, art. 1(2) (d).
[18] I.e. the Merchant Ship Search and Rescue Manual published in 1980 by IMO; see Merchant Shipping (Distress Signals and Prevention of Collisions) Regulations 1983, reg. 1(2) (d); as to IMO, see para. 1.03, *ante*.
[19] Merchant Shipping (Distress Signals and Prevention of Collisions) Regulations 1983, Sch. 1, Annex IV, s. 3(a).
[20] Ibid., Sch. 1, Annex IV, s. 3(b). For the meaning of "appropriate authority" see para. 1.07, note 9, *ante*.

4.06 *Rules for Distress Signals*

The Secretary of State[1] has made the following rules[2] prescribing the circumstances in which distress signals are to be used and the circumstances in which they are to be revoked.[3] No signal of distress[4] may be used by any vessel[5] unless the master[6] of the vessel so orders.[7] The master of the vessel must not order any signal of distress to be used by his vessel unless he is satisfied that his vessel is in serious and imminent danger, or that another ship or an aircraft is in serious and imminent danger and cannot itself send that signal;[8] he must also be satisfied that the vessel in danger (whether his own vessel or another vessel) or the aircraft in danger, as the case may be, requires immediate assistance in addition to any assistance then available to her.[9] The master of a vessel which has sent any signal of distress by means of radio, or other cause, must cause that signal to be revoked, by all appropriate means as soon as he is satisfied that the vessel or aircraft to which the signal relates is no longer in need of assistance as mentioned above.[10] The rules for signals of distress do not apply to seaplanes[11] and it is doubtful whether they apply to hovercraft.[12]

[1] As to the Secretary of State and his functions see para. 5.01, *post*.

[2] I.e. the Merchant Shipping (Signals of Distress) Rules 1977, S.I. 1977, No. 1010.

[3] As to the power to make such rules, see para. 1.05, text and note 10, *ante* Breach of the rules is an offence; see para. 1.10, text and notes 24-26, *ante*.

[4] "Signal of distress" means any of the distress signals prescribed in the Merchant Shipping (Distress Signals and Prevention of Collisions) Regulations 1983, S.I. 1983, No. 708, reg. 2(2), for use by vessels (other than seaplanes and hovercraft) as signals of distress (see para. 4.05, *ante*): Merchant Shipping (Signals of Distress) Rules 1977, r. 2; Merchant Shipping (Distress Signals and Prevention of Collisions) Regulations 1983, reg. 1(5) (d), Sch. 2, Part IV.

[5] For the meaning of "vessel" in the Merchant Shipping Acts, see para. 1.04, notes 15-17, *ante*. As to seaplanes and hovercraft, see the text and notes 11, 12, *infra*.

[6] For the meaning of "master" in the Merchant Shipping Acts see para. 1.10, note 5, *ante*.

[7] Merchant Shipping (Signals of Distress) Rules 1977, r. 1(1).

[8] Ibid., r. 3(2) (a).

[9] Ibid., r. 3(2) (b).

[10] Ibid., r. 3(3).

[11] See the Merchant Shipping Signals of Distress) Rules 1977, r. 2 (note 4, *supra*); Merchant Shipping (Distress Signals and Prevention of Collisions) Regulations 1983, reg. 2; Collision Rules (Seaplanes) Order 1983, S.I. 1983, No. 768, art. 4(b).

[12] The Merchant Shipping (Signals of Distress) Rules 1965, S.I. 1965, No. 1550, were made applicable to hovercraft by the Hovercraft (Application of Enactments) Order 1972, art. 8. The 1965 Rules were revoked by the Merchant Shipping (Signals of Distress) Rules 1977, r. 1(3), and subsequent Hovercraft (Application of Enactments) Amendment Orders have not made the 1977 Rules applicable to hovercraft. However, it may be that references in the Application of Enactments Order of 1972 to the 1965 Rules are now to be construed as references to the 1977 Rules. This is because both the 1972 Order and the 1977 Rules contained provisions applying the Interpretation Act 1889 to their own construction, as if they were Acts of Parliament; and the 1977 Rules provide that the 1965 Rules revoked by them are to be treated as an Act of Parliament; see the Merchant Shipping (Signals of Distress) Rules 1977, r. 1(2). It may therefore be that in spite of the fact that the Rules of 1977 are stated not to apply to hovercraft (see note 4, *supra*), they are nevertheless made applicable to hovercraft by the Interpretation Act 1978, s. 17(2)(a).

CHAPTER FIVE

ADMINISTRATION AND ENFORCEMENT

SECT. (1) Administration

5.01 *Administration by Department of Transport*

Under the Merchant Shipping Act 1894 it was provided that the Board of Trade was in general[1] to be the department to undertake the superintendence of all matters relating to merchant shipping and seamen and the Board was authorized to carry into execution the provisions of all statutes relating to merchant shipping for the time being in force.[2] The Board's functions relating to shipping and navigation were transferred to the Minister of Shipping in 1939,[3] and to the Minister of War Transport in 1941.[4] The Ministry of War Transport was dissolved in 1946 and all functions of the Minister were thereupon transferred to the Minister of Transport.[5] The functions of the Minister of Transport relating to shipping were transferred to the Board of Trade in 1965.[6] In 1968 the functions of the Board became exercisable by the President of the Board of Trade[7] and in 1970 all functions of the Board and its President were transferred to the Secretary of State[8] so as to be exercisable concurrently with the Board and its President, respectively.[9] Between 1970 and 1974 the shipping functions of the Secretary of State were exercised, as a matter of administrative arrangement, by the Secretary of State for Trade and Industry, assisted by the Department of Trade and Industry. In 1974, the functions of the Secretary of State for Trade and Industry and his department were subdivided [10] and from 1974-1983 the shipping functions were exercised, as a matter of administrative arrangement, by the Secretary of State for Trade, assisted by the Department of Trade. In 1983 the civil aviation and shipping functions of the Secretary of State were transferred to the Secretary of State for Transport.[11]

The Secretary of State for Transport has many shipping functions relating to matters described in this work. For example, he appoints surveyors,[12] inspectors[13] and the Coastguard.[14] He may make regulations as to entries in log books,[15] specifying charts, directions and information to be carried in ships[16] and the duties of surveyors.[17] He has functions with regard to investigations into shipping casualties.[18] He receives returns from surveyors,[19] courts of investigation,[20] death inquiries[21] and inquiries into conduct.[22] He may reissue and return a cancelled or suspended certificate.[23] Above all he may make safety regulations.[24]

---

[1] Certain functions were vested in the Admiralty and the Minister of Transport.
[2] Merchant Shipping Act 1894, s. 713.
[3] See the Minister of Shipping (Transfer of Functions) Order 1939, S.R. & O. 1939, No. 1470 (lapsed).
[4] See the Ministers of the Crown (Minister of War Transport) Order 1941, S.R. & O. 1941, No. 654.

[5] See the Ministry of War Transport (Dissolution) Order 1946, S.R. & O. 1946, No. 375.
[6] See the Transfer of Functions (Shipping and Construction of Ships) Order 1965, S.I. 1965, No. 145.
[7] Industrial Expansion Act 1968, s. 14(1).
[8] "Secretary of State" means one of Her Majesty's Principal Secretaries of State for the time being; Interpretation Act 1978, s. 5, Sch. 1; Secretary of State for Trade and Industry Order 1970, S.I. 1970, No. 1537, art. 1(2).
[9] Ibid., art. 2(1) (a), (b).
[10] See the Secretary of State (New Departments) Order 1974, S.I. 1974, No. 692.
[11] See the Transfer of Functions (Trade and Industry) Order 1983, S.I. 1983, No. 1127, art. 2(3). Any enactment, instrument, contract or other document passed, made or printed before the coming into operation of the order (11th August 1983) has effect, if it is connected with any civil aviation or shipping functions, as if any reference to the Secretary of State for Trade, the Department of Trade or an officer of that Minister or to the President of the Board of Trade or an officer of the Board were or included a reference to the Secretary of State for Transport, the Department of Transport or an officer of that Minister; ibid., art. 4(3) (a). The address of the Department of Transport, Marine Division, is Sunley House, 90 High Holborn, London WC1V 6LP.
[12] See para. 5.02, *post.*
[13] See para. 5.02, *post.*
[14] See para. 5.03, *post.*
[15] See para. 1.13, text and note 2, *ante.*
[16] See para. 5.05, *post.*
[17] See para. 5.02, *post.*
[18] See para. 1.13, text and notes 13-15, *ante,* 5.20, 5.21, *post.*
[19] See para. 5.06, *post.*
[20] See para. 5.21, *post.*
[21] See para. 5.22, *post.*
[22] See para. 5.22, *post.*
[23] See para. 5.23, *post.*
[24] See paras. 1.05 et seq., *ante.*

5.02 *Power to appoint surveyors and inspectors*

The Secretary of State for Transport[1] may, at such ports as he thinks fit, appoint either generally or for special purposes, and, on special occasion, any person he thinks fit to be a surveyor of ships,[2] who may be appointed either as a ship surveyor or as an engineer surveyor or as both.[3] The Secretary of State may appoint a surveyor-general of ships for the United Kingdom.[4] The Secretary of State may remove any surveyors of ships and fix and alter their remuneration.[5] He may also make regulations as to the performance of their duties.[6] The regulations may cover such matters as the manner in which surveys of ships are to be made, the notice to be given by them when surveys are required, the amount and payment of any travelling or other expenses incurred by them in the execution of their duties.[7] The regulations may also determine the persons by whom and the conditions under which the payment of expenses is to be made.[8] Surveyors of ships must perform their duties under the direction of the Secretary of State, and in accordance with the regulations made by him.[9]

The Secretary of State may also, as and when he thinks fit, appoint any person as an inspector to report to him whether the provisions of the Merchant Shipping Act 1894 or any regulations made under or by virtue of that Act,[10] or the terms of any approval, licence, consent, direction or exemption given by virtue of such regulations,[11] have been complied with.[12] An inspector may also be appointed to report to the Secretary of State upon the nature and causes of any accident or damage which any ship has sustained or caused, or is alleged to have sustained or caused or whether the hull and machinery of any steamship are sufficient and in good condition.[13]

[1] This provision, as originally enacted, referred to the Board of Trade. As to the devolution of functions on the Secretary of State see para. 5.01, *ante*.
[2] I.e. a surveyor for the purposes of the Merchant Shipipng Act 1894.
[3] Ibid., s. 724(1); Merchant Shipping Act 1906, s. 75. As to the powers of surveyors of ships, see para. 5.05, *post*. The governor of a British possession may appoint and remove local surveyors for the purposes of the Act to be carried into effect in that possession: Merchant Shipping Act 1894, s. 727.
[4] Ibid., s. 724(2). For the meaning of "the United Kingdom" see para. 1.08, note 19, *ante*.
[5] Ibid., s. 724(3).
[6] Ibid., s. 724(3). The regulations are contained in "Instructions to Surveyors" issued from time to time. The instructions are largely administrative and, although they are subject to the *ultra vires* principle, it may be that the rules as to sub-delegation do not apply to them with such force as they do to delegated legislation which creates a criminal offence; cf., para. 1.04, text and notes 6, 7, *ante*. For an example of such instructions see "Instructions to Surveyors on Lights and Signalling Equipment" available from H.M. Stationery Office.
[7] Ibid., s. 724(3).
[8] Ibid., s. 724(3).
[9] Ibid., s. 724(5).
[10] Collision regulations were formerly made under ibid., s. 418 and although s. 418 has been repealed as regards ships and hovercraft, it is still the enabling provision as regards collision regulations in their application to seaplanes; see para. 1.05, text and notes 30, 31, *ante*.
[11] The words in the text to this note were inserted by the Merchant Shipping Act 1979, s. 26.
[12] Merchant Shipping Act 1894, s. 728(b). As to the powers of inspectors see para. 5.07, *post*.
[13] Ibid., s. 728(a), (c). "Steamship" includes a ship propelled by electricity or other mechanical power; see s. 742.

5.03 *Functions of H.M. Coastguard*

The Coastguard consists of such numbers of officers and men as the Secretary of State for Transport[1] from time to time thinks fit.[2] It is raised, maintained, equipped and governed by the Secretary of State and employed as a coastwatching force for the performance of certain historic functions[3] and such other duties as may be determined by the Secretary of State.[4] Among such functions and duties are functions as receivers of wreck[5] and the duty to watch and protect shipwrecked property.[6] There are Coastguard look-out points at many places along the coast of the United Kingdom. There is a well-equipped Operations Centre of the Coastguard at Langdon Battery near Dover[7] which has a powerful radar scanner and which is linked to a second scanner at Dungeness. The Centre is also in constant touch with a radar station at Cap Gris Nez which is operated by the French Centre Régionel Opérationel de Sauvetage et Surveillance.[8] A 24-hour watch is kept from Langdon Battery over a substantial part of the Dover Strait, and enables the Coastguard to combine its traditional role of co-ordinating life-saving operations and coastwatching with an information service to mariners.

The main purpose of the information service is to assist mariners passing through the Dover Strait by giving them up-to-date information about visibility, buoyage and lights, the presence of hampered shipping and the positions, courses and speeds of ships which are not complying with the Dover Strait traffic separation scheme. The information is broadcast on VHF R/T Channel 10 at regular intervals of 30 minutes (10 and 40 minutes past each hour). When visibility falls below two miles additional broadcasts are made at 25 and 55 minutes past each hour, containing information as to the actual visibility reported by ships in the area. Broadcasts at intermediate times are made when deemed necessary.[9] A large measure of automatic data processing allows continuous tracking of ships and calculation of their courses and speeds. Ships which are seen from their echoes on the radar display to be contravening the traffic separation scheme are tracked by means of a computer and a drum-plotter on a tracing sheet on to which the computer can draw the principal features of the coast and of the traffic separation scheme.[10] The tracing sheet is then retained as a permanent record and can be produced in evidence at any subsequent proceedings.[11] In addition to the procedure for tracking, a separate system records on to videotapes photographs taken at five-second intervals of both radar outputs. The videotapes can be replayed immediately for the current purposes and are retained permanently by the Department of Transport. They may be inspected on payment of a fee and extracts produced if required.[12] The videotapes have many uses in determining the causes of collisions.[13]

Once a ship is seen from her track to be contravening the traffic separation scheme, she is then identified, either by the officers on duty at the Operations Centre or by aircraft summoned for the purpose, or by other ships which may be in the vicinity. As soon as identification has been reported to the officer preparing the tracing sheet, the name and track letters of the contravening ship are written on to the tracing sheet, together with a note of the wind, visibility and sea state in the vicinity.[14]

The facts are then reported to the Department of Transport, and the Secretary of State may, after further investigation, prosecute the offender or, if the ship is foreign, report the facts to the Government of the flag State.

[1] The management and control of the Coastguard was historically vested in the Admiralty but transferred to the Board of Trade in 1925: Coastguard Act 1925, s. 1(1). As to the devolution of the shipping functions of the Board of Trade on the Secretary of State see para. 5.01, *ante*.
[2] Coastguard Act 1925, s. 1(1).
[3] The historic functions include watching for ships in distress and for violations of the Customs laws.
[4] Coastguard Act 1925, s. 1(1).
[5] See the Merchant Shipping Act 1894, s. 566.
[6] See 574 H. of C. Official Report (5th Series) (Written Answers) Col. 55.
[7] The Operations Centre for the Dover Strait is controlled by H.M. Inspector of Coastguard, whose address is Coastguard Headquarters, Langdon Battery, Dover, Kent.
[8] The address of C.R.O.S.S. (Sector Manche) is Jobourg, Cherbourg, Normandy, France.
[9] Intermediate broadcasts are preceded by a warning call on Channel 16. Track letters are added to the sheet at the commencement of the track.
[10] As to the details of the Dover Strait traffic separation scheme see para. 2.07, *ante*, and Appendix II, *post*.
[11] As to the admissibility of the tracing sheets and the videotapes described in the text to note 13, *infra*, see para. 5.16, text and notes 2, 4 *post*.

[12] The current fees are £36.95p per hour's inspection.
[13] While the tapes provide irrefutable evidence of courses, speeds and positions, they are not evidence of the identity of any vessel. As to the admissibility of the tapes see para. 5.16, text and notes 4, 5, *post*.
[14] Identification is usually verified by visual observation of the aircraft circling above the contravening vessel or by watching the echoes of vessel and aircraft merge on the radar display.

5.04 *Powers of officers of Department of Transport and others*

Where any officer of the Department of Transport[1] or any of certain other prescribed persons,[2] has reason to suspect that the provisions of the Merchant Shipping Act 1894, or any law for the time being in force relating to merchant seamen or navigation, are not complied with, he may require the owner,[3] master[4] or any of the crew of any British ship[5] to produce any official log-books or other documents relating to the crew or any member of the crew in their respective possession or control.[6] He may also require any such master to produce a list of all persons on board his ship, and take copies of the official log-books or documents, or of any part of them.[7] He may muster the crew of any such ship and summon the master to appear and give any explanation concerning the ship or her crew or the official log-books or documents produced or required to be produced.[8]

If any person, on being duly required by an authorized officer,[9] fails without reasonable cause to produce to that officer any such official log-book or document as he is required to produce, he is liable on summarry conviction to a fine not exceeding level 3 on the standard scale, and if any person on being so required refuses to allow such a book or document to be inspected or copied, that person is guilty of an offence and liable on summary prosecution to a fine not exceeding level 5 on the standard scale.[10] He is also guilty of an offence, carrying the same penalty, if he impedes any muster of the crew duly required,[11] or refuses or neglects to give any explanation which he is required to give, or knowingly misleads or deceives any officer authorized to demand any such explanation.[12]

[1] This provision, as originally enacted, referred to the Board of Trade. As to the devolution of the functions of the Board on the Secretary of State and his Department see para. 5.01, *ante*. As to the power of the Secretary of State to appoint surveyors and inspectors see para. 5.02, *ante*.
[2] The prescribed persons are any commissioned officer of any of Her Majesty's ships on full pay, any British consular officer, the Registrar-General of Shipping and Seamen or his assistant, any chief officer of Customs in any place in Her Majesty's dominions, or any superintendent: Merchant Shipping Act 1894, s. 723(1). "Her Majesty's dominions" means territories under the sovereignty of the Crown; see *Halsbury's Laws of England*, 4th edn., vol. 6, para. 879. As to superintendents see para. 5.05, note 2, *post*.
[3] As to owners and their duties see para. 1.10, *ante*.
[4] For the meaning of "master" see para. 1.10, note 5, *ante*.
[5] For the meaning of "British ship" see para. 1.12, note 2, *ante*.
[6] Merchant Shipping Act 1894, s. 723(1) (a).
[7] Ibid., s. 723(1) (b).
[8] Merchant Shipping Act 1894, s. 723(1) (c), (d). As to the application of the Judges Rules to such questioning see para. 5.08, *post*.
[9] I.e. an officer authorized under the Merchant Shipping Act 1894, s. 723.

[10] Ibid., ss. 680(1) (b), 723(2); Merchant Shipping Act 1979, s. 43(3), Sch. 6, Part VI, para. 11; Criminal Justice Act 1982, ss. 37(2), 46(1), (4), 77, Sch. 14, para. 2. As to the standard scale, see para. 1.13, note 19, *ante*. As to the conduct of summary proceedings see paras. 5.15 et seq., *post*. For the meaning of "reasonable cause" see para. 5.06, note 8, *post*.
[11] I.e. required under the Merchant Shipping Act 1894, s. 723.
[12] Ibid., s. 723(2). "Neglects" implies failure to perform a duty which a person knows or ought to know; Re *Hughes, Rea* v. *Black* [1943] Ch. 196 at p. 298; [1943] 2 All E.R. 269 at p. 271, *per* Simonds, J. "Knowingly". Knowledge must be proved by the prosecution; see *Gaumont British Distributors Ltd.* v. *Henry* [1939] 2 K.B. 711; [1939] 2 All E.R. 808; *R.* v. *Hallam* [1957] 1 Q.B. 569; [1957] 1 All E.R. 665, C.C.A.; *Churchill* v. *Walton* [1967] 2 A.C. 224; [1967] 1 All E.R. 497, H.L. "To deceive" is to induce a man to believe a thing is true which is false, or a thing is false which is true, contrary to what a person practising the deceit knows or believes to be the case; see *Re London and Globe Finance Corporation Ltd.* [1903] 1 Ch. 728; [1900-3] All E.R. Rep. 891, at pp. 732, 891, respectively, *per* Buckley, J.;and *Welham* v *D.P.P.* [1961] A.C. 103; [1960] 1 All E.R. 805, at pp. 126, 127, 810. respectively.

5.05 *Powers of surveyors*

For the purpose of seeing that the Merchant Shipping Acts and regulations and rules made thereunder, or that the terms of any approval, licence, consent, direction or exemption given under the regulations, are duly complied with, a surveyor of ships,[1] a superintendent[2] or a duly authorized person[3] may at all reasonable times[4] go on board a ship[5] and inspect the ship and her equipment or any part of it, any articles on board and any document carried on board in pursuance of the Acts, regulations or rules.[6] These powers may be exercised outside the United Kingdom[7] in the case of a ship registered in the United Kingdom.[8] A person exercising these powers must not unnecessarily detain or delay a ship but may, if he considers it necessary in consequence of an accident[9] or for any other reason, require a ship to be taken into dock for a survey of her hull or machinery.[10] Failure to comply with such a requirement is an offence, as is obstruction of a person exercising the foregoing powers.[11] The offender is liable on summary conviction to a fine not exceeding level 5 on the standard scale.[12]

[1] As to the appointment of surveyors of ships see para. 5.02, *ante*.
[2] The Secretary of State for Transport appoints and removes mercantile marine superintendents who exercise the powers conferred on superintendents by the Merchant Shipping Acts: Merchant Shipping Act 1970, s. 81. The powers described in this paragraph, as originally enacted, were vested in the Board of Trade. As to the devolution of functions on the Secretary of State, see para. 5.01, *ante*.
[3] The Secretary of State has power to appoint any person, either generally or in a particular case, to exercise the powers described in this paragraph; see ibid., s. 76(1)(c).
[4] As to "reasonable times" see *Small* v. *Bickley* (1875) 32 L.T. 726.
[5] For the meaning of "ship" see para. 1.04, text and note 14, *ante*.
[6] Merchant Shipping Act 1970, s. 76(1); Merchant Shipping Act 1979, s. 37(5). The reference to the Merchant Shipping Acts includes here a reference to the Merchant Shipping Act 1979; s. 37(5). The Secretary of State has power to make rules specifying charts, directions and information to be carried in ships registered in the United Kingdom; see the Merchant Shipping Act 1970, s. 86(1).
[7] For the meaning of "the United Kingdom" see para. 1.08, note 19, *ante*.
[8] Merchant Shipping Act 1970, s. 76(1). Outside the United Kingdom the powers may also be exercised by proper officers; s. 76(1). "Proper officer" means a consular officer appointed by Her Majesty's Government in the United Kingdom and, in relation to a port in a country outside the United Kingdom which is not a foreign country, also an officer exercising in that port functions similar to those of a superintendent; ibid., s. 97(1).
[9] "An accident" has been defined as "an unlooked-for mishap or an untoward event" which is not expected or designed; see *Fenton* v. *Thorley & Co. Ltd.* [1903] A.C. 443, H.L. at p. 448, *per* Lord Macnaghten.

[10] Merchant Shipping Act 1970, s. 76(2).
[11] Ibid., s. 76(4). Obstruction can consist of anything which makes it more difficult for an authorised officer to carry out his duty; *Hinchcliffe* v. *Sheldon* [1955] 3 All E.R. 406. Physical violence is not required; *Borrow* v. *Howland* (1896) 74 L.T. 787. However, standing by and doing nothing is not obstruction unless there is a duty to act; *Swallow* v. *London County Council* [1916] 1 K.B. 224; [1914-15] All E.R. Rep. 403; cf., *Rice* v. *Connolly* [1966] 2 Q.B. 414; [1966] 2 All E.R. 649; *Baker* v. *Ellison* [1914] 2 K.B. 762.
[12] Merchant Shipping Act 1970, s. 76(4); Merchant Shipping Act 1979, s. 43(1), Sch. 6, Part IV; Criminal Justice Act 1982, ss. 37, 46(1), (4). As to the standard scale see para. 1.13, note 19, *ante*.

5.06 *Returns by surveyors*

Surveyors of ships[1] must make such returns to the Secretary of State for Transport[2] as he may require with respect to the nature and particulars of machinery and equipments of ships[3] surveyed by them.[4] The owner,[5] master[3] and engineer of any ship so surveyed must, on demand, give to the surveyors all such information and assistance within his power as they require for the purpose of those returns.[7] If any owner, master or engineer, on being applied to for that purpose, fails without reasonable cause[8] to give any such information or assistance, he is guilty of an offence and liable on summary conviction to a fine not exceeding level 3 on the standard scale.[9]

[1] As to the appointment of surveyors of ships see para. 5.02, *ante*. As to their powers see para. 5.05, *ante*.
[2] This provision, as originally enacted, referred to the Board of Trade. As to the devolution of functions on the Secretary of State see para. 5.01, *ante*.
[3] For the meaning of "ship" see para. 1.04, text and note 14, *ante*.
[4] Merchant Shipping Act 1894, s. 726(1). The returns also relate to build, dimensions, draught, burden, rate of sailing and room for fuel: s. 726(1).
[5] As to owners see para. 1.10, note 3, *ante*.
[6] For the meaning of "master" see para. 1.10, note 5, *ante*.
[7] Merchant Shipping Act 1894, s. 726(2).
[8] Ignorance of statutory provisions is not a reasonable excuse; cf., *Aldridge* v. *Warwickshire Coal Co. Ltd.* (1925) 133 L.T. 439, C.A. Whether a cause is reasonable is largely a question of fact; cf., *Leck* v. *Epsom Rural District Council* [1922] 1 K.B. 383; [1922] All E.R. Rep. 784.
[9] Merchant Shipping Act 1894, s. 726(3), 680(1) (b); Merchant Shipping Act 1979, s. 43(1), Sch. 6, Part II; Criminal Justice Act 1982, ss. 37, 46(1), (4), 77, Sch. 14, para. 2. As to the standard scale, see para. 1.13, note 19, *ante*.

5.07 *Powers of Department of Transport inspectors*

A duly appointed Department of Transport inspector[1] has the following powers: (1) he may at any reasonable time[2] enter any premises[3] in the United Kingdom[4] or board any ship[5] which is registered in the United Kingdom[6] wherever she may be and any other ship which is present in the United Kingdom or the territorial waters of the United Kingdom,[7] if he has reason to believe that it is necessary for him to enter the premises or board the ship for the purpose of performing his inspectorial functions;[8] (2) he may on entering premises or boarding a ship take with him any other duly authorized person[9] and any requisite equipment or materials;[10] (3) he may make such examination and investigation as he considers necessary;[11] (4) he may give a direction that any premises or ship which he has power to enter or board, or any part of them or any thing in them are to be left undisturbed for so long as is reasonably necessary for the purposes of his examination or investigation;[12] (5) he may take such measurements and photographs and make such recordings as he considers necessary for the purpose of his examination or investigation;[13] (6) he may take samples of any articles or substances found in any premises or ship which he is empowered to enter or board and of the atmosphere in or in the vicinity of any such premises or ship;[14] (7) he may, where it appears to him that any article or substance which he finds in the premises or ship has caused or is likely to cause danger to health or safety, have it dismantled or subjected to any process or test;[15] (8) he may take possession of the article or substance[16] and detain it for so long as is necessary (a) to examine it and dismantle, process or test it, (b) to ensure that it is not tampered with before his examination is completed, (c) to ensure that it is available for use as evidence in any proceedings for a merchant shipping offence;[17] (9) he may require any person who he has reasonable cause to believe is able to give any information relevant to his examination or investigation, to attend at a place and time specified by the inspector, to answer[18] such questions as the inspector thinks fit to ask and to sign a declaration of the truth of his answers;[19] (10) he may require the production of any statutory books or documents and any other books or documents which he considers it necessary for him to see for the purposes of his examination or inspection;[20] and (11) he may require any person to afford him such facilities and assistance[21] as the inspector considers necessary to enable him to exercise any of the powers described above.[22]

Any person who—(1) wilfully obstructs[23] a Department of Transport inspector[24] in the exercise of the powers described above;[25] or (2) without reasonable excuse[26] fails to comply with a statutory requirement duly imposed[27] or prevents another person from complying with such a requirement; or (3) makes a statement or signs a declaration which he knows is false,[28] or recklessly[29] makes a statement or signs a declaration which is false in purported compliance with a statutory requirement;[30] is guilty of an offence.[31] The offender is liable on summary conviction[32] to a fine not exceeding the statutory maximum,[33] or on conviction on indictment[34] to imprisonment for a term not exceeding two years or a fine or both.[35]

---

[1] I.e. an inspector appointed under the Merchant Shipping Act 1894, s. 728, as to which see para. 5.02, text and notes 10-13, *ante*.
[2] As to what constitutes a reasonable time, see *Small* v. *Bickley* (1875) 32 L.T. 726. In a situation which in the inspector's opinion is or may be dangerous, he may exercise his powers of entry and boarding at any time; Merchant Shipping Act 1979, s. 27(1) (a).
[3] "Premises" includes land, houses, buildings etc.; *Metropolitan Water Board* v. *Paine* [1907] 1 K.B. 285.
[4] For the meaning of "the United Kingdom" see para. 1.08, note 16, *ante*.
[5] For the meaning of "ship" see para. 1.04, text and note 14, *ante*.
[6] As to the registry of ships see the Merchant Shipping Act 1894, ss. 2-23; Merchant Shipping Act 1983.
[7] As to the territorial waters of the United Kingdom see para. 1.08, text and notes 16-26, *ante*.

[8] Merchant Shipping Act 1979, s. 27(1) (a). Nothing in this power, or in any of the others expounded in this paragraph, authorizes a person unnecessarily to detain a ship from proceeding on a voyage; ibid., s. 27(2).

[9] I.e. a person authorized for that purpose by the Secretary of State; ibid., s. 27(1)(b).

[10] Ibid., s. 27(1) (b). The equipment and materials in question are those required to assist him in performing his functions; s. 27(1) (b).

[11] I.e. necessary for the purpose of performing his functions; ibid., s. 27(1)(c).

[12] Ibid.; s. 27(1) (d). The direction not to disturb may be general or issued in particular respects; s. 27(1) (d).

[13] Ibid., s. 27(1) (e).

[14] Ibid., s. 27(1) (f). The Secretary of State may make provision by regulations for the procedure to be followed in taking samples and as to the way in which the samples taken are to be dealt with; s. 27(3). No such regulations have been made at the date at which this volume states the law.

[15] Ibid., s. 27(1) (g). The inspector may not damage or destroy the article or substance unless that is necessary in the circumstances; s. 27(1) (g). Where the inspector proposes to exercise the power conferred by s. 27(1) (g) he must, upon request by a person present who has responsibilities for the premises or ship, cause anything done under the power to be done in the presence of that person, unless the inspector considers that to do so would prejudice the person's safety; s. 27(4). He must also, before exercising the power under s. 27(1) (g), consult such persons as appear to him to be appropriate, to ascertain what dangers there may be in doing what the inspector proposes to do; s. 27(5).

[16] I.e. the article or substance mentioned in ibid., s. 27(1)(g).

[17] Ibid., s. 27(1) (h). The Merchant Shipping offences referred to are those contrary to the Merchant Shipping Acts or regulations made under the Acts; ibid., s. 27(1) (h). Where under the power conferred by s. 27(1) (h) an inspector takes possession of any article or substance found in any premises or ship, he must leave it there, either with a responsible person or, if that is impracticable, a notice fixed in a conspicuous position giving particulars of the article or substance sufficient to identify it; s. 27(6). The notice must state that the inspector has taken possession of it under his statutory power; s. 27(6). Before taking possession of any substance under this power, the inspector must, if practicable, take a sample of the substance and give a marked portion of the sample to a responsible person at the premises or on board the ship; s. 27(6).

[18] The answers must be given in the absence of persons other than any persons whom the inspector may allow to be present and a person nominated to be present by the person questioned; ibid., s. 27(1)(i)(ii). No answer given is admissible in evidence against that person or the husband or wife of that person in any proceeding except under s. 28(1) (c) (see the text to notes 28-30, infra) in respect of a statement in or a declaration relating to the answer; s. 27(7). The person nominated to be present under s. 27(1)(i)(ii) is entitled, when the questions are asked, to make representations to the inspector on behalf of the person who nominated him; s. 27(7). To some extent these provisions contradict the Judges' Rules, as to which see para. 5.08, post.

[19] Merchant Shipping Act 1979, s. 27(1) (i). As to the recovery of expenses incurred in complying with such requirements, see note 22, infra. Nothing in ibid., s. 27 is to be taken as compelling the production of a document which would be protected from discovery on grounds of legal professional privilege in a High Court action (s. 28(3)).

[20] Ibid., s. 27(1) (j). The inspector may also inspect and take copies of any of the books or documents or of any entry in them; s. 27(1) (j).

[21] I.e. facilities and assistance with respect to any matters or things within the person's control or in relation to which he has responsibilities; see ibid., s. 27(1) (k).

[22] Ibid., s. 27(1) (k). A person who complies with a requirement imposed on him under this provision or under s. 27(1) (i) (see the text and notes 18, 19, supra) is entitled to recover from the person who imposed the requirement, such sums as are prescribed by regulations made by the Secretary of State; s. 28(4). The regulations may make different provision for different circumstances; s. 28(4). Any payments made under s. 28(4) must be made out of money provided by Parliament; s. 28(4).

[23] As to what constitutes obstruction see para. 5.05, note 11, ante. "Wilful" has been held to mean deliberate and intentional, as distinct from accidental or inadvertent; R. v. Senior [1899] 1 Q.B. 283, at pp. 290, 291.

[24] Other persons who have the powers of Department of Transport inspectors, such as those holding preliminary inquiries (see para. 5.19, post) are within the protection afforded by this provision; see the Merchant Shipping Act 1979, s. 28(2).

[25] I.e. in the exercise of any power conferred by him by ibid., s. 27, as to which see supra.

[26] As to what constitutes a reasonable excuse, see para. 5.06, note 8, ante.

[27] I.e. a requirement imposed under the Merchant Shipping Act 1979, s. 27, as to which see *supra*.
[28] A statement or declaration may be false on account of what it omits even though it is literally true; *R.* v. *Lord Kylsant* [1932] 1 K.B. 442.
[29] As to what constitutes recklessness see *Derry* v. *Peek* (1889) 14 App. Cas. 337; [1886-90] All E.R. Rep. 1.
[30] I.e. in purported compliance with a requirement made under the Merchant Shipping Act 1979, s. 27(1) (i) (as to which see the text and notes 18, 19, *supra*); see ibid., s. 28(1) (c) which is expressed to be without prejudice to the generality of the provision noted as (2) in the text to notes 26, 27 *supra*.
[31] Ibid., s. 28(1). If the inspector is acting outside the scope of his powers, it is probable that no offence is committed; cf. *Codd* v. *Cabe* (1876) 40 J.P. 566; *R. Roxburgh* (1871) 12 Cox. C.C. 8; *R.* v. *Waterfield, R.* v. *Lynn* [1963] 3 All E.R. 659; [1964] 1 Q.B. 164; but see *Donelly* v. *Jackman* [1970] 1 All E.R. 987; *Squires* v. *Botwright* [1973] Crim. L.R. 106.
[32] As to summary trial see para. 5.15, *post*.
[33] This provision as enacted provided for a maximum fine on summary conviction of £1,000. Such references are now to be construed as references to the statutory maximum; Criminal Justice Act 1982, s. 49(1). As to what is the statutory maximum see para. 1.11, note 13, *ante*.
[34] As to trial on indictment see para. 5.14, *post*. As to the choice of summary trial or trial on indictment for offences triable either way see para. 5.13, *post*.
[35] Merchant Shipping Act 1979, s. 28(1).

5.08 *Questioning by surveyors and others*

As has been described, officers of the Department of Transport, surveyors and others have wide powers of interrogation, backed by penal sanctions.[1] When police officers question suspects, any answers obtained may not be admissible as evidence in subsequent proceedings unless the questioning was carried out in accordance with the Judges' Rules.[2] The Judges' Rules do not apply to investigations into civil matters but they do apply to questioning by persons other than police officers who have a duty to investigate offences.[3] It seems, therefore, that when surveyors and other Department of Transport personnel undertake questioning of suspects, they should so far as practicable apply the Judges' Rules.[4]

The Rules may be summarized as follows:— (1) When a police officer is trying to discover whether or by whom an offence has been committed he is entitled to question any person from whom he thinks that useful information may be obtained;[5] (2) As soon as he has evidence affording reasonable grounds for suspecting that a person has committed an offence, he must caution that person or cause him to be cautioned before putting to him any further questions relating to the offence; and when after being cautioned, a person is being questioned, or elects to make a statement, a record must be kept of the time and place at which the questioning or statement began and ended and of the persons present;[6] (3) Where a person is charged with or informed that he may be prosecuted for an offence he must be cautioned; and only in exceptional cases should questions relating to the offence be put to the accused after he has been charged or informed that he may be prosecuted;[7] (4) All written statements made after caution must be taken in accordance with detailed directions;[8] (5) If at any time after a person has been charged with, or has been informed that he may be prosecuted for an offence, the officer wishes to bring to the notice of that person a written statement by another person who has been charged with the same offence or informed that he may be prosecuted, he must hand to the first person a true copy of such written statement, but nothing must be said or done to invite any reply or comment.[9]

There are in addition certain general principles which apply to police questioning which, it is thought, would apply also to questioning by surveyors.[10] They may be summarized as follows:— (1) Citizens have a duty to help law enforcement agencies to discover and apprehend offenders; (2) Police officers, otherwise than by arrest, cannot compel any person against his will to come to or remain in a police station; (3) Every person should at every stage be entitled to communicate privately with a solicitor, except where unreasonable delay or hindrance is caused to the investigation or the administration of justice by his doing so; as soon as the officer has enough evidence to prefer a charge, he should without delay cause the suspect to be charged or informed that he may be prosecuted; (4) Every statement, oral or otherwise, must, to be admissible in evidence, have been made voluntarily.[11]

[1] See paras. 5.04, 5.05, 5.07, *ante.*
[2] See Home Office Circular No. 89/1978; *R.* v. *Collier, R.* v. *Stenning* [1965] 3 All E.R. 136 at p. 138, [1965] 1 W.L.R. 1470 at p. 1474, C.C.A.; cf., *R.* v. *Roberts* [1970] Crim. L.R. 464, C.A. The Judges' Rules are accompanied by administrative directions on interrogation and the taking of statements but failure to follow the directions does not necessarily render a statement obtained inadmissible; *R.* v. *Roberts (supra).*
[3] Judges' Rules, r. 6; see also *Walmsley* v. *Young* (1974) *The Times,* 10th July, D.C.; *R.* v. *Fallon* [1975] Crim. L.R. 341; cf., *R.* v. *Ovenell, R.* v. *Walter A. Cartwright Ltd.* [1969] 1 Q.B. 17: [1968] 1 All E.R. 933, C.A.
[4] A statement obtained in breach of the Rules may nevertheless be admitted in evidence if the judge decides that the statement was made voluntarily; *R.* v. *Prager* [1972] 1 A.. E.R. 1114 at p. 1118; [1972] 1 W.L.R. 260 at p. 266, C.A.; *R.* v. *Smith* [1961] 3 All E.R. 1972, C.C.A.; *R.* v. *Lemsatef* [1977] 2 All E.R. 835, C.A. Department of Transport inspectors have extensive powers of questioning, backed by criminal sanctions for disobedience. See para. 5.07, *ante.*
[5] Judges' Rules, r. 1.
[6] Ibid., r. 2.
[7] Ibid., r. 3.
[8] Ibid., r. 4. The detailed directions may be summarized as follows:— (1) If a person says that he wants to make a statement he must be told that it is intended to make a written record of what he says; (2) Any person writing his own statement must be allowed to do so without any prompting; (3) The person writing his own statement, if he is going to write it himself, must be asked to write out and sign a declaration before writing what he wants to say; (4) Whenever a police officer writes the statement he must take down the exact words spoken; (5) When the writing of a statement by a police officer is finished, the person making it must be asked to read it and make any corrections, alterations or additions he wishes. When he has finished reading it he must be asked to write and sign a certificate in the appropriate form at the end of the statement; (6) If the person who has made a statement refuses to read it or to write such certificate at the end of it or to sign it, the senior police officer present must record on the statement itself and in the presence of the person making it, what has happened.
[9] Judges' Rules, r. 5.
[10] Where the Judges' Rules do not apply, the application of these principles may determine whether a statement has been made voluntarily; *R.* v. *Collier, R.* v. *Stenning* [1965] 3 All E.R. 136, [1965] 1 W.L.R. 1470, C.C.A.
[11] For a detailed exposition of these principles, and of the Judges' Rules, see Archbold, *Criminal Pleading, Evidence and Practice,* 41st edn., paras. 15-45 et seq. New provisions as to questioning by police and confession evidence are before Parliament (November 1983); see the Police and Criminal Evidence Bill.

SECT. (2) Criminal proceedings

5.09 *Jurisdiction of court*

For the purpose of giving jurisdiction under the Merchant Shipping Act 1894, every offence is deemed to have been committed and every cause of complaint to have arisen either in the place in which it was actually committed or arose, or in any place in which the offender or person complained against may be.[1] Courts which have jurisdiction for any purpose in any coastal district also have jurisdiction over vessels on, or lying or passing off that coast, or being in or near adjoining bays, channels, lakes, rivers and navigable waters, and over the persons in or belonging to those vessels.[2] Any offence under the Act of 1894 is, in any British possession,[3] punishable by any court or magistrate by whom a similar offence is ordinarily punishable, or in such manner as may be determined by any Act or ordnance having the force of law in that possession.[4] Where any British subject[5] is charged with having committed any offence on board any British ship[6] on the high seas[7] or in any foreign port[8] or harbour or on board any foreign ship to which he does not belong, and that person is found within the jurisdiction of any court in Her Majesty's dominions,[9] that court will have jurisdiction to try the offence in certain circumstances.[10]

[1] Merchant Shipping Act 1894, s. 684. This provision obviates a difficulty which might otherwise prevent a British court from having jurisdiction to try a case. See, further, para. 5.12, *post*. It does not, however, empower a court to try the master or owner of a foreign ship for an offence committed outside British jurisdiction; see para. 1.08, *ante*.
[2] See the Merchant Shipping Act 1894, s. 685(1). This provision is additional to any jurisdiction or power of Magistrates' Courts; see s. 685(2).
[3] "British possession", in statutes passed after 1889, means, unless the contrary intention appears, any part of Her Majesty's dominions (see para. 5.04, note 2, *ante*) except the United Kngdom; Interpretation Act 1978, s. 5, Sch. 1. For the meaning of "the United Kingdom" see para. 1.08, note 16, *ante*.
[4] Merchant Shipping Act 1894, s. 711. Part XIII of the Act (ss. 680-712), except where otherwise provided, applies to the whole of Her Majesty's dominions; s. 712.
[5] For the meaning of "British ship" see para. 1.12, note 2, *ante*.
[6] As to "British subjects" see *Halsbury's Laws of England*, 4th edn., vol. 4, para. 903.
[7] "High seas" here means all oceans, seas, bays, channels, rivers, creeks and waters below low-water mark, and "where great ships can go", except only such parts of oceans , etc., as lie within the body of some county; *R.* v. *Liverpool Justices Ex parte Molyneux* [1972] 2 Q.B. 384; [1972] 2 All E.R. 471.
[8] For the meaning of "port" see para. 1.11, note 7, *ante*.
[9] For the meaning of "Her Majesty's dominions" see para, 5.04, note 2, *ante*.
[10] Merchant Shipping Act 1894, s. 686. For this provision to apply, the court in question must have had cogizance of the offence if it had been committed on board a British ship within the limits of its ordinary jurisdiction; s. 686. The provision applies also to a person who is not a British subject but who is charged with having committed any offence on board any British ship on the high seas; see s. 686(1). An offence in s. 686 means an offence under English law; *R.* v. *Kelly* [1981] 2 Lloyd's Rep. 384, H.L.; [1981] 2 All E.R. 1098 H.L.

5.10 *Time limit for proceedings*

Proceedings on indictment for the prosecution of an offence may be brought at any time after the commission of an offence.[1] There is no time limit. Nor is there any time limit for the initiation of summary proceedings under the Merchant Shipping Acts for the prosecution of an indictable offence.[2]

Summary proceedings instituted in the United Kingdom[3] for an offence which is triable only summarily must generally be commenced within six months after the commission of the offence;[4] otherwise there can be no conviction;[5] but if either or both of the parties to the proceedings happen during that time to be out of the United Kingdom, then the proceedings must be commenced within two months after they both first happen to arrive, or to be at one time, in the United Kingdom *and* before the expiry of three years beginning with the date of commission of the offence.[6] Notwithstanding this restriction,[7] provided proceedings are begun within three years beginning with the date of commission of the offence, summary proceedings may be commenced at any time before either (a) the expiry of six months beginning with the day when evidence which he considers sufficient to justify prosecution for the offence comes to the knowledge of the Secretary of State;[8] or (b) the expiry of two months after the end of this period and beginning with the day when the accused was first present in the United Kingdom if throughout the period he was absent from the United Kingdom.[9]

[1] See Archbold, *Criminal Pleading, Evidence and Practice*, 41st edn., para. 1-85.
[2] See the Merchant Shipping Act, s. 683(3); Merchant Shipping Act 1979, s. 42(1). An equivalent provision in the Magistrates' Courts Act 1980, s. 127(2), is stated not to apply to offences under the Merchant Shipping Acts; see the Merchant Shipping Act 1979, s. 42(4); Magistrates' Courts Act 1980, Sch. 7. As to the prosecution of offences which are triable "either way", see para. 5.13, *post*.
[3] For the meaning of "the United Kingdom" see para. 1.08, note 16, *ante*.
[4] See the Merchant Shipping Act 1894, s. 683(1). In construing the word "after" in this provision, the day upon which the offence was committed is not to be counted in compiling the period of six months; *Radcliffe* v. *Bartholomew* [1892] 1 Q.B. 161; [1891-4] All E.R. 829. But contrast the other time limits expounded *infra*.
[5] See the Merchant Shipping Act 1894, s. 683(1).
[6] Ibid., s. 683(1); Merchant Shipping Act 1979, s. 42(1). In construing the expression "beginning with" in this provision, the day from which the period runs *is* to be included; see *Hare* v. *Gocher* [1962] 2 Q.B. 641; [1962] 2 All E.R. 763. For the provisions imposing time limits for summary proceedings in British possessions, see the Merchant Shipping Act 1894, s. 683(2).
[7] I.e. notwithstanding the provisions of the Merchant Shipping Act 1894, s. 683(1) (as amended).
[8] Merchant Shipping Act 1979, s. 42(2) (a). For the meaning of "the Secretary of State" see para. 5.01, note 8, *ante*. A certificate of the Secretary of State stating that evidence came to his knowledge on a particular day is conclusive evidence of that fact; ibid., s. 42(3) (a). A document purporting to be a certificate of the Secretary of State and to be signed on his behalf is presumed to be such a certificate unless the contrary is proved; s. 42(3) (b).
[9] Ibid., s. 42(2) (b).

5.11 *Conveyance of offenders and witnesses*

When any complaint is made to any British consular officer[1] that any offence on the high seas[2] has been committed by any master[3] belonging to any British ship,[4] the consular officer may inquire into the case upon oath.[5] If the case so requires, he may take any steps in his power for the purpose of placing the offender under the necessary restraint and of sending him as soon as practicable in safe custody to the United Kingdom,[6] in any ship belonging to Her Majesty or to any of her subjects, for the proceedings.[7] The consular officer may order the master of any ship belonging to any subject of Her Majesty bound to the United Kingdom to receive and afford a passage and subsistence during the voyage to any such offender and to the witnesses.[8] The master of the ship must, on his ship's arrival in the United Kingdom, give the offender into police custody.[9] The offender must be taken by the police before a justice of the peace who must deal with the matter as in cases of offences committed upon the high seas.[10]

If any master of a ship, when required by any British consular officer to receive and afford passage and subsistence to any offender or witness, does not receive him and afford him passage and subsistence, or does not duly deliver the offender into police custody, he is guilty of an offence and liable on summary conviction to a fine not exceeding level 5 on the standard scale.[11] The expense of imprisoning any offender and of conveying him and the witnesses to the United Kingdom, except in the ships to which he or they belong, must be paid out of moneys provided by Parliament, where they are not paid as part of the costs of the prosecution.[12]

[1] "Consular officer", when used in relation to a foreign country, means the officer recognized by Her Majesty as a consular officer of that foreign country: Merchant Shipping Act 1894, s. 742.
[2] For the meaning of "high seas" cf., para. 5.09, note 7, *ante*.
[3] For the meaning of "master" see para. 1.10, note 5, *ante*. This provision formerly applied also to seamen and apprentices but the reference to them was removed by the Merchant Shipping Act 1970, s. 100(1), Sch. 3, para. 2.
[4] For the meaning of "British ship" see para. 1.12, note 2, *ante*.
[5] Merchant Shipping Act 1894, s. 689(1) (b). The powers described in this paragraph apply also to offences committed out of Her Majesty's dominions against person or property: see s. 689(1)(a). For the meaning of "Her Majesty's dominions", see para. 5.04, note 2, *ante*.
[6] For the meaning of "the United Kingdom" see para. 1.08, note 16, *ante*. There is also power of the conveyance to be to any British possession in which there is a court capable of taking cognizance of the offence: see the Merchant Shipping Act, s. 689(1).
[7] Ibid., s. 689(1).
[8] Ibid., s. 689(2). There are limits to the number of such passengers which the master can be compelled to receive and there are provisions for endorsing the ship's agreement; see s. 689(2). This provision also applies in the case of ships bound for a British possession which has jurisdiction; see s. 689(2).
[9] Ibid., s. 689(3). The same rule applies where the ship arrives in a British possession; see s. 689(3).
[10] Ibid., s. 689(3).
[11] Ibid., ss. 680(1) (b); 689(4); Merchant Shipping Act 1979, s. 43(1), Sch. 6, Part IV; Criminal Justice Act 1982, ss. 37, 46(1), (4). As to the standard scale, see para. 1.13, note 19, *ante*.
[12] Merchant Shipping Act 1894, s. 689(5). The same provision applies to the expense of conveyance to a British possession; see s. 689(5). As to costs following conviction, see para. 5.15, text and notes 11, 12, *post*.

5.12 *Service of summons and other documents*

Criminal proceedings for the offences which have been described[1] are almost invariably commenced by the issue of a summons requiring the attendance of the defendant before a Magistrates' Court.[2] There are general rules for the service of

summonses, and additional rules contained in the Merchant Shipping Act 1894 for the
service of documents for the purposes of that Act. In general a summons is served by
delivering it to the person to whom it is directed, or by leaving it for him with some
person at his last known or usual place of abode, or by sending it by registered post
or recorded delivery service addressed to him at his last or usual place of abode.[3]
Service of a summons or other document on a corporation may be effected by delivering it at, or sending it by post to, the registered office of the corporation, if that office
is in the United Kingdom.[4] If there is no registered office in the United Kingdom the
summons or document may be delivered at, or sent by post to, any place in the United
Kingdom where the corporation trades or conducts its business.[5]

   Where a document is to be served for the purposes of the Merchant Shipping Act
1894[6] on the master[7] of a ship,[8] where there is one, or on a person belonging to a ship,
the document may be left for him on board that ship with the person being or appearing to be in command or charge of the ship.[9] Where the document is to be served on
the master of a ship, where there is no master, and the ship is in the United Kingdom,
the document may be served on the managing owner.[10] If there is no managing owner,
it may be served on some agent of the owner residing in the United Kingdom, or,
where no such agent is known or can be found, it may be served by affixing a copy of
it to the mast of the ship.[11]

[1] See para. 1.10, text and notes 3-7, *ante*. See also paras. 1.11, text and notes 9, 10, *ante*; 5.04, text and
notes 9-12, *ante*; 5.05, text and notes 11, 12, *ante*; 5.06, text and notes 8, 9, *ante*; 5.07, text and notes
23-35, *ante*; 5.11, text and note 11, *ante*.
[2] This is so whether the offence is to be tried summarily before the magistrates or on indictment in the
Crown Court after committal proceedings before the magistrates.
[3] Magistrates' Courts Rules 1981, S.I. 1981, No. 552, r. 99(1). If at the hearing the defendant fails to
appear, unless he was served personally, it must be proved that the summons came to his knowledge:
see r. 99(2). As to "last place of abode" see *Hanrott's Trustees* v. *Evans* (1887) 4 T.L.R. 128; *R.* v.
Farmer [1892] 1 Q.B. 637, C.A.; *R.* v. *Webb* [1896] 1 Q.B. 487; *Re Follick, Ex parte Trustee* (1907)
97 L.T. 645; *Stylo Shoes Ltd.* v. *Prices Tailors Ltd.* [1960] Ch. 396; [1959] 3 All E.R. 901.
[4] Magistrates' Courts Rules 1981, r. 99(3), (4).
[5] Ibid., r. 99(3).
[6] Such documents would include summonses for offences under the Merchant Shipping Acts
generally. Notices under the Criminal Justice Act 1967, s. 9 are frequently served with a summons.
As to the effect of such notices see para. 5.16, text and note 10, *post*.
[7] For the meaning of "master" see para. 1.10, note 5, *ante*.
[8] For the meaning of "ship" see para. 1.04, text and note 14, *ante*.
[9] Merchant Shipping Act 1894, s. 696(1) (b).
[10] Ibid., s. 696(1) (c).
[11] Ibid., s. 696(1) (c). The provisions of s. 696(1) are permissive and other methods of service, provided
the document is duly received, will suffice; *Sharpley* v. *Manby* [1942] 1 K.B. 217; [1942] 1 All E.R. 66,
C.A.; *Stylo Shoes Ltd.* v. *Prices Tailors Ltd.* [1960] Ch. 396; [1959] 3 All E.R. 901.

5.13 *Summary proceedings or indictment*

   As has been seen, a master or owner may be prosecuted for breach of the collision
regulations either summarily or on indictment.[1] Where an information charges a
person with an offence which is thus triable either way, the Magistrates' Court dealing

with it must ask first the prosecutor and then the accused which of summary trial or trial by indictment appear more suitable.[2] The court then decides which is the more suitable, having regard to the nature of the case, the circumstances and the adequacy or otherwise of the court's summary powers.[3] If the court decides that summary trial is more suitable this is stated to the defendant and it is explained to him that he can either consent to be tried by the court or be tried (on indictment) by a jury.[4] If the defendant consents, then the case proceeds as a summary trial but the court can change to an indictment procedure at any time up to the close of the prosecution evidence.[5] If the court decides originally that the indictment procedure is more suitable, or if the defendant does not consent to summary trial, it announces the fact to the defendant and the hearing continues as a committal proceeding.[6] Where the magistrates have thus begun to hear a case as examining justices on indictment, they may, if the accused consents and it appears to the court, having regard to any representations made,[7] that the offence is after all more suitable for summary trial, proceed to try the case summarily.[8]

[1] See para. 1.10, text and notes 8, 9, *ante*.
[2] Magistrates' Courts Act 1980, s. 19(1) (2). This application is to be made before evidence is called; see ibid., s. 18(2).
[3] Ibid., s. 19(1), (3).
[4] See ibid., s. 20.
[5] See ibid., ss. 20(3) (a), 25(2).
[6] See ibid., ss. 20(3) (b), 21.
[7] I.e. representations made in the presence of the defendant by the prosecutor, or by the defendant; ibid., s. 25(3).
[8] See ibid., s. 25(3).

5.14 *Procedure on indictment*

As has been mentioned, the Magistrates' Court must decide whether a prosecution for breach of the collision regulations is more suitable to be tried summarily or by jury on indictment.[1] When a case is tried on indictment, the function of the magistrates is to decide whether there is a *prima facie* case to commit the defendant to the Crown Court for trial by judge and jury. The magistrates hear the evidence[2] upon which the prosecution's case is based, in the presence of the defendant, who may put questions to the witnesses.[3] If the court decides, on consideration of the evidence and of any statement of the defendant,[4] that there is sufficient evidence to put the defendant upon trial by jury for any indictable offence,[5] the court must commit him for trial.[6] Otherwise the court must discharge him.[7]

If a defendant is committed for trial, he must be sent to the Crown Court for trial of the indictment by judge and jury.[8]

[1] See para. 5.13, *ante*.
[2] Evidence need not necessarily be oral; see note 4, *infra*.

80

³ If written evidence is received (see note 4, *infra*) there will be no right to cross-examine the witness. There are provisions whereby facts may be formally admitted; see the Criminal Justice Act 1967, s. 10.
⁴ The court does not always consider the evidence. Where the defendant is legally represented by counsel or solicitor (whether the representative is present in court or not) and there is no objection from the representative, the court may commit for trial on the basis of written statements containing the evidence, without considering their contents; Magistrates' Courts Act 1980, ss. 6(2), 102; Criminal Justice Act 1982, s. 61.
⁵ The indictable offence may be a different one from that in respect of which the defendant was brought before the magistrates' court.
⁶ Magistrates' Courts Act 1980, s. 6(1).
⁷ See ibid., s. 6(1).
⁸ As it is very rare for any of the offences mentioned in this work to be committed for trial, the procedure in the Crown Court is not described. As to the trial of indictments generally, see Archbold, *Criminal Pleading, Evidence and Practice*, 41st edn., Chapter 4.

5.15 *Procedure on summary trial*

On any proceedings in a Magistrates' Court both parties may be represented by counsel or a solicitor.[1] Where a case is being dealt with summarily[2] and the defendant does not plead guilty, the prosecutor calls the evidence[3] for the prosecution, and before doing so may address the court.[4] At the conclusion of the evidence for the prosecution, the defendant may address the court, whether or not he afterwards makes an unsworn statement or calls evidence.[5] At the conclusion of the evidence, if any, for the defence, the prosecutor may call evidence to rebut that evidence.[6] At the conclusion of the evidence for the defence and any unsworn statement which the defendant may make and the evidence, if any, in rebuttal, the defendant may address the court if he has not already done so.[7] Either party may, with the leave of the court, address the court a second time but where the court grants leave to one party it must not refuse leave to the other.[8] Where both parties address the court twice, the prosecutor must address the court for the second time before the defendant does so.[9]

If at the conclusion of the case the court finds the defendant not guilty, then that concludes matters, except that the prosecution may appeal on a point of law,[10] and the magistrates have power to award costs against the prosecution.[11] If the defendant is found guilty, then the court pronounces sentence and has power to award costs against the defendant.[12] Where the court imposes a fine under the Merchant Shipping Act 1894 and no specific application is provided in that Act, the court may, if it thinks fit, direct the whole or any part of the fine to be applied in compensating any person for any wrong or damage which he may have sustained by the act or default in respect of which the fine is imposed.[13] The Department of Transport may suspend the certificate of a master who has been convicted of an offence and there may also be separate proceedings leading to the cancellation or suspension of a master's certificate.[14] The defendant may appeal to the Crown Court against conviction or sentence,[15] or on a point of law to the Queen's Bench Divisional Court.[16]

[1] Magistrates' Courts Act 1980, s. 122.
[2] As to the choice of summary procedure or trial on indictment see para. 5.13, *ante*. As to summary proceedings generally see *Stone's Justices' Manual*.
[3] Evidence must in general be sworn and given orally but written statements and documents may sometimes be admissible (see paras. 5.16, 5.17, *post*) and facts may sometimes be agreed without proof; see the Criminal Justice Act 1967, s. 10. Evidence is usually dispensed with if the plea is one of guilty.
[4] Magistrates' Courts Rules 1981, S.I. No. 552, r. 13(1).
[5] Ibid., r. 13(2).
[6] Ibid., r. 13(3).
[7] Ibid., r. 13(4).
[8] Ibid., r. 13(5).
[9] Ibid., r. 13(6).
[10] See note 16, *infra*.
[11] See the Costs in Criminal Cases Act 1973, s. 2(1).
[12] See ibid., s. 2(2). See also the Merchant Shipping Act 1894, s. 700. The same power applies if the defendant pleads guilty.
[13] Merchant Shipping Act 1894, s. 699(1). Subject to any such directions, fines are to be paid into the Exchequer; see s. 699(2).
[14] See paras. 5.20 et seq., *post*.
[15] Magistrates' Courts Act 1980, s. 108.
[16] Magistrates' Courts Act 1980, s. 111.

5.16 *Admissibility of documents generally*

As a general rule, documents are not admissible in criminal proceedings as evidence of facts stated in those documents, unless they are produced by their maker at the hearing.[1] However, there are numerous exceptions to this rule. In particular, trade or business records may be admissible, where the person who supplied the information has since died or is otherwise unable or unfit to attend court or cannot reasonably be expected to have any recollection of the matters dealt with.[2] Photographs are generally admissible if verified by their maker[3] and it has been held (in a civil case) that mechanically recorded film of radar echoes was admissible and constituted real evidence of the movement of those echoes.[4] If such film were to be produced in a criminal trial, the court would wish to be satisfied that the film was produced from proper custody, was a record of the echoes in the area in question at the relevant time and that it had not been tampered with.[5] A certified copy or extract of the particulars entered by the registrar in the register book on the registry of a ship, together with a certified statement showing the ownership of the ship at the time being, is admissible and is evidence of the facts stated in it.[6] The official log-book of any ship is admissible in evidence, as is any document purporting to be a copy of an entry in the log and to be certified as a true copy by the master of the ship.[7]

Statements made by the defendant under caution will generally be admissible in evidence.[8] When in any criminal proceedings in the United Kingdom a witness cannot be found in the United Kingdom, any deposition which the witness may previously have made on oath outside the United Kingdom in relation to the same subject matter is admissible in evidence provided that it was made in the presence of the defendant.[9]

Written statements by any person are admissible to the same extent as oral evidence to the same effect by that person if certain conditions are satisfied. The principal conditions are (1) that any such statement purports to be signed by the person who made it; (2) the statement contains a declaration by that person to the effect that it is true to the best of his knowledge and belief and that he made the statement knowing that, if it were tendered in evidence, he would be liable to prosecution if he wilfully stated in it anything which he knew to be false or did not believe to be true; (3) before the hearing at which the statement is tendered in evidence, a copy of the statement is served by or on behalf of the party proposing to tender it, on each of the other parties to the proceedings; (4) none of the other parties, or their solicitors, within seven days from the service of the copy of the statement, serves a notice on the party so proposing objecting to the statement being so tendered in evidence; (5) if the statement refers to any other documents as an exhibit, the copy of the statement required to be served on any other party must be accompanied by a copy of that document or by such information as may be necessary in order to enable the party on whom it is served to inspect that document or a copy of it.[10]

[1] As to documentary evidence generally see *Halsbury's Laws of England*, 4th edn., vol. 17, paras. 124 et seq. As to the Admiralty chart see para. 5.17, *post*. As to tracing sheets see para. 5.03, text and notes 10, 11, *ante*.
[2] Criminal Evidence Act 1965, s. 1. It seems that notes and tracing sheets made by H.M. Coastguard may come within the category of trade or business records: but cf., *R. v. Gwilliam* [1968] 3 All E.R. 821, [1968] 1 W.L.R. 1839, C.A. See also *R. v. Crayden* [1978] 2 All E.R. 701, C.A., (hospital not a "business"). The Criminal Evidence Act 1965 defines "business" as including any "public transport, public utility or similar undertaking carried on by a local authority . . . "; see ibid., s. 1(4).*
[3] See, e.g., *R. v. Tolson* (1864) 4 F. & F. 103.
[4] *The Statue of Liberty* [1968] 2 All E.R. 195, [1968] 1 W.L.R. 739. This ruling would appear to apply to the videotapes mentioned in para. 5.03, text to note 12, *ante*.
[5] See the following cases on the admissibility of tape recordings:— *R. v. Stevenson, R. v. Hulse, R. v. Whitney* [1971] 1 All E.R. 678; [1971] 1 W.L.R. 1; *R. v. Robson, R. v. Harris* [1972] 2 All E.R. 699; [1972] 1 W.L.R. 651. See also *R. v. Senat, R. v. Sin* (1968) 52 Cr. App. Rep. 282, C.A.
[6] See the Merchant Shipping Act 1894, ss. 11, 695(1), (2). As to the penalties for falsely certifying or forging certificates see s. 695(3), (4).
[7] See the Merchant Shipping Act 1970, s. 75(1) (b).
[8] As to the rules governing admissibility see para. 5.08, *ante*.
[9] See the Merchant Shipping Act 1894, s. 691(1). As to authentication and proof of signatures see s. 691(2), (3).
[10] See the Criminal Justice Act 1967, s. 9.
*These provisions are likely to be replaced by a rule of admissibility which is wider in scope; see the Police and Criminal Evidence Bill.

5.17 *Admissibility of the Admiralty chart*

The Admiralty chart is habitually admitted in evidence in both civil and criminal trials. It is used to provide evidence of the low-water line along the coast, and of the natural features of the coast, banks and islands.[1] It is also used as a visual means of checking whether a ship whose position has been ascertained was at a particular time subject to the provisions of a traffic separation scheme.[2] Without the Admiralty chart, none of these matters could be simply verified and the use of the chart avoids much unnecessary oral evidence by surveyors and others. The chart is admissible because it is a public document[3] and the courts take judicial notice of the features displayed upon it[4] and approve its use in determining such matters as the baselines and limits of territorial waters.[5] This practice has the backing of international law.[6] The features displayed upon the chart are not necessarily conclusive, however, and may be challenged by expert evidence.[7]

[1] See *Post Office* v. *Estuary Radio* [1967] 3 All E.R. 663 at pp. 683, 684.
[2] The Admiralty charts have printed on them the features of traffic separation schemes. As to the schemes see paras. 2.06, 2.07, *ante*.
[3] I.e. it is an official copy of a document made by a public officer (the Royal Navy Hydrographer) who is under a quasi-judicial duty to inquire, for the purpose of the public making use of it and being able to refer to it; *Sturla* v. *Freccia* (1880) 5 App. Cas. 623 at p. 643, *per* Lord Blackburn.
[4] See *Birrell* v. *Dryer* (1884) 9 App. Cas. 345 at p. 352.
[5] See *Post Office* v. *Estuary Radio* [1967] 3 All E.R. 663 at pp. 683, 684.
[6] See the Convention on the Territorial Sea and the Contiguous Zone (Geneva, 29th April 1958, T.S. 3 (1965); Cmnd. (2511), arts. 3, 4(b); and see now the United Nations Convention on the Law of the Sea (1982), U.N. Document A/CONF. 62/122 of 7th October 1982, Part II, s. 2, art. 16.
[7] *Post Office* v. *Estuary Radio* [1967] 3 All E.R. 663 at p. 675. As to the standard of proof in criminal matters see para. 5.18, text and notes 1-4, *post*.

5.18 *Burden of proof*

In criminal cases the burden of proving all the facts which constitute an offence lies upon the prosecution. Those facts must be proved beyond reasonable doubt but there is no absolute standard of proof[1] and what the courts will accept as sufficient proof depends in some degree on the gravity of the offence[2] and the attainability of absolute proof.[3] In most cases where a prosecution is brought for a breach of the collision regulations, the offence is tried summarily. Moreover, absolute proof of the physical features which constitute a baseline would involve expense and delay quite out of proportion to the subject matter. It is for these reasons that it is submitted that the Admiralty chart (with the most recent corrections endorsed upon it) should be regarded as constituting proof beyond reasonable doubt of the features shown on it, subject always to the right of either side to prove that the chart is erroneous.[4]

The burden upon the defence is to demonstrate that the prosecution has not established the facts beyond reasonable doubt. In many cases there are statutory defences, and if the defendant wishes to establish one of these or take advantage of any exception, exemption, proviso, excuse or qualification in relation to any offence under the Merchant Shipping Act 1894, he may do so by proving the necessary facts[5] on the preponderance of probability.[6] Therefore there is a less onerous burden upon the defence than upon the prosecution.[7]

[1] See *Bater* v. *Bater* [1950] 2 All E.R. 458 at p. 459, *per* Denning, L.J.
[2] See *Bater* v. *Bater*, *supra*, and *Hornal* v. *Neuburger Products Ltd.* [1956] 3 All E.R. 971 at p. 978, *per* Morris, L.J.
[3] *Hornal* v. *Neuberger Products Ltd.*, *supra*, at p. 977, *per* Hodson, L.J.
[4] See para. 5.17, text and notes 5-7, *ante*.
[5] See the Merchant Shipping Act 1894, s. 697.

[6] See *R.* v. *Carr-Briant* [1943] 2 All E.R. 156; *R.* v. *Dunbar* [1957] 3 All E.R. 737. This principle is of particular relevance in relation to the new statutory defence to a charge of contravening the Merchant Shipping (Distress Signals and Prevention of Collisions) Regulations 1983, S.I. 1983, No. 708; see para. 1.10, text and note 13, *ante*.
[7] Any exception, exemption, proviso, excuse or qualification, in relation to any offence under the Merchant Shipping Act 1894 need not be specified or negatived in any information or complaint and, if it is so specified or negatived, no proof in relation to the matter so specified or negatived is required on the part of the prosecution; see ibid., s. 697.

SECT. (3) Inquiries and Investigations

5.19 *Preliminary inquiries into shipping casualties, etc.*

The Secretary of State for Transport[1] may cause a preliminary inquiry to be held by a person appointed by him where any of the following casualties has occurred:— (1) the loss[2] or presumed loss, stranding, grounding, abandonment of or damage to a ship;[3] or (2) a loss of life or serious personal injury caused by fire on board or by any accident to a ship or ship's boat,[4] or by any accident occurring on board a ship or ship's boat; or (3) any damage caused by a ship.[5] At the time when the casualty occurred the ship must have been registered in the United Kingdom[6] or the ship or boat must have been in the United Kingdom or its territorial waters.[7] A person appointed to hold a preliminary inquiry[8] has the powers of a Department of Transport inspector[9] for the purpose of the inquiry.[10] Whether or not a preliminary inquiry into the casualty is held, the Secretary of State may cause a formal investigation into the casualty to be held by a Wreck Commissioner.[11]

[1] This provision, as originally enacted, referred to the Board of Trade. As to the devolution of the functions of the board on the Secretary of State, see para. 5.01, *ante*.
[2] "Loss" refers to physical loss; see *The Olympic* [1913] P. 92; [1911-13] All E.R. Rep. 469, C.A.; *The Woodhorn* (1891) 92 L.T. Jo. 113; *Horlock* v. *Beal* [1916] 1 A.C. 486; [1916-17] All E.R. Rep. 81.
[3] For the meaning of "ship" see para. 1.04, text and note 14, *ante*. As to the special provisions relating to hovercraft casualties, see the Hovercraft (Application of Enactments) Order 1972, S.I. 1972, No. 971, art. 9, Sch. 4, Part A.
[4] "Ship's boat" includes a life-raft; Merchant Shipping Act 1970, s. 97(1).
[5] Ibid., s. 55(1); Merchant Shipping Act 1979, s. 32(2) (a). Where an incident has occurred which the Secretary of State considers was or is capable of causing a casualty into which he could require an inquiry under the Merchant Shipping Act 1970, s. 55(1), the powers to hold an inquiry or an investigation or both which are conferred on him by s. 55(1), paras. (i), (ii), are exercisable in relation to that incident as if it were such a casualty; Merchant Shipping Act 1970, s. 55 (1A); Merchant Shipping Act 1979, s. 32(2) (b). As to investigations see para. 5.20, *post*.
[6] For the meaning of "the United Kingdom" see para. 1.08, note 16, *ante*.
[7] As to the territorial waters of the United Kingdom, see para. 1.08, text and notes 16-26, *ante*.
[8] I.e. appointed to hold a preliminary inquiry under the Merchant Shipping Act 1970, s. 55.
[9] I.e. the powers conferred by ibid., s. 27. As to this section, and as to Department of Transport inspectors and their powers, see para. 5.07, *ante*.
[10] Merchant Shipping Act 1970, s. 55(2).
[11] Ibid., s. 55(1), (ii). The formal investigation is held in England, Wales or Northern Ireland by a Wreck Commissioner and in Scotland by the Sheriff; ibid., s. 55(1), (ii). The Lord Chancellor may appoint such number of persons as he thinks fit to be Wreck Commissioners and may remove any Wreck Commissioners appointed by him; s. 82(1). The Lord Chancellor, with the consent of the Treasury, determines their remuneration and that of assessors which is paid out of moneys provided by Parliament; s. 83. As to assessors, see para. 5.20, note 6, *post*.

5.20 *Formal investigation into shipping casualties*

A Wreck Commissioner[1] holding a formal investigation[2] into a casualty[3] or incident[4] must conduct it in accordance with prescribed rules.[5] The rules must require him to have the assistance of one or more assessors, or not less than two assessors if any question as to the cancellation or suspension of an officer's certificate is likely to arise.[6] A Wreck Commissioner has the same powers as a Magistrates' Court to compel witnesses to attend and produce documents,[7] and he has power to administer oaths for the purposes of the investigation.[8] If, as a result of the investigation, the Wreck Commissioner is satisfied that an officer is unfit to discharge his duties[9] or has been seriously negligent[10] and in either case that this has caused or contributed to the casualty,[11] he may cancel or suspend any certificate issued to the officer[12] or censure him.[13] The Wreck Commissioner may also cancel or suspend the officer's certificate, or censure him, if he is satisfied, as a result of the investigation, that the officer failed in his duty to give assistance and information after a collision.[14] The Secretary of State has power to order a rehearing and there is a right of appeal to the High Court.[15]

If the Wreck Commissioner cancels or suspends the officer's certificate, the latter must deliver it forthwith[16] to the Wreck Commissioner or to the Secretary of State for Transport.[17] If the officer fails to deliver his certificate, he commits an offence and is liable on summary conviction to a fine not exceeding level 3 on the standard scale.[18]

The Wreck Commissioner may make such order as to the costs of the investigation as he thinks just.[19] He must make a report on the case to the Secretary of State for Transport.[20]

---

[1] As to Wreck Commissioners, see para. 5.19, note 11, *ante*. In Scotland formal investigations are conducted by the Sheriff; see para. 5.19, note 11, *ante*.

[2] I.e. a formal investigation under the Merchant Shipping Act 1970, s. 55; see para. 5.19, text and note 11, *ante*.

[3] As to the casualties into which an investigation may be held, see para 5.19, text and notes 2-5, *ante*. As to the special provision for hovercraft casualties, see the Hovercraft Application of Enactments Order 1972, S.I. 1972, No. 971, art. 9, Sch. 4, Part A.

[4] I.e. such an incident as is described in para. 5.19, note 5, *ante*. See also the Merchant Shipping Act 1979, s. 32(3).

[5] Merchant Shipping Act 1970, s. 56(1). The rules referred to are those made or deemed to have been made under ibid., s. 58(1); as to which see para. 5.21, *post*.

[6] Ibid., s. 56(1). Rules deemed to have been made under section 58 divide the list of assessors into four classes according to qualification:—(1) mercantile marine masters; (2) mercantile marine engineers; (3) naval officers; and (4) persons of fishery, naval architectural or other special skill or knowledge: see generally, the Shipping Casualties and Appeals and Re-hearings Rules 1923, S.R. & O. 1923, No. 752, Appendix, Part II. As to the payment of assessors, see para. 5.19, note 11, *ante*. The Rules of 1923 were made under the Merchant Shipping Act 1894, s. 466. This provision has now been repealed but the Rules continue to have effect as if made under the Merchant Shipping Act 1970, s. 58; see para. 5.21, note 10, *post*.

[7] I.e. the powers conferred by the Magistrates' Courts Act 1980, s. 97(1), (3), (4); see the Merchant Shipping Act 1970, s. 56(2); Magistrates' Courts Act 1980, Sch. 7.

[8] Merchant Shipping Act 1970, s. 56(2).

[9] I.e. unfit within the meaning of ibid., s. 52(1), (a), as to which see para. 5.22, text and note 13, *post*.
[10] I.e. seriously negligent within the meaning of ibid., s. 52(1) (a), as to which see para. 5.22, text and note 14, *post*.
[11] I.e. has failed in his duty under the Merchant Shipping Act 1894, s. 422, as to which see para. 1.11, text and notes 1-8, *ante*.
[12] I.e. any certificate issued under the Merchant Shipping Act 1970, s. 43. As to the manning of ships and the certification of officers and other crew members, see *Halsbury's Laws of England*, 4th edn., title SHIPPING, vol. 43, paras. 182 et seq.
[13] Ibid., s. 56(4).
[14] Merchant Shipping Act 1970, s. 56(4).
[15] As to rehearings and appeals, see para. 5.23, *post*.
[16] For the meaning of "forthwith" see *Re Southam, Ex parte Lamb* (1881) 19 Ch. D. 169, C.A., at p. 173.
[17] Merchant Shipping Act 1970, s. 56(4).
[18] Ibid., s. 59; Merchant Shipping Act 1979, s. 43(1), Sch. 6, Part II; Criminal Justice Act 1982, ss. 37, 46(1), (4). As to the standard scale, see para. 1.11, note 19, *ante*. This offence is also committed when an officer fails to deliver his certificate when required to do so under the Merchant Shipping Act 1970, s. 52, as to which see para. 5.22, text and notes 14, 22, *post*.
[19] Ibid., s. 56(5). Any costs which a person is ordered to pay under this provision may be recovered from him by the Secretary of State for Transport, s. 56(6).
[20] Ibid., s. 56(5). This provision, as originally enacted, referred to the Board of Trade. As to the devolution of the functions of the Board on the Secretary of State, see para. 5.01, *ante*.

5.21 *Procedure on formal investigation*

The Secretary of State for Transport[1] may make rules for the conduct of inquiries[2] and formal investigations[3] and for the conduct of any rehearing[4] which is not held by the High Court.[5] The rules may provide for the appointment and summoning of assessors, the manner in which any facts may be proved, the persons allowed to appear, and the notices to be given to persons affected.[6] A provision of the Merchant Shipping Act 1894, that if a charge is made against any person, he is to have the right to defend himself against the allegation, in person or otherwise, has been repealed without being replaced.[7] There are detailed rules as to service of notice of the investigation on masters,[8] owners[9] and others,[10] as to notices to produce documents,[11] the admissibility of affidavits in evidence[12] and as to adjournments.[13] The witnesses called by the Secretary of State give evidence first and may be cross-examined by the parties in such order as the judge directs; and they may be re-examined.[14] The questions regarding the casualty and the conduct of the certificated officers or other persons connected with it, upon which the opinion of the court is desired, are then stated in open court on behalf of the Secretary of State.[15] The court hears the parties upon the questions and determines them.[16] The parties may address the court, call or recall witnesses and generally adduce evidence.[17] When the evidence has been concluded, any of the parties may address the court on the evidence.[18] The Secretary of State has a right of reply on the whole case.[19] The judge may deliver the decision of the court either *viva voce* or in writing.[20] The Secretary of State has power to order a rehearing and there is a right of appeal when an officer's certificate has been cancelled.[21]

[1] This provision, as originally enacted, referred to the Board of Trade. As to the devolution of the functions of the Board on the Secretary of State, see para. 5.01, *ante*.

[2] I.e. inquiries under the Merchant Shipping Act 1970, ss. 52 and 54. As to inquiries into the fitness or conduct of officers, see para. 5.22, text and notes 12-24, *post*. Inquiries under s. 54 into the fitness or conduct of seamen other than officers are not dealt with in this work.

[3] I.e. formal investigations under ibid., s. 56, as to which see para. 5.20, *ante*.

[4] I.e. rehearings under ibid., s. 57, as to which see para. 5.23, text and notes 1-8, *post*.

[5] Ibid., s. 58(1).

[6] Ibid., s. 58(2). This provision is expressed to be without prejudice to the generality of s. 58(1).

[7] See the Merchant Shipping Act 1894, s. 466 (11); Merchant Shipping Act 1970, s. 100 (3), Sch. 5.

[8] For the meaning of "master" see para. 1.10, note 5, *ante*.

[9] For the meaning of "owner" see para. 1.10, note 3, *ante*.

[10] See the Shipping Casualties and Appeals and Re-hearings Rules 1923, S.R. & O. 1923, No. 752, r. 3. These rules, originally made under the Merchant Shipping Act 1894, s. 479 (repealed), now have effect as if made under the Merchant Shipping Act 1970, s. 58; Interpretation Act 1978, s. 17(2)(b).

[11] See ibid., rr. 6, 7.

[12] See ibid., r. 8.

[13] See ibid., r. 14.

[14] See ibid., r. 10.

[15] See ibid., r. 11.

[16] See ibid., r. 12.

[17] See ibid., r. 12.

[18] See ibid., r. 13.

[19] See ibid., r. 13.

[20] Ibid., r. 15.

[21] As to the cancellation or suspension of certificates see paras. 5.20, text and notes 9-13, 5.22, text and notes 18-21, *ante*. As to rehearings and appeals, see para. 5.23, *post*.

5.22 *Other inquiries*

In addition to preliminary inquiries[1] and formal investigations,[2] there are several other types of inquiry. For example, if any person dies in a ship[3] registered in the United Kingdom,[4] or the master[5] of or a seaman employed in such a ship dies in a country outside the United Kingdom, an inquiry into the cause of death must be held by a superintendent[6] or proper officer[7] at the next port[8] where the ship calls after the death.[9] The person holding the inquiry must make a report of his findings to the Secretary of State for Transport.[10] Also where any loss of life arises by reason of any casualty happening to or on board any boat belonging to a fishing vessel, the Secretary of State may, if he thinks fit, cause an inquiry to be made or a formal investigation to be held as in the case of a shipping casualty.[11]

If it appears to the Secretary of State[12] that an officer—

(1) is unfit to discharge his duties, whether by reason of incompetence or misconduct or for any other reason; or

(2) has been seriously negligent in the discharge or his duties; or

(3) has failed to fulfil his duty to give assistance and information[13] after a collision;

the Secretary of State may cause an inquiry to be held by one or more persons appointed by him.[14] The inquiry must be conducted in accordance with prescribed rules[15] which must require the persons holding the inquiry to do so with one or more assessors.[16] The persons holding the inquiry have all the powers of a Department of Transport inspector.[17] If they are satisfied that the officer is unfit [18] or has been seriously negligent[19] or has failed to give assistance and information,[20] they may cancel his certificate[21] or censure him.[22] They may also make such order as to the costs of the inquiry as they think just.[23] They must make a report on the case to the Secretary of State.[24] The Secretary of State may order a rehearing and there are rights of appeal.[25] Colonial courts are empowered to conduct investigations into shipping casualties and inquiries into the conduct of officers.[26]

[1] As to preliminary inquiries see para. 5.19, *ante*.

[2] As to formal investigations see para. 5.20, *ante*.

[3] For the meaning of "ship" see para. 1.04, text and note 14, *ante*.

[4] As to the registry of British ships see the Merchant Shipping Act 1894, ss. 2-23; and the Merchant Shipping Act 1983. For the meaning of "the United Kingdom" see para. 1.08, note 16, *ante*.

[5] For the meaning of "master" see para. 1.10, note 5, *ante*.

[6] As to superintendents see para. 5.05, note 2, *ante*.

[7] For the meaning of "proper officer" see para. 5.05, note 8, *ante*.

[8] For the meaning of "port" see para. 1.11, note 7, *ante*.

[9] See the Merchant Shipping Act 1970, s. 61(1). The scope of an inquiry under s. 61 has been enlarged to include deaths in boats and life-rafts, deaths following injury or disease or occurring on board where the person leaves the ship in consequence of the disease or injury and dies abroad, and possible deaths in or losses from ships, boats and life-rafts; s. 61(1), (1A), (1B); Merchant Shipping Act 1979, s. 29(1). The superintendent or proper officer holding the inquiry has all the powers of a Department of Transport inspector; s. 61(2). As to such powers see para. 5.07, *ante*. No inquiry may be held where an inquest is to be held; s. 61(4).

[10] Ibid., s. 61(3). This provision, as originally enacted, referred to the Board of Trade. As to the devolution of the functions of the Board on the Secretary of State see para. 5.01, *ante*.

[11] Merchant Shipping Act 1894, s. 468. This provision is prospectively repealed, as from a day to be appointed under the Merchant Shipping Act 1970, s. 101, Sch. 5.

[12] This provision, as originally enacted, referred to the Board of Trade. As to the devolution of the functions of the Board on the Secretary of State, see para. 5.01, *ante*.

[13] I.e. failed to comply with the provisions of s. 422 of the Merchant Shipping Act 1894, as to which see para. 1.11, *ante*.

[14] Merchant Shipping Act 1970, s. 52(1). If he does cause an inquiry to be held, the Secretary of State may, if he thinks fit, suspend any certificate issued to the officer under ibid., s. 43, pending the outcome of the inquiry, and require the officer to deliver it to him; s. 52(1). The suspension may, on the application of the officer, be terminated by the High Court; s. 52(2). Failure to deliver the certificate is an offence; see para. 5.20, text and note 18, *ante*.

[15] I.e. the rules prescribed under ibid., s. 58(1). Rules have been made under this provision, requiring among other things that (1) Notice of the inquiry is served by the Secretary of State on the officer concerned; (2) The inquiry is to be held in public; (3) The person holding the inquiry is to be assisted by one or more assessors; (4) The officer is to have the right to defend himself against the allegation, call and cross-examine witnesses and tender documents as evidence; (5) The person holding the inquiry must announce his decision at or as soon as possible after the end of the inquiry; see the Merchant Shipping (Section 52 Inquiries) Rules 1982, S.I. 1982, No. 1752, rr. 4-8.

[16] Merchant Shipping Act 1970, s. 52(3). As to assessors, see para. 5.20, note 6, *ante*. As to their remuneration, see para. 5.19, note 11, *ante*.

[17] Merchant Shipping Act 1970, s. 52(3); Merchant Shipping Act 1979, s. 37(4).

[18] See para. (1) of the text to note 13, *supra*. A single episode of incompetence or misconduct would not ordinarily justify a finding against a master with a clean record; see *The Empire Antelope, The Radchurch* [1943] P. 79.

[19] See para. (2) of the text to note 13, *supra*.

[20] See para. (3) of the text to note 13, *supra*.

[21] I.e. any certificate issued to him under the Merchant Shipping Act 1970, s. 43.

[22] Ibid., s. 52(4) (a). If the certificate is cancelled or suspended; the officer must deliver it forthwith to the persons holding the inquiry or to the Secretary of State, unless he has already done so under s. 52(1); s. 52(4). As to s. 52(1), see note 14, *supra*. Failure to deliver the certificate is an offence; see para. 5.20, text and note 18, *ante*.

23 Merchant Shipping Act 1970, s. 52(4) (b). The costs are recoverable by the Secretary of State from the person ordered to pay them; ibid., s. 52(5).
24 Ibid., s. 52(4) (c).
25 As to rehearings and appeals, see para. 5.23, *post*.
26 See the Merchant Shipping Act 1894, s. 478; and note 25, *infra*. The provisions of ss. 468, 478, do not apply in relation to hovercraft; see the Hovercraft (Application of Enactments) Order 1972, S.I. 1972, No. 971, art. 9, Sch. 4, Part A.

5.23 *Rehearings, appeals and restoration of certificate*

Where an inquiry has been held into the fitness or conduct of an officer,[1] or a formal investigation has been held into a shipping casualty,[2] the Secretary of State for Transport[3] may order the whole or part of the case to be reheard.[4] He must do so if new and important evidence which could not be produced at the inquiry or investigation has been discovered or if there appear to the Secretary of State to be other grounds for suspecting that a miscarriage of justice may have occurred.[5] The order may provide for the rehearing to be by the persons who held it, by a Wreck Commissioner[6] or by the High Court.[7] Any rehearing which is not held by the High Court must be conducted in accordance with the prescribed rules.[8] If there is no application for a rehearing, or if an application has been made and refused, and if those holding the inquiry or investigation have decided to cancel or suspend the certificate of any person[9] or have found any person at fault,[10] there is a right of appeal to the High Court.[11] This right is available to the person whose certificate has been suspended or who has been found at fault, or to any other person who had an interest in the inquiry, appeared at the hearing and is affected by the decision or finding.[12]

Where a certificate has been cancelled or suspended, the Secretary of State, if he is of the opinion that the justice of the case requires it, may reissue the certificate if it has been cancelled or reduce the period of suspension and return it if it has been suspended.[12] Alternatively he may grant a new certificate of the same or a lower grade in place of the cancelled or suspended certificate.[14]

1 I.e. an inquiry under the Merchant Shipping Act 1970, s. 52, as to which see para. 5.22, text and notes 12-24, *ante*.
2 I.e. a formal investigation under ibid., s. 55, as to which see paras. 5.20, 5.21, *ante*.
3 This provision, as originally enacted, referred to the Board of Trade. As to the devolution of the functions of the Board on the Secretary of State, see para. 5.01, *ante*
4 Merchant Shipping Act 1970, s. 57(1).
5 Ibid., s. 57(1) (a), (b).
6 As to Wreck Commissioners and their remuneration, see para. 5.19, note 11, *ante*.
7 Merchant Shipping Act 1970, s. 57(2) (a). Equivalent provisions relating to Scotland are made by s. 57(2) (b).
8 Ibid., s. 57(3). As to the rules prescribed for s. 52 inquiries, see para. 4.22, note 15, *ante*. As to the rules prescribed for formal investigations, see para. 4.21, text and notes 8-20, *ante*. The provisions of the Merchant Shipping Act 1970, s. 56 (as to which see para. 5.20, *ante*) apply to a rehearing of a formal investigation as they apply on the holding of a formal investigation; s. 57(3). Rules of courts made for the purpose of rehearings under s. 57 which are held by the High Court, or of appeals to the High Court, may require the court, subject to such exceptions, if any, as may be allowed by the

rules, to hold such a rehearing or hear such an appeal with the assistance of one or more assessors; s. 58(3). As to assessors, see para. 5.20, note 6. As to their remuneration, see para. 5.19, note 11, *ante*.
[9] As to the cancellation or suspension of certificates, see paras. 5.20, text and notes 9-12, 5.22, text and notes 18-22, *ante*.
[10] As to findings of fault and censure, see para. 5.20, text and note 13; 5.22, text and note 22, *ante*.
[11] See the Merchant Shipping Act 1970, 57(4). In Scotland, the right of appeal is to the Court of Session; ibid., s. 57(4).
[12] Ibid., s. 57(4).
[13] Ibid., s. 60.
[14] Ibid., s. 60.

SECT. (4) Compensation and damages

5.24 *Compensation and damages*

Where a breach of the collision regulations or rules for distress signals has occurred, a civil action for damages may lie in favour of a shipowner whose ship is damaged or lost as a result. This topic involves a wider area of duty than the duty to observe the rules and regulations and is exhaustively treated in leading works on collisions at sea.[1] Nevertheless, a brief summary of the civil liability of masters and owners is necessary for completeness.

The criminal liability of masters of ships for illegally using or displaying signals of distress has already been described.[2] The offending master is liable to a fine[3] and is further liable to pay compensation for any labour undertaken, risk incurred or loss sustained in consequence of the signal's having been supposed to be a signal of distress.[4] The compensation may, without prejudice to any other remedy, be recovered in the same manner as salvage.[5]

A master may be liable in damages for an act of negligence in the navigation of his ship, whether or not a breach of the collision regulations is involved.[6] There was formerly a statutory presumption of fault on the part of a master in breach of the collision regulations but this was repealed in 1911.[7] Until 1983 there remained a rebuttable presumption that damage to person or property, arising from the non-observance by any ship of the collision regulations, was occasioned by the wilful default of the person in charge of the deck of the ship at the time.[8] The presumption could be rebutted on showing to the satifaction of the court that the circumstances of the case made a departure from the regulation necessary.[9] In any event, the damage in question still had to *arise from* the non-observance. The injured party had to prove that the non-observance or some other unseamanlike act had some effect in causing the damage.[10] Even this presumption has been repealed with effect from 1st June 1983 so far as it related to vessels and hovercraft.[11] A master will not be liable for a wrong step taken in the agony of collision, unless the emergency was the fault of his ship.[12]

No liability will attach to him if he can show that the accident was inevitable.[13] He may be able to plead contributory negligence by another party.[14] In most cases, any civil action will be brought not against the master but against the owner, although the owner may be able to claim an indemnity from the master in respect of any damages or loss which the owner has had to pay as a result of the master's negligence.[15]

An owner is liable for the negligent acts of those employees of his who are in charge of his ship.[16] There is a presumption that those in charge of the ship are employed by the owner.[17] However, the owner is not generally[18] liable in negligence for damage caused by a ship unless either he is personally at fault[19] or he is the employer of the actual wrongdoer.[20] Moreover, an owner is not liable for the malicious or criminal acts of his employees when those employees are acting outside the scope of their employment.[21]

Civil actions arising out of collisions are generally brought in the Admiralty Court of the Queen's Bench Division of the High Court.[22] There are provisions for apportioning loss[23] and limiting liability.[24] A maritime lien attaches to a ship which has caused damage.[25] The lien is for the amount of the damage, and is enforced by an action *in rem*.[26] There are special rules of procedure respecting actions *in rem*.[27] Otherwise the burden of proof,[28] the standard of proof[29] and the rules of evidence are generally similar to those applied in other civil actions.[30]

---

[1] See *British Shipping Laws*—vol. 4, Marsden, *The Law of Collisions at Sea*, 11th edn.
[2] See para. 1.10, text and notes 24-26, *ante*.
[3] See para. 1.10, text and note 26, *ante*.
[4] Merchant Shipping (Safety Convention) Act 1949, s. 21(3); Merchant Shipping (Distress Signals and Prevention of Collisions) Regulations 1983, S.I. 1983, No. 708, reg. 1(5)(b), Sch. 2, Part I.
[5] Ibid., s. 21(3). As to the recovery of salvage see the Merchant Shipping Act 1894, s. 547 et seq.
[6] See *The Dundee* (1823) 1 Hag. Ad. 109, *per* Lord Stowell, at p. 120.
[7] This presumption had effect even although the infringement did not contribute to the collision; see the Merchant Shipping Act 1873, s. 17 (repealed), and the Merchant Shipping Act 1894, s. 419(4) (repealed). As to the abolition of the presumption see the Maritime Conventions Act 1911, s. 4.
[8] Merchant Shipping Act 1894, s. 419(3).
[9] Ibid., s. 419(3).
[10] See *The Tempus* [1913] P. 166, *per* Sir Samuel Evans, P., at p. 172.
[11] See the Merchant Shipping (Distress Signals and Prevention of Collisions) Regulations 1983, reg. 1(4)(a); Hovercraft (Application of Enactments) (Amendment) Order 1983, S.I. 1983, No. 769, art. 3(a)(i).
[12] See, e.g., *The Sisters* (1876) 1 P.D.117.
[13] See, e.g., *The Merchant Prince* [1892] P. 179, C.A.
[14] See the Maritime Conventions Act 1911, s. 1; and see *The Eurymedon* [1938] P. 41, C.A.
[15] See, e.g., *Green* v. *New River Co.* (1792) 4 T.R. 589; but see *Jones* v. *Manchester Corpn.* [1952] 2 Q.B. 852. See also *Lister* v. *Romford Ice and Cold Storage Co. Ltd.* [1957] A.C. 555; cf., *Morris* v. *Ford Motor Co. Ltd.* [1973] 2 All E.R. 1084, C.A.
[16] See *River Wear Commissioners* v. *Adamson* (1877) 2 App. Cas. 743; *Hibbs* v. *Ross* (1866) L.R. 1 Q.B. 534.
[17] *Joyce* v. *Capel* (1838) 8 C. & P. 370.
[18] A liability for damage to harbour works which is independent of fault attaches to owners under the Harbours Docks and Piers Clauses Act 1847, s. 74, where that provision is incorporated in a harbour authority's special Act.

[19] The owner may be at fault in giving a wrong helm order or personally making an error of navigation He may also be at fault in failing adequately to instruct and supervise his marine staff; see *The Dayspring* [1968] 2 Lloyd's Rep. 204; *The Lady Gwendolen* [1965] 1 Lloyd's Rep. 335, C.A.

[20] See *River Wear Commissioners* v. *Adamson* (1877) 2 App. Cas. 743, *per* Lord Cairns, C., at p. 751.

[21] See, e.g., *The Druid* (1842) 1 W. Rob. 391.

[22] See, generally, *British Shipping Laws*, vol. 1, Admiralty Practice. Such actions may in small cases be brought in County courts having Admiralty jurisdiction; see County Courts Act 1959, s. 56.

[23] See the Maritime Conventions Act 1911, s. 1.

[24] See the Merchant Shipping (Liability of Shipowners and Others) Act 1900.

[25] See *The Tolten* [1946] P. 135, C.A.

[26] An action *in rem* may become a combined personal action and action *in rem* if the owner enters an appearance; see *The Dupleix* [1912] P. 8.

[27] See, generally, R.S.C. Order 75.

[28] See *Morgan* v. *Sim, The City of London* (1857) 11 Moo. P.C. 307, at p. 312.

[29] The plaintiff must establish the facts upon which he relies on "the balance of probabilities"; see *Newis* v. *Lark* (1571) Plowd. 403, at p. 412; *Cooper* v. *Slade* (1858) 6 H.L. Cas. 746, at p. 772; *Bonnington Castings Ltd.* v. *Wardlaw* [1956] 1 A.C. 613, at p. 620, H.L.

[30] The rules of evidence in civil cases are in some respects more relaxed than in criminal cases; see the Civil Evidence Act 1968.

APPENDIX I

INTERNATIONAL REGULATIONS FOR PREVENTING COLLISIONS AT SEA, 1972

TABLE SHOWING DERIVATION

THIS COLUMN	THIS COLUMN
This column contains the 1972 Rules originally set out in the First Schedule to the Collision Regulations and Distress Signals Order 1977 (revoked) and now, in amended form implementing IMO Resolution A.464 (XII), in the First Schedule to the Merchant Shipping (Distress Signals and Prevention of Collisions) Regulations 1983. New or amended material is underlined.	Provision or rule from which rule in left column is derived. Author's comments are in square brackets. The Rules in this column are the 1960 Rules, i.e. the Rules set out in the First Schedule to the Collision Regulations (Ships and Seaplanes on the Water) and Signals of Distress (Ships) Order 1965, except where otherwise stated.

PART A. GENERAL

6.01   RULE 1
Application

(*a*) These Rules shall apply to all vessels upon the high seas and in all waters connected therewith navigable by seagoing vessels.

(*b*) Nothing in these Rules shall interfere with the operation of special rules made by an appropriate authority for roadsteads, harbours, rivers, lakes or inland waterways connected with the high seas and navigable by seagoing vessels. Such special rules shall conform as closely as possible to these Rules.

(*c*) Nothing in these Rules shall interfere with the operation of any special rules made by the Government of any State with respect to additional station or signal lights, shapes or whistle signals for ships of war and vessels proceeding under convoy, or with respect to additional station or signal lights or shapes for fishing vessels engaged in fishing as a fleet. These additional station or signal lights, shapes or whistle signals shall, so far as possible, be such that they cannot be mistaken for any light, shape or signal authorized elsewhere under these Rules.

(*d*) Traffic separation schemes may be adopted by the Organization for the purpose of these Rules.

RULE 1

(*a*) These Rules shall be followed by all vessels and seaplanes upon the high seas and in all waters connected therewith navigable by seagoing vessels, except as provided in Rule 30.

RULE 30
Reservation of Rules for Harbours and Inland Navigation

Nothing in these Rules shall interfere with the operation of a special rule duly made by local authority relative to the navigation of any harbour, river, lake, or inland water, including a reserved seaplane area.

RULE 13

(*a*) Nothing in these Rules shall interfere with the operation of any special rules made by the Government or any nation with respect to additional station and signal lights for ships of war, for vessels sailing under convoy, for fishing vessels engaged in fishing as a fleet or for seaplanes on the water.

RULE 28

(*d*) Nothing in these Rules shall interfere with the operation of any special rules made by the Government of any nation with respect to the use of additional whistle signals between ships of war or vessels sailing under convoy.

(*e*) Whenever the Government concerned shall have determined that a vessel of special construction or purpose cannot comply fully with the provisions of any of these Rules with respect to the number, position, range or arc of visibility of lights or shapes, as well as to the disposition and characteristics of sound-signalling appliances, without interfering with the special function of the vessel, such vessel shall comply with such other provisions in regard to the number, position, range or arc of visibility of lights or shapes, as well as to the disposition and characteristics of sound-signalling appliances, as her Government shall have determined to be the closest possible compliance with these Rules in respect of that vessel.

RULE 13
(*b*) Whenever the Government concerned shall have determined that a naval or other military vessel or waterborne seaplane of special construction or purpose cannot comply fully with the provisions of any of these Rules with respect to the number, position, range or arc of visibility of lights or shapes, without interfering with the military function of the vessel or seaplane, such vessel or seaplane shall comply with such other provisions in regard to the number, position, range or arc of visibility of lights or shapes as her Government shall have determined to be the closest possible compliance with these Rules in respect of that vessel or seaplane.

6.02   ### RULE 2
Responsibility
(*a*) Nothing in these Rules shall exonerate any vessel, or the owner, master or crew thereof, from the consequences of any neglect to comply with these Rules or of the neglect of any precaution which may be required by the ordinary practice of seamen, or by the special circumstances of the case.

RULE 29
Nothing in these Rules shall exonerate any vessel, or the owner, master or crew thereof, from the consequences of any neglect to carry lights or signals, or of any neglect to keep a proper look-out, or of the neglect of any precaution which may be required by the ordinary practice of seamen, or by the special circumstances of the case.

(*b*) In construing and complying with these Rules due regard shall be had to all dangers of navigation and collision and to any special circumstances, including the limitations of the vessels involved, which may make a departure from these Rules necessary to avoid immediate danger.

RULE 27
In obeying and construing these Rules due regard shall be had to all dangers of navigation and collision, and to any special circumstances, including the limitations of the craft involved, which may render a departure from the above Rules necessary in order to avoid immediate danger.

6.03   ### RULE 3
General definitions
For the purpose of these Rules, except where the context otherwise requires:
(*a*) The word "vessel" includes every description of water craft, including non-displacement craft and seaplanes, used or capable of being used as a means of transportation on water.

RULE 1(c)
(*c*) In the following Rules, except where the context otherwise requires:—
(i) the word "vessel" includes every description of water craft, other than a seaplane on the water, used or capable or being used as a means of transportation on water;

RULE 18
(*b*) For the purposes of this Rule and Rules 19 to 29 inclusive, except Rule 20(*c*) and Rule 28, a seaplane on the water shall be deemed to be a vessel, and the expression "power-driven vessel" shall be construed accordingly.

(*b*) The term "power-driven vessel" means any vessel propelled by machinery

RULE 1(c)
(iii) the term "power-driven vessel" means any vessel propelled by machinery;

(*c*) The term "sailing vessel" means any vessel under sail provided that propelling machinery, if fitted, is not being used.

(iv) every power-driven vessel which is under sail and not under power is to be considered a sailing vessel, and every vessel under power whether under sail or not, is to be considered a power-driven vessel;

(*d*) The term "vessel engaged in fishing" means any vessel fishing with nets, lines, trawls or other fishing apparatus which restrict manoeuvrability, but does not include a vessel fishing with trolling lines or other fishing apparatus which do not restrict manoeuvrability.

(xiv) the term "engaged in fishing" means fishing with nets, lines or trawls, but does not include fishing with trolling lines.

(*e*) The word "seaplane" includes any aircraft designed to manoeuvre on the water.

(ii) the word "seaplane" includes a flying boat and any other aircraft designed to manoeuvre on the water;

(*f*) The term "vessel not under command" means a vessel which through some exceptional circumstance is unable to manoeuvre as required by these Rules and is therefore unable to keep out of the way of another vessel.

———————

(*g*) The term "vessel restricted in her ability to manoeuvre" means a vessel which from the nature of her work is restricted in her ability to manoeuvre as required by these Rules and is therefore unable to keep out of the way of another vessel. The term "vessels restricted in their ability to manoeuvre" shall include but not be limited to:

  (i) a vessel engaged in laying, servicing or picking up a navigation mark, submarine cable or pipeline;

  (ii) a vessel engaged in dredging, surveying or underwater operations;

  (iii) a vessel engaged in replenishment or transferring persons, provisions or cargo while underway;

  (iv) a vessel engaged in the launching or recovery of aircraft;

  (v) a vessel engaged in mineclearance operations;

  (vi) a vessel engaged in a towing operation such as severely restricts the towing vessel and her tow in their ability to deviate from their course.

———————

(*h*) The term "vessel constrained by her draught" means a power-driven vessel which because of her draught in relation to the available depth of water is severely restricted in her ability to deviate from the course she is following.

———————

(*i*) The word "underway" means that a vessel is not at anchor, or made fast to the shore, or aground.

(v) a vessel or seaplane on the water is "under way" when she is not at anchor, or made fast to the shore, or aground;

(*j*) The words "length" and "breadth" of a vessel mean her length overall and greatest breadth.

(vii) the length and breadth of a vessel shall be her length overall and largest breadth;

(*k*) Vessels shall be deemed to be in sight of one another only when one can be observed visually from the other.

(ix) vessels shall be deemed to be in sight of one another only when one can be observed visually from the other;

(*l*) The term "restricted visibility" means any condition in which visibility is restricted by fog, mist, falling snow, heavy rainstorms, sandstorms or any other similar causes.

RULE 15
(c) In fog, mist, falling snow, heavy rainstorms, or any other condition, similarly restricting visibility, whether by day or night . . .

PART B. STEERING AND SAILING RULES

Section I. Conduct of vessels in any condition of visibility

6.04   RULE 4
Application
Rules in this Section apply in any condition of visibility.

6.05   RULE 5
Look-out
Every vessel shall at all times maintain a proper look-out by sight and hearing as well as by all available means appropriate in the prevailing circumstances and conditions so as to make a full appraisal of the situation and of the risk of collision.

RULE 29
Nothing in these Rules shall exonerate any vessel, or the owner, master or crew thereof, from the consequences of . . . any neglect to keep a proper look-out . . .

6.06   RULE 6
Safe speed
Every vessel shall at all times proceed at a safe speed so that she can take proper and effective action to avoid collision and be stopped within a distance appropriate to the prevailing circumstances and conditions.
In determining a safe speed the following factors shall be among those taken into account:
(*a*) By all vessels:
    (i) the state of visibility;
    (ii) the traffic density including concentrations of fishing vessels or any other vessels;
    (iii) the manoeuvrability of the vessel with special reference to stopping distance and turning ability in the prevailing conditions;
    (iv) at night the presence of background light such as from shore lights or from back scatter of her own lights;
    (v) the state of wind, sea and current, and the proximity of navigational hazards;
    (vi) the draught in relation to the available depth of water.

[Cf. 1960 Rule 16, opposite 1972 Rule 19(b)]

(b) Additionally, by vessels with operational radar:
   (i) the characteristics, efficiency and limitations of the radar equipment;
   (ii) any constraints by the radar range scale in use;

   (iii) the effect on radar detection of the sea state, weather and other sources of interference;

   (iv) the possibility that small vessels, ice and other floating objects may not be detected by radar at an adequate range;
   (v) the number, location and movement of vessels detected by radar;

   (vi) the more exact assessment of the visibility that may be possible when radar is used to determine the range of vessels or other objects in the vicinity.

Annex—Recommendations
(2) . . . small vessels, small icebergs and similar floating objects may not be detected by radar . . .

. . . Radar indications of one or more vessels in the vicinity may mean that "moderate speed" should be slower than a mariner without radar might consider moderate in the circumstances.

6.07   RULE 7
                Risk of collision
(a) Every vessel shall use all available means appropriate to the prevailing circumstances and conditions to determine if risk of collision exists. If there is any doubt such risk shall be deemed to exist.

(b) Proper use shall be made of radar equipment if fitted and operational, including long-range scanning to obtain early warning of risk of collision and radar plotting or equivalent systematic observation of detected objects.

[See generally the Annex to the 1960 Rules]

(c) Assumptions shall not be made on the basis of scanty information, especially scanty radar information.

Annex—Recommendation (1)
(1) Assumptions made on scanty information may be dangerous and should be avoided.

(d) In determining if risk of collision exists the following considerations shall be among those taken into account:
   (i) such risk shall be deemed to exist if the compass bearing of an approaching vessel does not appreciably change;
   (ii) such risk may sometimes exist even when an appreciable bearing change is evident, particularly when approaching a very large vessel or a tow or when approaching a vessel at close range.

PART D. *Preliminary*
2. *Risk of collision can, when circumstances permit, be ascertained by carefully watching the compass bearing of an approaching vessel. If the bearing does not appreciably change, such risk should be deemed to exist.*

6.08   RULE 8
            Action to avoid collision
(a) Any action taken to avoid collision shall, if the circumstances of the case admit, be positive, made in ample time and with due regard to the observance of good seamanship.

PART D. *Preliminary*
1. *In obeying and construing these Rules, any action taken should be positive, in ample time, and with due regard to the observance of good seamanship.*

(b) Any alteration of course and/or speed to avoid collision shall, if the circumstances of the case admit, be large enough to be readily apparent to another vessel observing visually or by radar; a succession of small alterations of course and/or speed should be avoided.

(c) If there is sufficient sea room, alteration of course alone may be the most effective action to avoid a close-quarters situation provided that it is made in good time, is substantial and does not result in another close quarters situation.

(d) Action taken to avoid collision with another vessel shall be such as to result in passing at a safe distance . . . *

(d) . . . The effectiveness of the action shall be carefully checked until the other vessel is finally past and clear.

[* Rule 8(d) is printed here in two separate paragraphs to show in the right-hand column the separate provenance of the two sentences.]

(e) If necessary to avoid collision or allow more time to assess the situation, a vessel shall slacken her speed or take all way off by stopping or reversing her means of propulsion.

6.09   RULE 9
                   Narrow channels
(a) A vessel proceeding along the course of a narrow channel or fairway shall keep as near to the outer limit or fairway which lies on her starboard side as is safe and practicable.

(b) A vessel of less than 20 metres in length or a sailing vessel shall not impede the passage of a vessel which can safely navigate only within a narrow channel or fairway.

Annex—Recommendations
(5) Alteration of course . . . may be . . . most effective to avoid a close quarters situation provided that . . . (c) it is substantial. A succession of small alterations of course should be avoided.

(7) An alteration of speed, either alone or in conjunction with an alteration of course, should be substantial. A number of small alterations of speed should be avoided.

Annex—Recommendations
(5) Alteration of course alone may be the most effective action to avoid close quarters provided that:—
(a) There is sufficient sea room.
(b) It is made in good time.
(c) It is substantial.
(d) It does not result in a close quarters situation with other vessels.

Annex—Recommendations
(4) When action has been taken under Rule 16(c) to avoid a close quarters situation, it is essential to make sure that such action is having the desired effect. Alterations of course or speed or both are matters as to which the mariner must be guided by the circumstances of the case.

RULE 23
Every power-driven vessel which is directed by these Rules to keep out of the way of another vessel shall, on approaching her, if necessary, slacken her speed or stop or reverse.

Annex—Recommendations
(8) If a close quarters situation is imminent, the most prudent action may be to take all way off the vessel.

RULE 25
(a) In a narrow channel every power-driven vessel when proceeding along the course of the channel shall, when it is safe and practicable, keep to that side of the fairway or mid-channel which lies on the starboard side of such vessel.

(c) In a narrow channel a power-driven vessel of less than 65 feet in length shall not hamper the safe passage of a vessel which can navigate only inside such channel.

RULE 20
(b) This Rule [RULE 20 (a)—power to give way to sail] shall not give to a sailing vessel the right to hamper, in a narrow channel, the safe passage of a power driven vessel which can navigate safely only inside such channel.

(*c*) A vessel engaged in fishing shall not impede the passage of any other vessel navigating within a narrow channel or fairway.

(*d*) A vessel shall not cross a narrow channel or fairway if such crossing impedes the passage of a vessel which can safely navigate only within such channel or fairway. The latter vessel may use the sound signal prescribed in Rule 34 (d) if in doubt as to the intention of the crossing vessel.

(*e*) (i) In a narrow channel or fairway when overtaking can take place only if the vessel to be overtaken has to take action to permit safe passing, the vessel intending to overtake shall indicate her intention by sounding the appropriate signal prescribed in Rule 34 (*c*) (i). The vessel to be overtaken shall, if in agreement, sound the appropriate signal prescribed in Rule 34 (*c*) (ii) and take steps to permit safe passing. If in doubt she may sound the signals prescribed in Rule 34 (d).
(ii) This Rule does not relieve the overtaking vessel of her obligation under Rule 13.

(*f*) A vessel nearing a bend or an area of a narrow channel or fairway where other vessels may be obscured by an intervening obstruction shall navigate with particular alertness and caution and shall sound the appropriate signal prescribed in Rule 34 (*e*).

(*g*) Any vessel shall, if the circumstances of the case admit, avoid anchoring in a narrow channel.

6.10   RULE 10
              Traffic separation schemes
(*a*) This Rule applies to traffic separation schemes adopted by the Organization:

(*b*) A vessel using a traffic separation scheme shall:
    (i) proceed in the appropriate traffic lane in the general direction of traffic flow for that lane;

    (ii) so far as practicable keep clear of a traffic separation line or separation zone;

RULE 26
... This Rule [Rule 26—other vessels to keep out of the way of vessels engaged in fishing] shall not give to any vessel engaged in fishing the right of obstructing a fairway used by vessels other than fishing vessels.

[Many river by-laws have provisions to this effect. See also the rules of good seamanship.]

25 (*b*) Whenever a power-driven vessel is nearing a bend in a channel where a vessel approaching from the other direction cannot be seen, such power-driven vessel, when she shall have arrived within one-half ($\frac{1}{2}$) mile of the bend, shall give a signal by one prolonged blast on her whistle which signal shall be answered by a similar blast given by any approaching power-driven vessel that may be within hearing around the bend. Regardless of whether an approaching vessel on the farther side of the bend is heard, such bend shall be rounded with alertness and caution.

The Collision Regulations (Traffic Separation Schemes) Order 1972, Schedule, Part I. (The Separation Rules)

THE SEPARATION RULES—RULE 3
Except as provided in these Regulations a ship shall navigate in a traffic lane only in a direction generally parallel—
    (*a*) when the traffic lane adjoins a traffic separation line, to that line, or
    (*b*) when the traffic lane adjoins a traffic separation zone, to the adjoining side of that zone
keeping such line or zone on its port hand.

THE SEPARATION RULES—RULE 4
Except as provided in these Regulations a ship shall not navigate in a traffic separation zone or a boundary separation zone.

(iii) normally join or leave a traffic lane at the termination of the lane, but when joining or leaving from either side shall do so at as small an angle to the general direction of traffic flow as practicable.

(c) A vessel shall so far as practicable avoid crossing traffic lanes, but if obliged to do so shall cross as nearly as practicable at right angles to the general direction of traffic flow.

THE SEPARATION RULES—RULE 5

A ship may cross a traffic lane, a traffic separation zone or a boundary separation zone at right angles or as near thereto as is reasonably practicable.

(d) Inshore traffic zones shall not normally be used by through traffic which can safely use the appropriate traffic lane within the adjacent traffic separation scheme. However, vessels of less than 20 metres in length and sailing vessels may under all circumstances use inshore traffic zones.

(e) A vessel other than a crossing vessel or a vessel joining or leaving a lane shall not normally enter a separation zone or cross a separation line except:

(i) in cases of emergency to avoid immediate danger;

(ii) to engage in fishing within a separation zone.

THE SEPARATION RULES—RULE 4

Except as provided in these Regulations a ship shall not navigate in a traffic separation zone or a boundary separation zone.

(f) A vessel navigating in areas near the terminations of traffic separation schemes shall do so with particular caution.

(g) A vessel shall so far as practicable avoid anchoring in a traffic separation scheme or in areas near its terminations.

(h) A vessel not using a traffic separation scheme shall avoid it by as wide a margin as is practicable.

(i) A vessel engaged in fishing shall not impede the passage of any vessel following a traffic lane.

THE SEPARATION RULES—RULE 7

Nothing in these Regulations shall apply to a fishing vessel when actually engaged in fishing . . .

(j) A vessel of less than 20 metres in length or a sailing vessel shall not impede the safe passage of a power-driven vessel following a traffic lane.

(k) A vessel restricted in her ability to manoeuvre when engaged in an operation for the maintenance of safety of navigation in a traffic separation scheme is exempted from complying with this Rule to the extent necessary to carry out the operation.

(l) A vessel restricted in her ability to manoeuvre when engaged in an operation for the laying, servicing or picking up of a submarine cable, within a traffic separation scheme, is exempted from complying with this Rule to the extent necessary to carry out the operation.

Section II. Conduct of vessels in sight of one another

6.11   RULE 11
Application
Rules in this section apply to vessels in sight of one another.

1960 RULES
PART D—*Preliminary*
4. Rules 17 to 24 apply only to vessels in sight of one another.

6.12   RULE 12
Sailing vessels
(*a*) When two sailing vessels are approaching one another, so as to involve risk of collision, one of them shall keep out of the way of the other as follows:
  (i) when each has the wind on a different side, the vessel which has the wind on the port side shall keep out of the way of the other;
  (ii) when both have the wind on the same side, the vessel which is to windward shall keep out of the way of the vessel which is to leeward;
  (iii) if a vessel with the wind on the port side sees a vessel to windward and cannot determine with certainty whether the other vessel has the wind on the port or on the starboard side, she shall keep out of the way of the other.

(*b*) For the purposes of this Rule the windward side shall be deemed to be the side opposite to that on which the mainsail is carried or, in the case of a square-rigged vessel, the side opposite to that on which the largest fore-and-aft sail is carried.

RULE 17
(*a*) When two sailing vessels are approaching one another, so as to involve risk of collision, one of them shall keep out of the way of the other as follows:—
  (i) When each has the wind on a different side, the vessel which has the wind on the port side shall keep out of the way of the other.
  (ii) When both have the wind on the same side, the vessel which is to windward shall keep out of the way of the vessel which is to leeward

(*b*) For the purposes of this Rule the windward side shall be deemed to be the side opposite to that on which the mainsail is carried or, in the case of a square-rigged vessel, the side opposite to that on which the largest fore-and-aft sail is carried.

6.13   RULE 13
Overtaking
(*a*) Notwithstanding anything contained in the Rules of Part B, Sections I and II, any vessel overtaking any other shall keep out of the way of the vessel being overtaken.

(*b*) A vessel shall be deemed to be overtaking when coming up with another vessel from a direction more than 22.5 degrees abaft her beam, that is, in such a position with reference to the vessel she is overtaking, that at night she would be able to see only the sternlight of that vessel but neither of her sidelights.

(*c*) When a vessel is in any doubt as to whether she is overtaking another, she shall assume that this is the case and act accordingly.

(*d*) Any subsequent alteration of the bearing between the two vessels shall not make the overtaking vessel a crossing vessel within the meaning of these Rules or relieve her of the duty of keeping clear of the overtaken vessel until she is finally past and clear.

RULE 24
(*a*) Notwithstanding anything contained in these Rules, every vessel overtaking any other shall keep out of the way of the overtaken vessel.

RULE 24
(*b*) Every vessel coming up with another vessel from any direction more than 22½ degrees (2 points) abaft her beam, *i.e.*, in such a position, with reference to the vessel which she is overtaking, that at night she would be unable to see either of that vessel's sidelights, shall be deemed to be an overtaking vessel; . . .

RULE 24
(*c*) If the overtaking vessel cannot determine with certainty whether she is forward of or abaft this direction from the other vessel, she shall assume that she is an overtaking vessel and keep out of the way.

RULE 24
(*b*) . . . and no subsequent alteration of the bearing between the two vessel shall make the overtaking vessel a crossing vessel within the meaning of these Rules, or relieve her of the duty of keeping clear of the overtaken vessel until she is finally past and clear.

6.14

RULE 14
Head-on situation

(*a*) When two power-driven vessels are meeting on reciprocal or nearly reciprocal courses so as to involve risk of collision each shall alter her course to starboard so that each shall pass on the port side of the other.

(*b*) Such a situation shall be deemed to exist when a vessel sees the other ahead or nearly ahead and by night she could see the masthead lights of the other in a line or nearly in a line and/or both sidelights and by day she observes the corresponding aspect of the other vessel.

(*c*) When a vessel is in any doubt as to whether such a situation exists she shall assume that it does exist and act accordingly.

6.15

RULE 15
Crossing situation

When two power-driven vessels are crossing so as to involve risk of collision, the vessel which has the other on her own starboard side shall keep out of the way and shall, if the circumstances of the case admit, avoid crossing ahead of the other vessel.

6.16

RULE 16
Action by give-way vessel

Every vessel which is directed to keep out of the way of another vessel shall, so far as possible, take early and substantial action to keep well clear.

6.17

RULE 17
Action by stand-on vessel

(*a*) (i) Where one of two vessels is to keep out of the way the other shall keep her course and speed.

(ii) The latter vessel may however take action to avoid collision by her manoeuvre alone, as soon as it becomes apparent to her that the vessel required to keep out of the way is not taking appropriate action in compliance with these Rules.

RULE 18

(*a*) When two power-driven vessels are meeting end on, or nearly end on, so as to involve risk of collision, each shall alter her course to starboard, so that each may pass on the port side of the other . . .

RULE 18

(*a*) . . . This Rule only applies to cases where vessels are meeting end on, or nearly end on, in such a manner as to involve risk of collision, and does not apply to two vessels which must, if both keep on their respective courses, pass clear of each other. The only cases to which it does apply are when each of two vessels is end on, or nearly end on, to the other; in other words, to cases in which, by day, each vessel sees the masts of the other in a line, or nearly in a line, with her own; and by night, to cases in which each vessel is in such a position as to see both the sidelights of the other. It does not apply, by day, to cases in which a vessel sees another ahead crossing her own course; or, by night, to cases where the red light of one vessel is opposed to the red light of the other or where the green light of one vessel is opposed to the green light of the other or where a red light without a green light or a green light without a red light is s(en ahead, or where both green and red lights are seen anywhere but ahead.

RULE 19

When two power-driven vessels are crossing, so as to involve risk of collision, the vessel which has the other on her own starboard side shall keep out of the way of the other.

RULE 22

Every vessel which is directed by these Rules to keep out of the way of another vessel shall . . . if the circumstances of the case admit, avoid crossing ahead of the other.

RULE 22

Every vessel which is directed by these Rules to keep out of the way of another vessel shall, so far as possible, take positive early action to comply with this obligation, and shall, if the circumstances of the case admit, avoid crossing ahead of the other.

RULE 21

Where by any of these Rules one of two vessels is to keep out of the way, the other shall keep her course and speed . . .

(*b*) When, from any cause, the vessel required to keep her course and speed finds herself so close that collision cannot be avoided by the action of the give-way vessel alone, she shall take such action as will best aid to avoid collision.

(*c*) A power-driven vessel which takes action in a crossing situation in accordance with sub-paragraph (*a*) (ii) of this Rule to avoid collision with another power-driven vessel shall, if the circumstances of the case admit, not alter course to port for a vessel on her own port side.

(*d*) This Rule does not relieve the give-way vessel of her obligation to keep out of the way

6.18 RULE 18
Responsibilities between vessels
Except where Rules 9, 10 and 13 otherwise require:
(*a*) A power-driven vessel underway shall keep out of the way of:
  (i) a vessel not under command;
  (ii) a vessel restricted in her ability to manoeuvre;
  (iii) a vessel engaged in fishing;
  (iv) a sailing vessel.

(*b*) A sailing vessel underway shall keep out of the way of:
  (i) a vessel not under command;
  (ii) a vessel restricted in her ability to manoeuvre;
  (iii) a vessel engaged in fishing.

(*c*) A vessel engaged in fishing when underway shall, so far as possible, keep out of the way of:
  (i) a vessel not under command;
  (ii) a vessel restricted in her ability to manoeuvre.

(*d*) (i) Any vessel other than a vessel not under command or a vessel restricted in her ability to manoeuvre shall, if the circumstances of the case admit, avoid impeding the safe passage of a vessel constrained by her draught, exhibiting the signals in Rule 28.
  (ii) A vessel constrained by her draught shall navigate with particular caution having full regard to her special condition.

(*e*) A seaplane on the water shall, in general, keep well clear of all vessels and avoid impeding their navigation. In circumstances, however, where risk of collision exists, she shall comply with the Rules of this Part

RULE 21
... When, from any cause, the latter vessel finds herself so close that collision cannot be avoided by the action of the giving-way vessel alone, she also shall take such action as will best aid to avert collision (see Rules 27 and 29).)

RULE 26
All vessels not engaged in fishing, except vessels to which the provisions of Rule 4 apply shall, when under way, keep out of the way of vessels engaged in fishing.

RULE 20
(*a*) When a power-driven vessel and a sailing vessel are proceeding in such directions as to involve risk of collision, except as provided for in Rules 24 and 26, the power-driven vessel shall keep out of the way of the sailing vessel.

RULE 26
All vessels not engaged in fishing, except vessels to which provisions of Rule 4 apply, shall, when under way, keep out of the way of vessels engaged in fishing.

RULE 20
(*c*) A seaplane on the water shall, in general, keep well clear of all vessels and avoid impeding their navigation. In circumstances, however where risk of collision exists, she shall comply with these Rules.

Section III. Conduct of vessels in restricted visibility

6.19   RULE 19
Conduct of vessels in restricted visibility
(*a*) This Rule applies to vessels not in sight of one another when navigating in or near an area of restricted visibility.

(*b*) Every vessel shall proceed at a safe speed adapted to the prevailing circumstances and conditions of restricted visibility. A power-driven vessel shall have her engines ready for immediate manoeuvre.

(*c*) Every vessel shall have due regard to the prevailing circumstances and conditions of restricted visibility when complying with the Rules of Section I of this Part.

(*d*) A vessel which detects by radar alone the presence of another vessel shall determine if a close-quarters situation is developing and/or risk of collision exists. If so she shall take avoiding action in ample time, provided that when such action consists of an alteration of course, so far as possible the following shall be avoided:
(i) an alteration of course to port for a vessel forward of the beam, other than for a vessel being overtaken;
(ii) an alteration of course towards a vessel abeam or abaft the beam.

(*e*) Except where it has been determined that a risk of collision does not exist, every vessel which hears apparently forward of her beam the fog signal of another vessel, or which cannot avoid a close-quarters situation with another vessel forward of her beam, shall reduce her speed to the minimum at which she can be kept on her course. She shall if necessary take all her way off and in any event navigate with extreme caution until danger of collision is over.

RULE 16
(*a*) Every vessel, or seaplane when taxi-ing on the water, shall, in fog, mist, falling snow, heavy rain-storms or any other condition similarly restricting visibility, go at a moderate speed, having careful regard to the existing circumstances and conditions.

———————

———————

RULE 16
(*b*) A power-driven vessel hearing, apparently forward of her beam, the fog-signal of a vessel the position of which is not ascertained, shall, so far as the circumstances of the case admit stop her engines, and then navigate with caution until danger of collision is over.

RULE 16
(*c*) A power-driven vessel which detects the presence of another vessel forward of her beam before hearing her fog signal or sighting her visually may take early and substantial action to avoid a close quarters situation but, if this cannot be avoided, she shall, so far as the circumstances of the case admit, stop her engines in proper time to avoid collision and then navigate with caution until danger of collision is over.

PART C. LIGHTS AND SHAPES

6.20   RULE 20
Application
(*a*) Rules in this Part shall be complied with in all weathers.

(*b*) The Rules concerning lights shall be complied with from sunset to sunrise, and during such times no other lights shall be exhibited, except such lights

RULE 1
(*b*) The Rules concerning lights shall be complied with in all weathers . . .

(*b*) . . . from sunset to sunrise, and during such times no other lights shall be exhibited, except such lights as cannot be mistaken for the prescribed

as cannot be mistaken for the lights specified in these Rules or do not impair their visibility or distinctive character, or interfere with the keeping of a proper look-out.

(*c*) The lights prescribed by these Rules shall, if carried, also be exhibited from sunrise to sunset in restricted visibility and may be exhibited in all other circumstances when it is deemed necessary.

(*d*) The Rules concerning shapes shall be complied with by day.

(*e*) The lights and shapes specified in these Rules shall comply with the provisions of Annex I to these Regulations.

lights or do not impair their visibility or distinctive character, or interfere with the keeping of a proper look-out . . .

(*b*) . . . The lights prescribed by these Rules may also be exhibited from sunrise to sunset in restricted visibility and in all other circumstances when it is deemed necessary.

———————

———————

Rule 21
Definitions

(*a*) "Masthead light" means a white light placed over the fore and aft centreline of the vessel showing an unbroken light over an arc of the horizon of 225 degrees and so fixed as to show from right ahead to 22.5 degrees abaft the beam on either side of the vessel.

[This definition is similar to one included in 1960 Rule 2(a)(i). See this column opposite 1972 Rule 23(a) (i).]

(*b*) "Sidelights" means a green light on the starboard side and a red light on the port side each showing an unbroken light over an arc of the horizon of 112.5 degrees and so fixed as to show the light from right ahead to 22.5 degrees abaft the beam on its respective side. In a vessel of less than 20 metres in length the sidelights may be combined in one lantern carried on the fore and aft centreline of the vessel.

[See this column opposite 1972 Rule 23(a) (iii).]

(*c*) "Sternlight" means a white light placed as nearly as practicable at the stern showing an unbroken light over an arc of the horizon of 135 degrees and so fixed as to show the light 67.5 degrees from right aft on each side of the vessel.

[See this column opposite 1972 Rule 23(a) (iv).]

(*d*) "Towing light" means a yellow light having the same characteristics as the "sternlight" defined in paragraph (*c*) of this Rule.

———————

(*e*) "All-round light" means a light showing an unbroken light over an arc of the horizon of 360 degrees.

———————

(*f*) "Flashing light" means a light flashing at regular intervals at a frequency of 120 flashes or more per minute.

———————

6.22   RULE 22
                   Visibility of lights
    The lights prescribed in these Rules shall have an
intensity as specified in Section 8 of Annex I to these
Regulations so as to be visible at the following
minimum ranges:
    (*a*) In vessels of 50 metres or more in length:
        —a masthead light, 6 miles;
        —a sidelight, 3 miles;
        —a sternlight, 3 miles;
        —a towing light, 3 miles;
        —a white, red, green or yellow all-round light,
        3 miles.

    (*b*) In vessels of 12 metres or more in length but
    less than 50 metres in length:
        —a masthead light, 5 miles; except that where
    the length of the vessel is less than 20 metres,
    3 miles;
        —a sidelight, 2 miles;
        —a sternlight, 2 miles;
        —a towing light, 2 miles;
        —a white, red, green or yellow all-round light,
        2 miles.

    (*c*) In vessels of less than 12 metres in length:
        —a masthead light, 2 miles;
        —a sidelight, 1 mile;
        —a sternlight, 2 miles;
        —a towing light, 2 miles;
        —a white, red, green or yellow all-round light,
        2 miles.

    (*d*) In inconspicuous, partly submerged vessels or
    objects being towed:
        —a white all-round light, 3 miles.

[(*a*) See opposite 1972 Rule 23(a)(i)
See opposite 1972 Rule 23(a) (iii)
See opposite 1972 Rule 23(a) (iv)]

6.23   RULE 23
             Power-driven vessels underway
    (*a*) a power-driven vessel underway shall exhibit:
        (i) a masthead light forward;

        (ii) a second masthead light abaft of and
        higher than the forward one; except that a
        vessel of less than 50 metres in length
        shall not be obliged to exhibit such light
        but may do so;

                        RULE 2
    (*a*) A power-driven vessel when under way shall
carry:—
        (i) On or in front of the foremast, or if a
        vessel without a foremast then in the
        forepart of the vessel a white light so
        constructed as to show an unbroken light
        over an arc of the horizon of 225 degrees
        (20 points of the compass), so fixed as to
        show the light 112½ degrees (10 points)
        on each side of the vessel, that is, from
        right ahead to 22½ degrees (2 points)
        abaft the beam on either side and of such
        a character as to be visible at a distance
        of at least 5 miles.

        (ii) Either forward of or abaft the white light
        prescribed in sub-section (i) a second white
        light similar in construction and character
        to that light. Vessels of less than 150 feet
        in length shall not be required to carry
        this second white light but may do so.

(iii) These two white lights shall be so placed in a line with and over the keel that one shall be at least 15 feet higher than the other and in such a position that the forward light shall always be shown lower than the after one. The horizontal distance distance between the two white lights shall be at least three times the vertical distance. The lower of these two white light or, if only one is carried, then that light, shall be placed at a height above the hull of not less than 20 feet, and, if the breadth of the vessel exceeds 20 feet, then at a height above the hull not less than such breadth, so however that the light need not be placed at a greater height above the hull than 40 feet. In all circumstances the light or lights, as the case may be, shall be so placed as to be clear of and above all other lights and obstructing super-structures.

(iii) sidelights;

(iv) On the starboard side a green light so constructed as to show an unbroken light over an arc of the horizon of $112\frac{1}{2}$ degrees (10 points of the compass), so fixed as to show the light from right ahead to $22\frac{1}{2}$ degrees (2 points) abaft the beam on the starboard side, and of such a character as to be visible at a distance of at least 2 miles.

(v) On the port side a red light so constructed as to show an unbroken light over an arc of the horizon of $112\frac{1}{2}$ degrees (10 points of the compass), so fixed as to show the light from right ahead to $22\frac{1}{2}$ degrees (2 points) abaft the beam on the port side, and of such a character as to be visible at a distance of at least 2 miles.

(vi) The said green and red sidelights shall be fitted with inboard screens projecting at least 3 feet forward from the light, so as to prevent these lights from being seen across the bows.

RULE 10

(iv) a sternlight.

(a) Except where otherwise provided in these Rules, a vessel when under way shall carry at her stern a white light, so constructed that it shall show an unbroken light over an arc of the horizon of 135 degrees (12 points of the compass), so fixed as to show the light $67\frac{1}{2}$ degrees (6 points) from right aft on each side of the vessel, and of such a character as to be visible at a distance of at least 2 miles.

(b) An air-cushion vessel when operating in the non-displacement mode shall, in addition to the lights prescribed in paragraph (a) of this Rule, exhibit an all-round flashing yellow light.

(c) (i) A power-driven vessel of less than 12 metres in length may in lieu of the lights prescribed in paragraph (a) of this Rule exhibit an all-round white light and sidelights;

(ii) A power-driven vessel of less than 7 metres in length and whose maximum speed does not exceed 7 knots may, in lieu of the lights prescribed in paragraph (a) of this Rule, exhibit an all-round white light and shall, if practicable, also exhibit sidelights;

(iii) the masthead light or all-round white light on a power-driven vessel of less than 12 metres in length may be displaced from the fore and aft centreline of the vessel if centreline fitting is not practicable, provided that the sidelights are combined in one lantern which shall be carried on the fore and aft centreline of the vessel or located as nearly as practicable in the same fore and aft line as the masthead light or the all-round white light.

RULE 7

Power-driven vessels of less than 65 feet in length, vessels under oars or sails of less than 40 feet in length, and rowing boats, when under way shall not be required to carry the lights prescribed in Rules 2, 3 and 5, but if they do not carry them they shall be provided with the following lights:—

(a) Power-driven vessels of less than 65 feet in length, except as provided in sections (b) and (c), shall carry:—
  (i) In the forepart of the vessel, where it can best be seen, and at a height above the gunwale of not less than 9 feet, a white light constructed and fixed as prescribed in Rule 2(a)(i) and of such a character as to be visible at a distance of at least 3 miles.
  (ii) Green and red sidelights constructed and fixed as prescribed in Rule 2(a)(iv) and (v), and of such a character as to be visible at a distance of at least 1 mile, or a combined lantern showing a green light and a red light from right ahead to 22½ degrees (2 points) abaft the beam on their respective sides. Such a lantern shall be carried not less than 3 feet below the white light.

6.24   RULE 24
              Towing and pushing
(a) A power-driven vessel when towing shall exhibit:
  (i) instead of the light prescribed in Rule 23(a)(i) or (a)(ii), two masthead lights in a vertical line. When the length of the tow, measuring from the stern of the towing vessel to the after end of the tow exceeds 200 metres, three such lights in a vertical line;
  (ii) sidelights;

RULE 3

(a) A power-driven vessel when towing or pushing another vessel or seaplane shall, in addition to her sidelights, carry two white lights in a vertical line one over the other, not less than 6 feet apart, and when towing and the length of the tow, measuring from the stern of the towing vessel to the stern of the last vessel towed, exceeds 600 feet, shall carry three white lights in a vertical line one over the other, so that the upper and the lower lights shall be the same distance from, and not less than 6 feet above or below, the middle light. Each of these lights shall be of the same construction and character and one of them shall be carried in the same position as the while light prescribed in Rule 2(a) (i). None of these lights shall be carried at a height of less than 14 feet above the hull. In a vessel with a single mast, such lights may be carried on the mast.

(iii) a sternlight;

(b) The towing vessel shall also show either the stern light prescribed in Rule 10 or in lieu of that light a small white light abaft the funnel or after mast for the tow to steer by, but such light shall not be visible forward of the beam.

(iv) a towing light in a vertical line above the sternlight;

_____

(v) when the length of the tow exceeds 200 metres, a diamond shape where it can best be seen.

(c) Between sunrise and sunset a power-driven vessel engaged in towing, if the length of tow exceeds 600 feet, shall carry, where it can best be seen, a black diamond shape at least 2 feet in diameter.

(b) When a pushing vessel and a vessel being pushed ahead are rigidly connected in a composite unit they shall be regarded as a power-driven vessel and exhibit the lights prescribed in Rule 23.

_____

(c) A power-driven vessel when pushing ahead or towing alongside, except in the case of a composite unit, shall exhibit:

(i) instead of the light prescribed in Rule 23(a)(i) or (a)(ii), two masthead lights in a vertical line;

_____

(ii) sidelights;

(iii) a sternlight.

(d) A power-driven vessel to which paragraph (a) or (c) of this Rule apply shall also comply with Rule 23(a)(ii).

_____

RULE 5

(e) A vessel or object being towed, other than those mentioned in paragraph (g) of this Rule, shall exhibit:

(a) . . . any vessel or seaplane being towed shall carry the same lights as are prescribed in Rule 2 for a power-driven vessel or a seaplane under way, respectively, with the exception of the white lights prescribed therein, which they shall never carry. They shall also carry stern lights as prescribed in Rule 10, provided that vessels towed, except the last vessel of a tow, may carry, in lieu of such stern light, a small white light as prescribed in Rule 3(b).

(i) sidelights;

(ii) a sternlight;

(iii) when the length of the tow exceeds 200 metres, a diamond shape where it can best be seen.

(d) Between sunrise and sunset a vessel being towed, if the length of the tow exceeds 600 feet, shall carry where it can best be seen a black diamond shape at least 2 feet in diameter.

(f) Provided that any number of vessels being towed alongside or pushed in a group shall be lighted as one vessel,

(c) A vessel being pushed ahead shall carry, at the forward end, on the starboard side a green light and on the port side a red light, which shall have the same characteristics as the lights prescribed in Rule 2(a)(iv) and (v) and shall be screened as provided in Rule 2(a)(vi), provided that any number of vessels pushed ahead in a group shall be lighted as one vessel.

(i) a vessel being pushed ahead, not being part of a composite unit, shall exhibit at the forward end, sidelights;

(ii) a vessel being towed alongside shall exhibit a sternlight and at the forward end, sidelights.

(*g*) An inconspicuous, partly submerged, vessel or object, or combination of such vessels or objects being towed, shall exhibit:

    (i) if it is less than 25 metres in breadth, one all-round white light at or near the forward end and one at or near the after end except that dracones need not exhibit a light at or near the forward end;

    (ii) if it is 25 metres or more in breadth, two additional all-round white lights at or near the extremities of its breadth;

    (iii) if it exceeds 100 metres in length, additional all-round white lights between the lights prescribed in sub-paragraphs (i) and (ii) so that the distance between the lights shall not exceed 100 metres;

    (iv) a diamond shape at or near the aftermost extremity of the last vessel or object being towed and if the length of the tow exceeds 200 metres an additional diamond shape where it can best be seen and located as far forward as practicable.

(*h*) Where from any sufficient cause it is impracticable for a vessel or object being towed to exhibit the lights prescribed in paragraph (*e*) or (*g*) of this Rule, all possible measures shall be taken to light the vessel or object towed or at least to indicate the presence of such vessel or object.

(*i*) Where from any sufficient cause it is impracticable for a vessel not normally engaged in towing operations to display the lights prescribed in paragraph (*a*) or (*c*) of this Rule, such vessel shall not be required to exhibit those lights when engaged in towing another vessel in distress or otherwise in need of assistance. All possible measures shall be taken to indicate the nature of the relationship between the towing vessel and the vessel being towed as authorized by Rule 36, in particular by illuminating the towline.

6.25   RULE 25
Sailing vessels underway and vessels under oars
(*a*) A sailing vessel underway shall exhibit:
(i) sidelights;
(ii) a sternlight.

(*b*) In a sailing vessel of less than 20 metres in length the lights prescribed in paragraph (*a*) of this Rule may be combined in one lantern carried at or near the top of the mast where it can best be seen.

RULE 5
(*a*) A sailing vessel under way . . . shall carry the same lights as are prescribed in Rule 2 for a power-driven vessel . . . , with the exception of the white lights prescribed therein, which they shall never carry. They shall also carry stern lights as prescribed in Rule 10 . . .

RULE 7
(*d*) Vessels of less than 40 feet in length, under oars or sails, except as provided in section (*f*), shall, if they do not carry the sidelights, carry, where it can best be seen, a lantern showing a green light on one side and a red light on the other, of such a character as

to be visible at a distance of at least 1 mile, and so fixed that the green light shall not be seen on the port side, nor the red light on the starboard side. Where it is not possible to fix this light, it shall be kept ready for immediate use and shall be exhibited in sufficient time to prevent collision and so that the green light shall not be seen on the port side nor the red light on the starboard side.

(c) A sailing vessel underway may, in addition to the lights prescribed in paragraph (a) of this Rule, exhibit at or near the top of the mast, where they can best be seen, two all-round lights in a vertical line, the upper being red and the lower green, but these lights shall not be exhibited in conjunction with the combined lantern permitted by paragraph (b) of this Rule.

Rule 5
(b) In addition to the lights prescribed in section (a), a sailing vessel may carry on the top of the foremast two lights in a vertical line one over the other, sufficiently separated so as to be clearly distinguished. The upper light shall be red and the lower light shall be green. Both lights shall be constructed and fixed as prescribed in Rule 2(a) (i) and shall be visible at a distance of at least 2 miles.

(d) (i) A sailing vessel of less than 7 metres in length shall, if practicable, exhibit the lights prescribed in paragraph (a) or (b) of this Rule, but if she does not, she shall have ready at hand an electric torch or lighted lantern showing a white light which shall be exhibited in sufficient time to prevent collision.

[See below]

(ii) A vessel under oars may exhibit the lights prescribed in this Rule for sailing vessels, but if she does not, she shall have ready at hand an electric torch or lighted lantern showing a white light which shall be exhibited in sufficient time to prevent collision.

Rule 7
(f) Small rowing boats, whether under oars or sail, shall only be required to have ready at hand an electric torch or a lighted lantern, showing a white light, which shall be exhibited in sufficient time to prevent collision.

(e) A vessel proceeding under sail when also being propelled by machinery shall exhibit forward where it can best be seen a conical shape, apex downwards.

Rule 14
A vessel proceeding under sail, when also being propelled by machinery, shall carry in the daytime forward, where it can best be seen, one black conical shape, point downwards, not less than 2 feet in diameter at its base.

6.26 **Rule 26**
Fishing vessels
(a) A vessel engaged in fishing, whether underway or at anchor, shall exhibit only the lights and shapes prescribed at this Rule.

Rule 9
(b) Vessels engaged in fishing, when under way or at anchor, shall show only the lights and shapes prescribed in this Rule, which lights and shapes shall be visible at a distance of at least 2 miles.

(b) A vessel when engaged in trawling, by which is meant the dragging through the water of a dredge net or other apparatus used as a fishing appliance, shall exhibit:
  (i) two all-round lights in a vertical line, the upper being green and the lower white, or a shape consisting of two cones with their apexes together in a vertical line one above the other; a vessel of less than 20 metres in length may instead of this shape exhibit a basket;
  (ii) a masthead light abaft of and higher than the all-round green light; a vessel of less than 50 metres in length shall not be obliged to exhibit such a light but may do so;

Rule 9
(c) (i) Vessels when engaged in trawling, by which is meant the dragging of a dredge net or other apparatus through the water, shall carry two lights in a vertical line, one over the other, not less than 4 feet nor more than 12 feet apart. The upper of these lights shall be green and the lower light white and each shall be visible all round the horizon. The lower of these two lights shall be carried at a height above the sidelights not less than twice the distance between the two vertical lights.

(iii) when making way through the water, in addition to the lights prescribed in this paragraph, sidelights and a sternlight.

(c) A vessel engaged in fishing, other than trawling, shall exhibit:

(i) two all-round lights in a vertical line, the upper being red and the lower white, or a shape consisting of two cones with apexes together in a vertical line one above the other; a vessel of less than 20 metres in length may instead of this shape exhibit a basket;

(ii) when there is outlying gear extending more than 150 metres horizontally from the vessel, an all-round white light or a cone apex upwards in the direction of the gear;

(iii) when making way through the water, in addition to the lights prescribed in this paragraph, sidelights and a sternlight.

(d) A vessel engaged in fishing in close proximity to other vessels engaged in fishing may exhibit the additional signals described in Annex II to these Regulations.

(e) A vessel when not engaged in fishing shall not exhibit the lights or shapes prescribed in this Rule, but only those prescribed for a vessel of her length.

6.27   RULE 27
Vessels not under command or restricted in their ability to manoeuvre

(a) A vessel not under command shall exhibit:

(i) two all-round red lights in a vertical line where they can best be seen;

(ii) two balls or similar shapes in a vertical line where they can best be seen;

See Rule 9(e) below

RULE 9
(d) Vessels when engaged in fishing, except vessels engaged in trawling, shall carry the lights prescribed in section (c)(i) except that the upper of the two vertical lights shall be red. Such vessels if of less than 40 feet in length may carry the red light at a height of not less than 9 feet above the gunwale and the white light not less than 3 feet below the red light.

RULE 9
(h) By day vessels when engaged in fishing shall indicate their occupation by displaying where it can best be seen a black shape consisting of two cones each not less than 2 feet in diameter with their points together one above the other. Such vessels if of less than 65 feet in length may substitute a basket for such black shape. If their outlying gear extends more than 500 feet horizontally into the seaway vessels engaged in fishing shall display in addition one black conical shape, point upwards, in the direction of the outlying gear.

RULE 9
(e) Vessels referred to in sections (c) and (d), when making way through the water, shall carry the sidelights or lanterns prescribed in Rule 2(a)(iv) and (v) or Rule 7(a)(ii) or (d), as appropriate, and the sternlight prescribed in Rule 10. When not making way through the water they shall show neither the sidelights nor the stern light.

———————

RULE 9
(a) Fishing vessels when not engaged in fishing shall show the lights or shapes for similar vessels of their length.

RULE 4
(a) A vessel which is not under command shall carry, where they can best be seen, and, if a power-driven vessel, in lieu of the lights prescribed in Rule 2(a) (i) and (ii), two red lights in a vertical line one over the other not less than 6 feet apart, and of such a character as to be visible all round the horizon at a distance of at least 2 miles. By day, she shall carry in a vertical line one over the other not less than 6 feet apart, where they can best be seen, two black balls or shapes each not less than 2 feet in diameter.

(b) A seaplane on the water which is not under command may carry, where they can best be seen, and in lieu of the light prescribed in Rule 2(b) (i), two red lights in a vertical line, one over the other, not less than 3 feet apart, and of such a character as to be visible all round the horizon at a distance of at least

2 miles, and may by day carry in a vertical line one over the other not less than 3 feet apart, where they can best be seen, two black balls or shapes, each not less than 2 feet in diameter.

(iii) when making way through the water, in addition to the lights prescribed in this paragraph, sidelights and a sternlight.

(e) The vessels and seaplanes referred to in this Rule, when not making way through the water, shall show neither the coloured sidelights nor the stern light, but when making way they shall show them.

(b) A vessel restricted in her ability to manoeuvre, except a vessel engaged in mineclearance operations, shall exhibit:
   (i) three all-round lights in a vertical line where they can best be seen. The highest and lowest of these lights shall be red and the middle light shall be white;
   (ii) three shapes in a vertical line where they can best be seen. The highest and lowest of these shapes shall be balls and the middle one a diamond;

(c) A vessel engaged in laying or in picking up a submarine cable or navigation mark, or a vessel engaged in surveying or underwater operations, or a vessel engaged in replenishment at sea, or in the launching or recovery of aircraft when from the nature of her work she is unable to get out of the way of approaching vessels, shall carry, in lieu of the lights prescribed in Rule 2(a) (i) and (ii), or Rule 7(a) (i), three lights in a vertical line one over the other so that the upper and lower lights shall be the same distance from, and not less than 6 feet above or below, the middle light. The highest and lowest of these lights shall be red, and the middle light shall be white, and they shall be of such a character as to be visible all round the horizon at a distance of at least 2 miles. By day, she shall carry in a vertical line one over the other not less than 6 feet apart, where they can best be seen, three shapes each not less than 2 feet in diameter, of which the highest and lowest shall be globular in shape and red in colour, and the middle one diamond in shape and white.

(iii) when making way through the water, a masthead light or lights, sidelights and a sternlight, in addition to the lights prescribed in sub-paragraph (i);
   (iv) when at anchor, in addition to the lights or shapes prescribed in sub-paragraphs (i) and (ii), the light, lights or shape prescribed in Rule 30.

[See 1960 Rule 4(e) above]

RULE 11
(d) A vessel engaged in laying or in picking up a submarine cable or navigation mark, or a vessel engaged in surveying or underwater operations, when at anchor, shall carry the lights or shapes prescribed in Rule 4(c) in addition to those prescribed in the appropriate preceding sections of this Rule.

(c) A power-driven vessel engaged in a towing operation such as severely restricts the towing vessel and her tow in their ability to deviate from their course shall, in addition to the lights or shapes prescribed in Rule 24(a), exhibit the lights or shapes prescribed in sub-paragraphs (b)(i) and (ii) of this rule.

(d) A vessel engaged in dredging or underwater operations, when restricted in her ability to manoeuvre, shall exhibit the lights and shapes prescribed in sub-paragraphs (b)(i), (ii) and (iii) of this Rule and shall in addition, when an obstruction exists, exhibit:
   (i) two all-round red lights or two balls in a vertical line to indicate the side on wich the obstruction exists;

[See 1960 Rule 4(c) above]

(ii) two all-round green lights or two diamonds in a vertical line to indicate the side on which another vessel may pass;

(iii) when at anchor the lights or shapes prescribed in this paragraph instead of the lights or shapes prescribed in Rule 30.

[See 1960 Rule 11(*d*) above]

(*e*) Whenever the size of a vessel engaged in diving operations makes it impracticable to exhibit all lights and shapes prescribed in paragraph (*d*) of this Rule, the following shall be exhibited:

(i) three all-round lights in a vertical line where they can best be seen. The highest and lowest of these lights shall be red and the middle light shall be white;

(ii) a rigid replica of the International Code flag "A" not less than 1 metre in height shall be exhibited. Measures shall be taken to ensure its all-round visibility.

RULE 4

(*f*) A vessel engaged in mineclearance operations shall, in addition to the lights prescribed for a power-driven vessel in Rule 23 or to the lights or shape prescribed for a vessel at anchor in Rule 30 as appropriate, exhibit three all-round green lights or three balls. One of these lights or shapes shall be exhibited near the foremast head and one at each end of the fore yard. These lights or shapes indicate that it is dangerous for another vessel to approach within 1000 metres of the mineclearance vessel.

(*d*)(i) A vessel engaged in minesweeping operations shall carry at the fore truck a green light, and at the end or ends of the fore yard on the side or sides on which danger exists, another such light or lights. These lights shall be carried in addition to the light prescribed in Rule 2(*a*)(i) or Rule 7(*a*)(i), as appropriate, and shall be of such a character as to be visible all round the horizon at a distance of at least 2 miles. By day she shall carry black balls, not less than 2 feet in diameter, in the same position as the green lights.

(ii) The showing of these lights or balls indicates that it is dangerous for other vessels to approach closer than 3,000 feet astern of the minesweeper or 1,500 feet on the side or sides on which danger exists.

RULE 7

(*g*) Vessels of less than 12 metres in length except those engaged in diving operations, shall not be required to exhibit the lights and shapes prescribed in this Rule.

(*g*) The vessels and boats referred to in this Rule [lights and shapes for small vessels] shall not be required to carry the lights or shapes prescribed in Rules 4(*a*) and 11(*e*) and the size of their day signals may be less than is prescribed in Rules 4(*c*) and 11(*c*).

RULE 4

(*h*) The signals prescribed in this Rule are not signals of vessels in distress and requiring assistance. Such signals are contained in Annex IV to these Regulations.

(*g*) These signals are not signals of vessels in distress and requiring assistance. Such signals are contained in Rule 31.

6.28   RULE 28

Vessels constrained by their draught

A vessel constrained by her draught may, in addition to the lights prescribed for power-driven vessels in Rule 23, exhibit where they can best be seen three all-round red lights in a vertical line, or a cylinder.

6.29   RULE 29
                 Pilot vessels
(*a*) A vessel engaged on pilotage duty shall exhibit:
  (i) at or near the masthead, two all-round lights
      in a vertical line, the upper being white and the
      lower red;

  (ii) when underway, in addition, sidelights and a
       sternlight;

  (iii) when at anchor, in addition to the lights
        prescribed in sub-paragraph (i), the light,
        lights or shapes prescribed in Rule 30 for
        vessels at anchor.

(*b*) A pilot vessel when not engaged on pilotage
duty shall exhibit the lights or shapes prescribed for a
similar vessel of her length.

6.30   RULE 30
       Anchored vessels and vessels aground
(*a*) A vessel at anchor shall exhibit where it can
best be seen:
  (i) in the fore part, an all-round white light or one
      ball;
  (ii) at or near the stern and at a lower level than
       the light prescribed in sub-paragraph (i), an
       all-round white light.

(*b*) A vessel of less than 50 metres in length may
exhibit an all-round white light where it can best be
seen instead of the lights prescribed in paragraph (*a*)
of this Rule.

RULE 8
(*a*) A power-driven pilot-vessel when engaged on
pilotage duty and under way:—
  (i) Shall carry a white light at the masthead at a
      height of not less than 20 feet above the hull,
      visible all round the horizon at a distance of at
      least 3 miles and at a distance of 8 feet below it
      a red light similar in construction and character.
      If such a vessel is of less than 65 feet in length
      she may carry the white light at a height of not
      less than 9 feet above the gunwale and the red
      light at a distance of 4 feet below the white light.
  (ii) Shall carry the sidelights or lanterns prescribed
       in Rule 2(*a*)(iv) and (v) or Rule 7(*a*)(ii) or (*d*),
       as appropriate, and the stern light prescribed in
       Rule 10.

[Note Rule 8(*b*) contains other (obsolete) rules for
sailing pilot vessels.]

RULE 8
(*c*) A pilot-vessel when engaged on pilotage duty
and not under way shall carry the lights and show the
flares prescribed in sections (*a*)(i) and (iii) or (*b*)(i)
and (iii), as appropriate, and if at anchor shall also
carry the anchor lights prescribed in Rule 11.

RULE 8
(*d*) A pilot-vessel when not engaged on pilotage
duty shall show the lights or shapes for a similar vessel
of her length.

RULE 11
(*b*) A vessel of 150 feet or more in length, when at
anchor, shall carry near the stem of the vessel, at a
height of not less than 20 feet above the hull, one such
light, and at or near the stern of the vessel and at such
a height that it shall be not less than 15 feet lower than
the forward light, another such light. Both these
lights shall be visible at a distance of at least 3 miles
and so placed as to be as far as possible visible all
round the horizon.
(*c*) Between sunrise and sunset every vessel when at
anchor shall carry in the forepart of the vessel, where
it can best be seen, one black ball not less than 2 feet
in diameter.

RULE 11
(*a*) A vessel of less than 150 feet in length, when at
anchor, shall carry in the forepart of the vessel, where
it can best be seen, a white light visible all round the
horizon at a distance of at least 2 miles. Such a vessel
may also carry a second white light in the position
prescribed in section (*b*) of this Rule but shall not be
required to do so. The second white light, if carried,
shall be visible at a distance of at least 2 miles and so
placed as to be as far as possible visible all round the
horizon.

(c) A vessel at anchor may, and a vessel of 100 metres and more in length shall, also use the available working or equivalent lights to illuminate her decks.

(d) A vessel aground shall exhibit the lights prescribed in paragraph (a) or (b) of this Rule and in addition, where they can best be seen:
  (i) two all-round red lights in a vertical line;
  (ii) three balls in a vertical line.

(e) A vessel of less than 7 metres in length, when at anchor, not in or near a narrow channel, fairway or anchorage, or where other vessels normally navigate, shall not be required to exhibit the lights or shape prescribed in paragraphs (a) and (b) of this Rule.

(f) A vessel of less than 12 metres in length, when aground, shall not be required to exhibit the lights or shapes prescribed in sub-paragraphs (d)(i) and (ii) of this Rule.

6.31   RULE 31
Seaplanes

Where it is impracticable for a seaplane to exhibit lights and shapes of the characteristics or in the positions prescribed in the Rules of this Part she shall exhibit lights and shapes as closely similar in characteristics and position as is possible.

PART D. SOUND AND LIGHT SIGNALS

6.32   RULE 32
Definitions

(a) The word "whistle" means any sound signalling appliance capable of producing the prescribed blasts and which complies with the specifications in Annex III to these Regulations.

(b) The term "short blast" means a blast of about one second's duration.

(c) The term "prolonged blast" means a blast of from four to six seconds' duration.

6.33   RULE 33
Equipment for sound signals

(a) A vessel of 12 metres or more in length shall be provided with a whistle and a bell and a vessel of 100 metres or more in length shall, in addition, be provided with a gong, the tone and sound of which cannot be confused with that of the bell. The whistle, bell and gong shall comply with the specifications in Annex III to these Regulations. The bell or gong or both may be replaced by other equipment having the same respective sound characteristics, provided that manual sounding of the prescribed signals shall always be possible.

RULE 11

(e) A vessel aground shall carry the light or lights prescribed in sections (a) or (b) and the two red lights prescribed in Rule 4(a). By day she shall carry, where they can best be seen, three black balls, each not less than 2 feet in diameter, placed in a vertical line one over the other, not less than 6 feet apart.

RULE 7

(g) The vessels and boats referred to in this Rule [lights and shapes for small vessels] shall not be required to carry the lights or shapes prescribed in Rules 4(a) and 11(e) and the size of their day signals may be less than is prescribed in Rules 4(c) and 11(c).

RULE 1

(a) ... Where, as a result of their special construction, it is not possible for seaplanes to comply fully with the provisions of Rules specifying the carrying of lights and shapes, these provisions shall be followed as closely as circumstances permit.

RULE 1

(c) (xiii) the word "whistle" means any appliance capable of producing the prescribed short and prolonged blasts;

RULE 1

(c) (xi) the term "short blast" means a blast of about one second's duration;

(xii) the term "prolonged blast" means a blast of from four to six seconds' duration;

RULE 15

(a) A power-driven vessel of 40 feet or more in length shall be provided with an efficient whistle, sounded by steam or by some substitute for steam, so placed that the sound may not be intercepted by any obstruction, and with an efficient fog horn to be sounded by mechanical means, and also with an efficient bell. A sailing vessel of 40 feet or more in length shall be provided with a similar fog horn and bell.

(*b*) A vessel of less than 12 metres in length shall not be obliged to carry the sound signalling appliances prescribed in paragraph (*a*) of this Rule but if she does not, she shall be provided with some other means of making an efficient sound signal.

6.34   RULE 34
         Manoeuvring and warning signals
(*a*) When vessels are in sight of one another, a power-driven vessel underway, when manoeuvring as authorized or required by these Rules, shall indicate that manoeuvre by the following signals on her whistle:
  —one short blast to mean "I am altering my course to starboard";
  —two short blasts to mean "I am altering my course to port";
  —three short blasts to mean "I am operating astern propulsion".

(*b*) Any vessel may supplement the whistle signals prescribed in paragraph (*a*) of this Rule by light signals, repeated as appropriate, whilst the manoeuvre is being carried out:
  (i) these light signals shall have the following significance:
    —one flash to mean "I am altering my course to starboard";
    —two flashes to mean "I am altering my course to port";
    —three flashes to mean "I am operating astern propulsion";
  (ii) the duration of each flash shall be about one second, the interval between flashes shall be about one second, and the interval between successive signals shall be not less than ten seconds;
  (iii) the light used for this signal shall, if fitted, be an all-round white light, visible at a minimum range of 5 miles, and shall comply with the provisions of Annex I to these Regulations.

(*c*) When in sight of one another in a narrow channel or fairway:
  (i) a vessel intending to overtake another shall in compliance with Rule 9(*e*)(i) indicate her intention by the following signals on her whistle:
    —two prolonged blasts followed by one short blast to mean "I intend to overtake you on your starboard side";
    —two prolonged blasts followed by two short blasts to mean "I intend to overtake you on your port side".
  (ii) the vessel about to be overtaken when acting in accordance with Rule 9(*e*)(i) shall indicate her agreement by the following signal on her whistle:
    —one prolonged, one short, one prolonged and one short blast, in that order.

RULE 28
(*a*) When vessels are in sight of one another, a power-driven vessel under way in taking any course authorized or required by these Rules, shall indicate that course by the following signals on her whistle, namely:—
One short blast to mean "I am altering my course to starboard".
Two short blasts to mean "I am altering my course to port".
Three short blasts to mean "My engines are going astern".

RULE 28
(*c*) Any whistle signal mentioned in this Rule may be further indicated by a visual signal consisting of a white light visible all round the horizon at a distance of at least 5 miles, and so devised that it will operate simultaneously and in conjunction with the whistle-sounding mechanism and remain lighted and visible during the same period as the sound signal.

(*d*) When vessels in sight of one another are approaching each other and from any cause either vessel fails to understand the intentions or actions of the other, or is in doubt whether sufficient action is being taken by the other to avoid collision, the vessel in doubt shall immediately indicate such doubt by giving at least five short and rapid blasts on the whistle. Such signal may be supplemented by a light signal of at least five short and rapid flashes.

(*e*) A vessel nearing a bend or an area of a channel or fairway where other vessels may be obscured by an intervening obstruction shall sound one prolonged blast. Such signal shall be answered with a prolonged blast by any approaching vessel that may be within hearing around the bend or behind the intervening obstruction.

(*f*) If whistles are fitted on a vessel at a distance apart of more than 100 metres, one whistle only shall be used for giving manoeuvring and warning signals.

6.35   RULE 35
Sound signals in restricted visibility
In or near an area of restricted visibility, whether by day or night, the signals prescribed in this Rule shall be used as follows:
    (*a*) A power-driven vessel making way through the water shall sound at intervals of not more than 2 minutes one prolonged blast.

    (*b*) A power-driven vessel underway but stopped and making no way through the water shall sound at intervals of not more than 2 minutes two prolonged blasts in succession with an interval of about 2 seconds between them.

    (*c*) A vessel not under command, a vessel restricted in her ability to manoeuvre, a vessel constrained by her draught, a sailing vessel, a vessel engaged in fishing and a vessel engaged in towing or pushing another vessel shall, instead of the signals prescribed in paragraphs (*a*) or (*b*) of this Rule, sound at intervals of not more than 2 minutes three blasts in succession, namely one prolonged followed by two short blasts.

RULE 28
(*b*) Whenever a power-driven vessel which, under these Rules, is to keep her course and speed, is in sight of another vessel and is in doubt whether sufficient action is being taken by the other vessel to avert collision, she may indicate such doubt by giving at least five short and rapid blasts on the whistle. The giving of such a signal shall not relieve a vessel of her obligations under Rules 27 and 29 or any other Rule, or of her duty to indicate any action taken under these Rules by giving the appropriate sound signals laid down in this Rule.

RULE 25
(*b*) Whenever a power-driven vessel is nearing a bend in a channel where a vessel approaching from the other direction cannot be seen, such power-driven vessel, when she shall have arrived within one-half ($\frac{1}{2}$) mile of the bend, shall give a signal by one prolonged blast on her whistle which signal shall be answered by a similar blast given by any approaching power-driven vessel that may be within hearing around the bend. Regardless of whether an approaching vessel on the farther side of the bend is heard, such bend shall be rounded with alertness and caution.

———

RULE 15
(*c*) In fog, mist, falling snow, heavy rainstorms, or any other condition similarly restricting visibility, whether by day or night, the signals prescribed in this Rule shall be used as follows:—
    (i) A power-driven vessel making way through the water shall sound at intervals of not more than 2 minutes a prolonged blast.

    (ii) A power-driven vessel under way, but stopped and making no way through the water, shall sound at intervals of not more than 2 minutes two prolonged blasts, with an interval of about 1 second between them.

    (iii) A sailing vessel under way shall sound, at intervals of not more than 1 minute, when on the starboard tack one blast, when on the port tack two blasts in succession, and when with the wind abaft the beam three blasts in succession.

(v) A vessel when towing, a vessel engaged in laying or in picking up a submarine cable or navigation mark, and a vessel under way which is unable to get out of the way of an approaching vessel through being not under command or unable to manoeuvre as required by these Rules shall, instead of the signals prescribed in sub-sections (i), (ii) and (iii) sound, at intervals of not more than 1 minute, three blasts in succession, namely, one prolonged blast followed by two short blasts.

(viii) A vessel engaged in fishing when under way or at anchor shall at intervals of not more than 1 minute sound the signal prescribed in sub-section (v). A vessel when fishing with trolling lines and under way shall sound the signals prescribed in sub-sections (i), (ii) or (iii) as may be appropriate.

[See Rule 15 (c) (v), (viii) above]

(*d*) A vessel engaged in fishing, when at anchor, and a vessel restricted in her ability to manoeuvre when carrying out her work at anchor, shall instead of the signals prescribed in paragraph (*g*) of this Rule sound the signal prescribed in paragraph (*c*) of this Rule.

(*e*) A vessel towed or if more than one vessel is towed the last vessel of the tow, if manned, shall at intervals of not more than 2 minutes sound four blasts in succession, namely one prolonged followed by three short blasts. When practicable, this signal shall be made immediately after the signal made by the towing vessel.

(vi) A vessel towed, or, if more than one vessel is towed, only the last vessel of the tow, if manned, shall, at intervals of not more than 1 minute, sound four blasts in succession, namely, one prolonged blast followed by three short blasts. When practicable, this signal shall be made immediately after the signal made by the towing vessel.

(*f*) When a pushing vessel and a vessel being pushed ahead are rigidly connected in a composite unit they shall be regarded as a power-driven vessel and shall give the signals prescribed in paragraphs (*a*) or (*b*) of this Rule.

Rule 15

(*g*) A vessel at anchor shall at intervals of not more than one minute ring the bell rapidly for about 5 seconds. In a vessel of 100 metres or more in length the bell shall be sounded in the forepart of the vessel and immediately after the ringing of the bell the gong shall be sounded rapidly for about 5 seconds in the after part of the vessel. A vessel at anchor may in addition sound three blasts in succession, namely one short, one prolonged and one short blast, to give warning of her position and of the possibility of collision to an approaching vessel.

(iv) A vessel when at anchor shall at intervals of not more than 1 minute ring the bell rapidly for about 5 seconds. In vessels of more than 350 feet in length the bell shall be sounded in the forepart of the vessel, and in addition there shall be sounded in the after part of the vessel, at intervals of not more than 1 minute for about 5 seconds, a gong or other instrument, the tone and sounding of which cannot be confused with that of the bell. Every vessel at anchor may in addition, in accordance with Rule 12, sound three blasts in succession, namely, one short, one prolonged, and one short blast, to give warning of her position and of the possibility of collision to an approaching vessel.

(*h*) A vessel aground shall give the bell signal and if required the gong signal prescribed in paragraph (*g*)* of this Rule and shall, in addition, give three separate and distinct strokes on the bell immediately before and after the rapid ringing of the bell. A vessel aground may in addition sound an appropriate whistle signal.

(*i*) A vessel of less than 12 metres in length shall not be obliged to give the above-mentioned signals but, if she does not, shall make some other efficient sound signal at intervals of not more than 2 minutes.

(*j*) A pilot vessel when engaged on pilotage duty may in addition to the signals prescribed in paragraphs (*a*), (*b*) or (*g*)* of this Rule sound an identity signal consisting of four short blasts.

[*The references to paragraph (*g*) were inserted to rectify an error in IMO Resolution A.464 (XII) (see T.S. Misc. No. 10 (1983); Cmnd. 8846). However, the second correction has not been implemented in the Schedule to the Merchant Shipping (Distress Signals and Prevention of Collisions) (Overseas Territories) Order 1983, S.I. 1983, No. 762 which refers in Rule 35 (j) to paragraph (*f*) and which is in all other respects identical to Sch. 1 of the Merchant Shipping (Distress Signals and Prevention of Collisions) Regulations 1983, S.I. 1983, No. 708.]

(vii) A vessel aground shall give the bell signal and, if required, the gong signal, prescribed in sub-section (iv) and shall, in addition, give 3 separate and distinct strokes on the bell immediately before and after such rapid ringing of the bell.

(ix) A vessel of less than 40 feet in length, a rowing boat, or a seaplane on the water, shall not be obliged to give the above-mentioned signals but if she does not, she shall make some other efficient sound signal at intervals of not more than 1 minute.

(x) A power-driven pilot-vessel when engaged on pilotage duty may, in addition to the signals prescribed in sub-sections (i), (ii) and (iv), sound an identity signal consisting of 4 short blasts.

6.36   RULE 36
Signals to attract attention
If necessary to attract the attention of another vessel any vessel may make light or sound signals that cannot be mistaken for any signal authorized elsewhere in these Rules, or may direct the beam of her searchlight in the direction of the danger, in such a way as not to embarrass any vessel. Any light to attract the attention of another vessel shall be such that it cannot be mistaken for any aid to navigation. For the purpose of this Rule the use of high intensity intermittent or revolving lights, such as strobe lights, shall be avoided.

RULE 12
Every vessel or seaplane on the water may, if necessary in order to attract attention, in addition to the lights which she is by these Rules required to carry, show a flare-up light or use a detonating or other efficient sound signal that cannot be mistaken for any signal authorised elsewhere under these Rules.

6.37   RULE 37
Distress signals
When a vessel is in distress and requires assistance she shall use or exhibit the signals described in Annex IV to these Regulations.

RULE 31
Distress signals
(*a*) When a vessel or seaplane on the water is in distress and requires assistance from other vessels or from the shore, the following shall be the signals to be used or displayed by her, either together or separately, namely:—

PART E. EXEMPTIONS

6.38   RULE 38

Exemptions

Any vessel (or class of vessels) provided that she complies with the requirements of the International Regulations for Preventing Collisions at Sea, 1960, the keel of which is laid or which is at a corresponding stage of construction before the entry into force of these Regulations may be exempted from compliance therewith as follows:

(a) The installation of lights with ranges prescribed in Rule 22, until four years after the date of entry into force of these Regulations.

(b) The installation of lights with colour specifications as prescribed in Section 7 of Annex I to these Regulations, until four years after the date of entry into force of these Regulations.

(c) The repositioning of lights as a result of conversion from Imperial to metric units and rounding off measurement figures, permanent exemption.

(d) (i) The repositioning of masthead lights on vessels of less than 150 metres in length, resulting from the prescriptions of Section 3(a) of Annex I to these Regulations, permanent exemption.

(ii) The repositioning of masthead lights on vessels of 150 metres or more in length, resulting from the prescriptions of Section 3(a) of Annex I to these Regulations, until nine years after the date of entry into force of these Regulations.

(e) The repositioning of masthead lights resulting from the prescriptions of Section 2(b) of Annex I to these Regulations, until nine years after the date of entry into force of these Regulations.

(f) The repositioning of sidelights resulting from the prescriptions of Sections 2(g) and 3(b) of Annex I to these Regulations until nine years after the date of entry into force of these Regulations.

(g) The requirements for sound signal appliances prescribed in Annex III to these Regulations until nine years after the date of entry into force of these Regulations.

(h) The repositioning of all-round lights resulting from the prescription of Section 9(b) of Annex I to these Regulations, permanent exemption.

ANNEX I

6.39   **Positioning and technical details of lights and shapes**

1. *Definition*

The term "height above the hull" means height above the uppermost continuous deck. This height shall be measured from the position vertically beneath the location of the light.

RULE 1

(c) (vi) the term "height above the hull" means height above the uppermost continuous deck;

2. *Vertical positioning and spacing of lights*

(*a*) On a power-driven vessel of 20 metres or more in length the masthead lights shall be placed as follows:

    (i) the forward masthead light, or if only one masthead light is carried, then that light, at a height above the hull of not less than 6 metres, and, if the breadth of the vessel exceeds 6 metres, then at a height above the hull not less than such breadth, so however that the light need not be placed at a greater height above the hull than 12 metres;

    (ii) when two masthead lights are carried the after one shall be at least 4·5 metres vertically higher than the forward one.

(*b*) The vertical separation of masthead lights of power-driven vessels shall be such that in all normal conditions of trim the after light will be seen over and separate from the forward light at a distance of 1,000 metres from the stem when viewed from sea level.

(*c*) The masthead light of a power-driven vessel of 12 metres but less than 20 metres in length shall be placed at a height above the gunwale of not less than 2·5 metres.

(*d*) A power-driven vessel of less than 12 metres in length may carry the uppermost light at a height of less than 2·5 metres above the gunwale. When however a masthead light is carried in addition to sidelights and a sternlight, then such masthead light shall be carried at least 1 metre higher than the sidelights.

(*e*) One of the two or three masthead lights prescribed for a power-driven vessel when engaged in towing or pushing another vessel shall be placed in the same position as either the forward masthead light or the after masthead light: provided that, if carried on the aftermast, the lowest after masthead light shall be at least 4.5 metres vertically higher than the forward masthead light.

    (*f*) (i) The masthead light or lights prescribed in Rule 23(*a*) shall be so placed as to be above and clear of all other lights and obstructions except as described in sub-paragraph (ii).

    (ii) When it is impracticable to carry the all-round lights prescribed by Rule 27(*b*)(i) or Rule 28 below the masthead lights, they may be carried above the after masthead light(s) or vertically in between the forward masthead light(s) and after masthead light(s), provided that in the latter case the requirement of Section 3(*c*) of this Annex shall be complied with.

(*g*) The sidelights of a power-driven vessel shall be placed at a height above the hull not greater than three-quarters of that of the forward masthead light. They shall not be so low as to be interfered with by deck lights.

[See the prescribed distances in 1960 Rule 2(*a*), opposite 1972 Rule 23(*a*) (ii)]

————

————

————

RULE 7
(*c*) Power-driven vessels of less than 40 feet in length may carry the white light at a less height than 9 feet above the gunwale but it shall be carried not less than 3 feet above the sidelights or the combined lantern prescribed in section (*a*) (ii).

[See 1960 Rule 3(*a*) opposite 1972 Rule 24(*a*)(i), (ii)]

[See 1960 Rule 2(*a*)(iii), opposite 1972 Rule 23(*a*)(ii).]

————

(*h*) The sidelights, if in a combined lantern and carried on a power-driven vessel of less than 20 metres in length, shall be placed not less than 1 metre below the masthead light.

(*i*) When the Rules prescribe two or three lights to be carried in a vertical line, they shall be spaced as follows:

   (i) on a vessel of 20 metres in length or more such lights shall be spaced not less than 2 metres apart, and the lowest of these lights shall, except where a towing light is required, be placed at a height of not less than 4 metres above the hull;

  (ii) on a vessel of less than 20 metres in length such lights shall be spaced not less than 1 metre apart and the lowest of these lights shall, except where a towing light is required, be placed at a height of not less than 2 metres above the hull;

 (iii) when three lights are carried they shall be equally spaced.

(*j*) The lower of the two all-round lights prescribed for a vessel when engaged in fishing shall be at a height above the sidelights not less than twice the distance between the two vertical lights.

(*k*) The forward anchor light prescribed in Rule 30(*a*)(i), when two are carried, shall not be less than 4.5 metres above the after one. On a vessel of 50 metres or more in length this forward anchor light shall be placed at a height of not less than 6 metres above the hull.

3. *Horizontal positioning and spacing of lights*

(*a*) When two masthead lights are prescribed for a power-driven vessel, the horizontal distance between them shall not be less than one-half of the length of the vessel but need not be more than 100 metres. The forward light shall be placed not more than one-quarter of the length of the vessel from the stem.

(*b*) On a power-driven vessel of 20 metres or more in length the sidelights shall not be placed in front of the forward masthead lights. They shall be placed at or near the side of the vessel.

(*c*) When the lights prescribed in Rule 27(*b*)(i) or Rule 28 are placed vertically between the forward masthead light(s) and the after masthead light(s) these all-round lights shall be placed at a horizontal distance of not less than 2 metres from the fore and aft centreline of the vessel in the athwartship direction.

4. *Details of location of direction-indicating lights for fishing vessels, dredgers and vessels engaged in underwater operations*

(*a*) The light indicating the direction of the outlying gear from a vessel engaged in fishing as prescribed in Rule 26(*c*)(ii) shall be placed at a horizontal distance of not less than 2 metres and not more than 6 metres away from the two all-round red and white lights.

[See 1960 Rule 7(*a*)(ii), opposite 1972 Rule 23(*c*).]

[See 1960 Rules:
  3(*a*) opposite 1972 Rule 24(*a*)(i), (ii)
  4(*a*) opposite 1972 Rule 27(*a*)(i)
  4(*c*) opposite 1972 Rule (27(*b*)(i)
  5(*b*) opposite 1972 Rule 25(*c*)
  9(*c*)(i) opposite 1972 Rule 26(*b*)(i), (ii).]

[See 1960 Rule 9(*c*)(i), opposite 1972 Rule 26(*b*)(i), (ii).]

[See 1960 Rule 11(*b*), opposite 1972 Rule 30(*a*).]

[See 1960 Rule 2(*a*)(iii), opposite 1972 Rule 23(*a*)(ii).]

———————

———————

RULE 9

(*f*) Vessels referred to in Section (*d*) with outlying gear extending more than 500 feet horizontally into the seaway shall carry an additional all-round white light at a horizontal distance of not less than 6 feet nor more than 20 feet away from the vertical lights in the

This light shall be placed not higher than the all-round white light prescribed in Rule 26(*c*)(i) and not lower than the sidelights.

(*b*) The lights and shapes on a vessel engaged in dredging or underwater operations to indicate the obstructed side and/or the side on which it is safe to pass, as prescribed in Rule 27(*d*)(i) and (ii), shall be placed at the maximum practical horizontal distance, but in no case less than 2 metres, from the lights or shapes prescribed in Rule 27(*b*)(i) and (ii). In no case shall the upper of these lights or shapes be at a greater height than the lower of the three lights or shapes prescribed in Rule 27(*b*)(i) and (ii).

5. *Screens for sidelights*

The sidelights of vessels of 20 metres or more in length shall be fitted with inboard screens painted matt black, and meeting the requirements of Section 9 of this Annex. On vessels of less than 20 metres in length the sidelights, if necessary to meet the requirements of Section 9 of this Annex, shall be fitted with inboard matt black screens. With a combined lantern using a single vertical filament and a very narrow division between the green and red sections, external screens need not be fitted.

6. *Shapes*

(*a*) Shapes shall be black and of the following sizes:
   (i) a ball shall have a diameter of not less than 0·6 metre;
   (ii) a cone shall have a base diameter of not less than 0·6 metre and a height equal to its diameter;
   (iii) a cylinder shall have a diameter of at least 0·6 metre and a height of twice its diameter;
   (iv) a diamond shape shall consist of two cones as defined in (ii) above having a common base.

(*b*) The vertical distance between shapes shall be at least 1.5 metres.

(*c*) In a vessel of less than 20 metres in length shapes of lesser dimensions but commensurate with the size of the vessel may be used and the distance apart may be correspondingly reduced.

7. *Colour specification of lights*

The chromaticity of all navigation lights shall conform to the following standards, which lie within the boundaries of the area of the diagram specified for each colour by the International Commission on Illumination (CIE).

The boundaries of the area for each colour are given by indicating the corner co-ordinates, which are as follows:

direction of the outlying gear. This additional white light shall be placed at a height not exceeding that of the white light prescribed in Section (*c*)(i) and not lower than the sidelights.

————

RULE 2(*a*) (vi)

(vi) The said green and red sidelights shall be fitted with inboard screens projecting at least 3 feet forward from the light, so as to prevent these lights from being seen across the bows.

[See 1960 Rule 3(*c*), opposite 1960 Rule 24(*a*)(v)
4(*a*), opposite 1960 Rule 27(*a*)(ii)
4(*c*), opposite 1960 Rule 27(*b*)(ii)
4(*d*)(i), opposite 1960 Rule 27(*f*)
5(*b*), opposite 1960 Rule 24(*e*)(iii)
9(*h*), opposite 1960 Rule 26(*c*)(i), (ii).]

————

(i) *White*

| x | 0·525 | 0·525 | 0·452 | 0·310 | 0·310 | 0·443 |
| y | 0·382 | 0·440 | 0·440 | 0·348 | 0·283 | 0·382 |

(ii) *Green*

| x | 0·028 | 0·009 | 0·300 | 0·203 |
| y | 0·385 | 0·723 | 0·511 | 0·356 |

(iii) *Red*

| x | 0·680 | 0·660 | 0·735 | 0·721 |
| y | 0·320 | 0·320 | 0·265 | 0·259 |

(iv) *Yellow*

| x | 0·612 | 0·618 | 0·575 | 0·575 |
| y | 0·382 | 0·382 | 0·425 | 0·406 |

8. *Intensity of lights*

(a) The minimum luminous intensity of lights shall be calculated by using the formula:

$$I = 3·43 \times 10^6 \times T \times D^2 \times K^{-D}$$

where I is luminous intensity in candelas under service conditions,

T is threshold factor 2×10^{-7} lux,

D is range of visibility (luminous range) of the light in nautical miles,

K is atmospheric transmissivity.

For prescribed lights the value of K shall be 0·8, corresponding to a meteorological visibility of approximately 13 nautical miles.

(b) A selection of figures derived from the formula is given in the following table:

Range of visibility (luminous range) of light in nautical miles D	Luminous intensity of light in candelas for K=0·8 I
1	0·9
2	4·3
3	12
4	27
5	52
6	94

Note: The maximum luminous intensity of navigation lights should be limited to avoid undue glare. This shall not be achieved by a variable control of the luminous intensity.

9. *Horizontal sectors*

(a) (i) In the forward direction, sidelights as fitted on the vessel shall show the minimum required intensities. The intensities shall decrease to reach practical cut-off between 1 degree and 3 degrees outside the prescribed sectors.

(ii) For sternlights and masthead lights and at 22·5 degrees abaft the beam for sidelights, the minimum required intensities shall be maintained over the arc of the horizon up to 5 degrees within the limits of the sectors prescribed in Rule 21. From 5 degrees within the prescribed sectors the intensity may decrease by 50 per cent up to the prescribed limits; it shall decrease steadily to reach practical cut-off at not more than 5 degrees outside the prescribed sectors.

(*b*) All-round lights shall be so located as not to be obscured by masts, topmasts or structures within angular sectors of more than 6 degrees, except anchor lights prescribed in Rule 30, which need not be placed at an impracticable height above the hull.

[Note: for a recent case on para. 9(*b*) see *The Coral I* [1982] 1 Lloyd's Rep. 441.]

10. *Vertical sectors*

(*a*) The vertical sectors of electric lights as fitted with the exception of lights on sailing vessels shall ensure that:
  (i) at least the required minimum intensity is maintained at all angles from 5 degrees above to 5 degrees below the horizontal;
  (ii) at least 60 per cent of the required minimum intensity is maintained from 7·5 degrees above to 7·5 degrees below the horizontal.

(*b*) In the case of sailing vessels the vertical sectors of electric lights as fitted shall ensure that:
  (i) at least the required minimum intensity is maintained at all angles from 5 degrees above to 5 degrees below the horizontal;
  (ii) at least 50 per cent of the required minimum intensity is maintained from 25 degrees above to 25 degrees below the horizontal.

(*c*) In the case of lights other than electric these specifications shall be met as closely as possible.

11. *Intensity of non-electric lights*

Non-electric lights shall so far as practicable comply with the minimum intensities, as specified in the Table given in Section 8 of this Annex.

12. *Manoeuvring light*

Notwithstanding the provisions of paragraph 2(*f*) of this Annex the manoeuvring light described in Rule 34(*b*) shall be placed in the same fore and aft vertical plane as the masthead light or lights and, where practicable, at a minimum height of 2 metres vertically above the forward masthead light, provided that it shall be carried not less than 2 metres vertically above or below the after masthead light. On a vessel where only one masthead light is carried the manoeuvring light, if fitted, shall be carried where it can best be seen, not less than 2 metres vertically apart from the masthead light.

13. *Approval*

The construction of lights and shapes and the installation of lights on board the vessel shall be to the satisfaction of the appropriate authority of the State whose flag the vessel is entitled to fly.

ANNEX II
6.40
Additional signals for fishing vessels fishing in close proximity

1. *General*

The lights mentioned herein shall, if exhibited in pursuance of Rule 26(*d*), be placed where they can best be seen. They shall be at least 0·9 metre apart but at a lower level than lights prescribed in Rule 26(*b*)(i) and (*c*)(i). The lights shall be visible all round the horizon at a distance of at least 1 mile but at a lesser distance than the lights prescribed by these Rules for fishing vessels.

2. *Signals for trawlers*

(*a*) Vessels when engaged in trawling, whether using demersal or pelagic gear, may exhibit:
   (i) when shooting their nets:
         two white lights in a vertical line;
   (ii) when hauling their nets:
         one white light over one red light in a vertical line;
   (iii) when the net has come fast upon an obstruction:
         two red lights in a vertical line.

(*b*) Each vessel engaged in pair trawling may exhibit:
   (i) by night, a searchlight directed forward and in the direction of the other vessel of the pair;
   (ii) when shooting or hauling their nets or when their nets have come fast upon an obstruction, the lights prescribed in 2(*a*) above.

[Cf. 1960 Rule 9(g), which permits, *inter alia*, vessels engaged in fishing to direct their searchlight in the direction of a danger threatening the approaching vessel.]

3. *Signals for purse seiners*

Vessels engaged in fishing with purse seine gear may exhibit two yellow lights in a vertical line. These lights shall flash alternately every second and with equal light and occultation duration. These lights may be exhibited only when the vessel is hampered by its fishing gear.

ANNEX III
6.41
Technical details of sound signal appliances

1. *Whistles*

(*a*) *Frequencies and range of audibility*

The fundamental frequency of the signal shall lie within the range 70-700 Hz.

The range of audibility of the signal from a whistle shall be determined by those frequencies, which may include the fundamental and/or one or more higher frequencies, which lie within the range 180-700 Hz ($\pm$1 per cent) and which provide the sound pressure levels specified in paragraph 1(*c*) below.

(*b*) *Limits of fundamental frequencies*

To ensure a wide variety of whistle characteristics, the fundamental frequency of a whistle shall be between the following limits:

(i) 70-200 Hz, for a vessel 200 metres or more in length;

(ii) 130-350 Hz, for a vessel 75 metres but less than 200 metres in length;

(iii) 250-700 Hz, for a vessel less than 75 metres in length.

(c) Sound signal intensity and range of audibility

A whistle fitted in a vessel shall provide, in the direction of maximum intensity of the whistle and at a distance of 1 metre from it, a sound pressure level in at least one 1/3rd-octave band within the range of frequencies 180-700 Hz ($\pm$ 1 per cent) of not less than the appropriate figure given in the table below.

Length of vessel in metres	1/3rd-octave band level at 1 metre in dB referred to $2 \times 10^{-5} \ N/m^2$	Audibility range in nautical miles
200 or more	143	2
75 but less than 200	138	1.5
20 but less than 75	130	1
Less than 20	120	0.5

The range of audibility in the table above is for information and is approximately the range at which a whistle may be heard on its forward axis with 90 per cent probability in conditions of still air on board a vessel having average background noise level at the listening posts (taken to be 68 dB in the octave band centred on 250 Hz and 63 dB in the octave band centred on 500 Hz).

In practice the range at which a whistle may be heard is extremely variable and depends critically on weather conditions; the values given can be regarded as typical but under conditions of strong wind or high ambient noise level at the listening post the range may be much reduced.

(d) Directional properties

The sound pressure level of a directional whistle shall be not more than 4 dB below the prescribed sound pressure level on the axis at any direction in the horizontal plane within $\pm$ 45 degrees of the axis. The sound pressure level at any other direction in the horizontal plane shall be not more than 10 dB below the prescribed sound pressure level on the axis, so that the range in any direction will be at least half the range on the forward axis. The sound pressure level shall be measured in that 1/3rd-octave band which determines the audibility range.

(e) Positioning of whistles

When a directional whistle is to be used as the only whistle on a vessel, it shall be installed with its maximum intensity directed straight ahead.

A whistle shall be placed as high as practicable on a vessel, in order to reduce interception of the emitted sound by obstructions and also to minimize hearing damage risk to personnel. The sound pressure level of the vessel's own signal at listening posts shall not exceed 110 dB(A) and so far as practicable should not exceed 100 dB(A).

(f) Fitting of more than one whistle

If whistles are fitted at a distance apart of more than 100 metres, it shall be so arranged that they are not sounded simultaneously.

(g) Combined whistle systems

If due to the presence of obstructions the sound field of a single whistle or of one of the whistles referred to in paragraph 1(f) above is likely to have a zone of greatly reduced signal level, it is recommended that a combined whistle system be fitted so as to overcome this reduction. For the purposes of the Rules a combined whistle system is to be regarded as a single whistle. The whistles of a combined system shall be located at a distance apart of not more than 100 metres and arranged to be sounded simultaneously. The frequency of any one whistle shall differ from those of the others by at least 10 Hz.

2. Bell or gong
(a) Intensity of signal

A bell or gong, or other device having similar sound characteristics shall produce a sound pressure level of not less than 110 dB at a distance of 1 metre from it.

(b) Construction

Bells and gongs shall be made of corrosion-resistant material and designed to give a clear tone. The diameter of the mouth of the bell shall be not less than 300 mm. for vessels of more than 20 metres in length, and shall be not less than 200 mm. for vessels of 12 metres or more but of less than 20 metres in length.

Where practicable, a power-driven bell striker is recommended to ensure constant force but manual operation shall be possible. The mass of the striker shall be not less than 3 per cent of the mass of the bell.

3. Approval

The construction of sound signal appliances, their performance and their installation on board the vessel shall be to the satisfaction of the appropriate authority of the State whose flag the vessel is entitled to fly.

ANNEX IV

6.42

Distress signals

1. The following signals, used or exhibited either together or separately, indicate distress and need of assistance:

(a) a gun or other explosive signal fired at intervals of about a minute;

(b) a continuous sounding with any fog-signalling apparatus;

(c) rockets or shells, throwing red stars fired one at a time at short intervals;

(d) a signal made by radiotelegraphy or by any other signalling method consisting of the group ... ▬ ▬ ▬ ... (SOS) in the Morse Code;

(e) a signal sent by radiotelephony consisting of the spoken word "Mayday";

(f) the International Code Signal of distress indicated by N.C.;

(g) a signal consisting of a square flag having above or below it a ball or anything resembling a ball;

(h) flames on the vessel (as from a burning tar barrel, oil barrel, etc.);

(i) a rocket parachute flare or a hand flare showing a red light;

(j) a smoke signal giving off orange-coloured smoke;

(k) slowly and repeatedly raising and lowering arms outstretched to each side;

(l) the radiotelegraph alarm signal;

(m) the radiotelephone alarm signal;

(n) signals transmitted by emergency position-indicating radio beacons.

2. The use or exhibition of any of the foregoing signals except for the purpose of indicating distress and need or assistance and the use of other signals which may be confused with any of the above signals is prohibited.

3. Attention is drawn to the relevant sections of the International Code of Signals, the Merchant Ship Search and Rescue Manual and the following signals:

(a) a piece of orange-coloured canvas with either a black square and circle or other appropriate symbol (for identification from the air);

(b) a dye marker.

1960 RULE 31

(a) When a vessel or seaplane on the water is in distress and requires assistance from other vessels or from the shore, the following shall be the signals to be used or displayed by her, either together or separately, namely:—

(i) A gun or other explosive signal fired at intervals of about a minute.

(ii) A continuous sounding with any fog-signalling apparatus.

(iii) Rockets or shells, throwing red stars fired one at a time at short intervals.

(iv) A signal made by radiotelegraphy or by any other signalling method consisting of the group ... ▬ ▬ ▬ ... in the Morse Code.

(v) A signal sent by radiotelephony consisting of the spoken word "Mayday".

(vi) The International Code Signal of distress indicated by N.C.

(vii) A signal consisting of a square flag having above or below it a ball or anything resembling a ball.

(viii) Flames on the vessel (as from a burning tar barrel, oil barrel, &c.).

(ix) A rocket parachute flare or a hand flare showing a red light.

(x) A smoke signal giving off a volume of orange-coloured smoke.

(xi) Slowly and repeatedly raising and lowering arms outstretched to each side.

NOTE to RULE 31(a)

NOTE.—*Vessels in distress may use the radiotelegraph alarm signal or the radiotelephone alarm signal to secure attention to distress calls and messages. The radiotelegraph alarm signal, which is designed to actuate the radiotelegraph auto alarms of vessels so fitted, consists of a series of twelve dashes, sent in 1 minute, the duration of each dash being 4 seconds, and the duration of the interval between 2 consecutive dashes being 1 second. The radiotelephone alarm signal consists of 2 tones transmitted alternately over periods of from 30 seconds to 1 minute.*

RULE 31

(b) The use of any of the foregoing signals, except for the purpose of indicating that a vessel or seaplane is in distress, and the use of any signals which may be confused with any of the above signals, is prohibited.

———

APPENDIX II

17. TRAFFIC SEPARATION SCHEMES—INFORMATION CONCERNING SCHEMES SHOWN ON ADMIRALTY CHARTS.

Former Notice 17/82 cancelled.

Note:—With effect from 22nd May 1982, IMCO became the International Maritime Organization (IMO).

7.01

1. In 1961, the Institutes of Navigation of France, the Federal Republic of Germany and the United Kingdom, carried out a study of measures for separating traffic in areas where statistics indicated an increased risk of collision. The first traffic separation scheme was implemented in the Dover Strait in 1967. Since then, a large number of similar routeing schemes have been established throughout the world and the details are shown on Admiralty charts and referred to in Admiralty Sailing Directions. For further information about Ships' Routeing, see the Mariner's Handbook, Chapter 4, Section 4.

7.02

2. The International Maritime Organization (IMO) is the body responsible for establishing and recommending measures on an international level concerning ships' routeing. Where schemes lie wholly within territorial waters, decisions concerning routeing rest with the national government but such schemes may also be submitted for IMO approval and adoption.

7.03

3. The details of schemes adopted by IMO are set out in the IMO publication "Ships' Routeing", the 4th edition of which was issued in 1979, and in subsequent IMO Resolutions. See also sub-paragraph 6(c) below. Compliance with Rule 10 of the International Regulations for Preventing Collisions at Sea, 1972, is mandatory for all ships when operating in or near schemes which have been adopted by IMO; this Rule is reproduced as an Annex to this notice. In some schemes, special provisions are included, governing their use by all ships or by specified classes of ships. On the charts, relevant information is given or there is a recommendation to chart users to consult Admiralty Sailing Directions for details.

7.04

4. While vessels using the traffic lanes in schemes adopted by IMO must, in particular, comply with Rule 10 of the International Collision Regulations, they are not thereby given any right of way over crossing vessels; the other Steering and Sailing Rules still apply in all respects, particularly if risk of collision is involved.

7.05

5. It is UK hdyographic policy to insert on Admiralty charts not only the IMO-adopted schemes but also the routes established by coastal states or other competent national authorities concerned with the safety of navigation. On the charts, the IMO-adopted schemes are not differentiated from the other routeing schemes; however, it is intended that all charts

showing traffic separation schemes should carry a reference to this Annual Notice. The portrayal of national traffic separation schemes on Admiralty charts is solely for the safety and convenience of shipping and implies no recognition of the international validity of the relevant regulations (see Mariner's Handbook Chapter 1, Section 1).

7.06

6. The list which follows contains details of all the traffic separation schemes at present included in the Admiralty chart series, or in the process of being inserted. Several facts about each scheme are given:

    (a) The regional headings, and the reference numbers of the headings, correspond to the standard Geographical Index which appears in each weekly edition of Admiralty Notices to Mariners.

    (b) The geographical positions quoted are approximate and, with the place names, are given merely to indicate the general location of the scheme and to facilitate its identification on the charts. If an extensive area is involved, the geographical co-ordinates of the extreme ends of the separation zones or lines are given.

    (c) All IMO-adopted schemes are marked * in the margin; any changes during the year are announced in Admiralty Notices to Mariners. For the other schemes, the originating authority is given, where this is known.

    (d) In each case, only the principal Admiralty charts on which the details of the scheme are shown, are quoted. Separate latticed versions are not listed. Chart numbers marked thus † indicate that action is in hand to insert new or amended traffic separation schemes on these charts, by issue of Notice to Mariners, or by inclusion in New Edition or New Charts.

    (e) In some cases, the volumes of the Admiralty Sailing Directions which contain details of the scheme are quoted under the heading "Remarks".

List of Traffic Separation Schemes shown on Admiralty Charts.

7.07 (2) BRITISH ISLES (including English Channel and western part of southern North Sea for which the English Channel Passage Planning Guide—Cart 5500—is recommended as an additional reference).

* At North Hinder,
    51° 49'·1 N., 2° 45'·8 E. to 51° 28'·0 N., 2° 07'·1 E.
    Charts 3371, 1610, 1406.
Major changes to this scheme took effect an 11th May 1983 [See Admiralty Notice to Mariners No. 1106 of 1983].

* At West Hinder,
    51° 22'·0 N., 2° 42'·7 E. to 51° 20'·0 N., 2° 10'·6 E.
    Charts 323, 1872, 1406.

* In the Strait of Dover and adjacent waters,
    51° 28'·0 N., 2° 07'·1 E. to 50° 27'·0 N., 0° 00'·0
    Charts 323, 1892, 2451, 1610, 1406.

* Off Casquets,
    49° 57'·0 N., 2° 39'·0 W.
    Charts 2656, 2675.

* Off Land's End, between Seven Stones and Longships,
  50° 03'·0 N., 5° 58'·0 W.
  Charts 1148, 2565, 2655.

* South of the Scilly Isles.
  49° 40'·0 N., 6° 24'·0 W.
  Charts 2565, 2655, 2649, 2675.

* West of the Scilly Isles,
  49° 58'·0 N., 6° 43'·0 W.
  Charts 2565, 2649, 2675.

* Off Fastnet Rock,
  51° 19'·3 N., 9° 30'·6 W.
  Charts 2424, 1123, 2649.

* Off Smalls,
  51° 44'·9 N., 5° 49'·4 W.
  Charts 1478, 1123.

* Off Tuskar Rock,
  52° 08'·5 N., 6° 03'·8 W.
  Charts 1787, 1410, 1123.

* Off Skerries,
  53° 22'·8 N., 4° 52'·0 W. to 53° 32'·1 N., 4° 31'·6 W.
  Charts 1977, 1411, 1826.

* Off Chicken Rock, Calf of Man,
  53° 57'·9 N., 5° 00'·3 W.
  Charts 2093, 1411.

* In the North Channel,
  55° 20'·6 N., 6° 02'·3 W.
  Charts 2798, 2724, 2635.

7.08 (3) U.S.S.R., NORTH COAST, NORWAY, FAROE ISLANDS AND ICELAND.

Off Mys Zimnegorskiy,
65° 21'·0 N., 39° 28'·3 E.
Charts 2272, 2273, 3180.
Government of U.S.S.R.

Off Ostrov Sosnovets,
66° 17'·3 N., 40° 32'·2 E.
Charts 2271, 2272, 3180.
Government of U.S.S.R.

Off Mys Orlov Terskiy,
67° 27'·5 N., 41° 22'·8 E.
Charts 2270, 3280, 3181.
Government of U.S.S.R.

Off Svyatonosskiy Poluostrov,
68° 15'·2 N., 39° 50'·8 E.
Charts 2269, 3180.
Government of U.S.S.R.

Entrance to Kol'skiy Zaliv,
69° 20'·4 N., 33° 33'·9 E.
Charts 2966, 2333.
Government of U.S.S.R.

Kárskiye Voróta Strait,
70° 25'·0 N., 57° 59'·0 E.
Chart 3035.
Government of U.S.S.R.

* Off Feistein,
58° 38'·0 N., 5° 08'·0 E.
Charts 2281, 2182c.

Oslo Fjord—South-East of Lille Færder,
59° 00'·6 N., 10° 35'·9 E.
Chart 3708.
Government of Norway.

Oslo Fjord—East of Fulehuk,
59° 09'·6 N., 10° 39'·2 E.
Chart 3159.
Government of Norway.

Oslo Fjord—East of Bastøy,
59° 20'·1 N., 10° 36'·0 E.
Chart 3159.
Government of Norway.

Oslo Fjord—West of Jeløya,
59° 30'·8 N., 10° 35'·4 E.
Charts 3154, 3159.
Government of Norway.

7.09 (4) BALTIC SEA.

* Off Sommers Island (Ostrov Sommers),
60° 11'·7 N., 27° 46'·4 E.
Charts 2393, 2264.

* Off Hogland (Gogland) Island (Ostrov Gogland),
  60° 02′·0 N., 27° 12′·8 E.
  Charts 2393, 2264, 2248.

* Off Rodsher Island (Ostrov Rodsher),
  60° 00′·4 N., 26° 40′·4 E.
  Charts 2357, 2248.

* Off Kalbådagrund Lighthouse,
  59° 53′·0 N., 25° 38′·6 E.
  Charts 2356, 2248.

* Off Porkkala Lighthouse,
  50′ 44′·9 N., 24° 21′·4 E.
  Charts 2241, 2248.

* Off Hankoniemi Peninsula (Hanko),
  59° 31′·6 N., 22° 41′·4 E.
  Charts 2241, 2297.

* Off Kōpu Peninsula (Hiiumaa Island) (Poolsaar),
  59° 07′·6 N., 21° 41′·7 E.
  Charts 2222, 2241.

* Off Gotland Island,
  56° 47′·5 N., 18° 22′·4 E.
  Charts 2288, 2816.

* Off Öland Island,
  56° 04′·2 N., 16° 41′·0 E.
  Charts 2251, 2816.

* In the Approaches to Rostock,
  54° 17′·7 N., 12° 00′·0 E.
  Chart 2365.

* South of Gedser,
  54° 26′·0 N., 12° 10′·0 E.
  Chart 2365.

* Between Korsoer and Sprogoe (Korsør and Sprogø),
  55° 20′·0 N., 11° 02′·0 E.
  Charts 2596, 2597, 2118.

* In the Sound,
  56° 03′·2 N., 12° 39′·4 E.
  Charts 2594, 2115.

* Off Falsterborev,
  55° 18′·6 N., 12° 39′·2 E.
  Charts 2595, 2115, 2360.

* Off Kiel Lighthouse,
  54° 29′·5 N., 10° 17′·6 E.
  Charts 33, 2116

Approaches to Gdansk and Gdynia,
54° 32'·0 N., 18° 48'·5 E.
Charts 2384, 2369, 2288.
Government of Poland.

In the Approaches to Tallinn,
59° 36'·9 N., 24° 40'·0 E.
Charts 2227, 2241, 2248.
Government of U.S.S.R.

7.10 (5) NORTH SEA AND NORTH AND WEST COASTS OF DENMARK, GERMANY, NETHERLANDS AND BELGIUM.

* In the Approaches to River Elbe,
  54° 00'·0 N., 8° 09'·7 E.
  Charts 3261, 1875.

* Off Terschelling and in the German Bight (Deutsche Bucht),
  53° 58'·0 N., 7° 37'·5 E. to 53° 28'·9 N., 4° 46'·2 E.
  Charts 2593, 3761, 1405.

* Deutsche Bucht Light-vessel, Western Approach,
  54° 08'·4 N., 6° 01'·6 E. to 54° 10'·7 N., 7° 21'·8 E.
  Charts 1405, 2182a, 2182b.

* In the Approach to River Jade,
  54° 05'·1 N., 7° 32'·1 E.
  Charts 3761†, 1405†.

* Off Texel,
  52° 56'·7 N., 4° 08'·8 E.
  Charts 2322, 2593, 1405, 1408.

* In the Approaches to Hook of Holland (from north and west),
  52° 01'·2 N., 3° 53'·6 E.
  Charts 122†, 2322, 3371, 1406, 1408, 5500.
  Major changes to this scheme took effect on 11th May 1983.

7.11 (6) FRANCE AND SPAIN, NORTH AND WEST COASTS, AND PORTUGAL.

* Off Ushant (Ile d'Ouessant),
  48° 30'·8 N., 5° 14'·0 W. to 48° 49'·0 N., 5° 46'·9 W.
  Charts 2643, 2644, 20, 2655, 2649, 2675.

* Off Berlenga,
  39° 25'·0 N., 9° 50'·0 W.
  Charts 1515, 1507, 87.

* Off Cape Roca (Cabo da Roca),
  38° 47'·0 N., 9° 50'·; W.
  Charts 1515, 87.

* Off Cape S. Vicente (Cabo de São Vicente),
  36° 54'·4 N., 9° 06'·6 W.
  Charts 1514, 92, 1228, 87.

* At Banco del Hoyo,
  35° 55'·8 N., 6° 08'·9 W.
  Charts 142, 92.

7.12 (8) MEDITERRANEAN AND BLACK SEAS

* In the Strait of Gibraltar,
  35° 59'·1 N., 5° 25'·6 W. to 35° 56'·3 N., 5° 45'·0 W.
  Charts 142, 773, 92.

* Off Cani Island (Iles Cani),
  37° 31'·7 N., 10° 07'·6 E.
  Charts 2121, 2122.

* Off Cape Bon (Cap Bon),
  37° 11'·7 N., 11° 06'·3 E.
  Chart 2122.

  In Vela Vrata,
  45° 07'·8 N., 14° 15'·8 E.
  Charts 2719, 204.
  Government of Yugoslavia.

* Saronicos Gulf (in the Approaches to Piraeus Harbour) (Saronikós Kolpós, in the
  Approaches to Piraiévs).
  37° 45'·1 N., 23° 40'·9 E.
  Chart 1657.

  Between Burgas and Nos Kaliakra,
  42° 30'·0 N., 27° 36'·0 E. to 43° 26'·0 N., 28° 41'·0 E.
  Chart 2230.
  Government of Bulgaria.

* In the Approaches to the Ports of Odessa and Il'ichevsk,
  46° 15'·3 N., 30° 55'·7 E.
  Charts 2206, 2212, 2213, 2231, 2232.

* Between the Ports of Odessa and Il'ichevsk,
  46° 22'·5 N., 30° 47'·2 E.
  Charts 2206, 2212, 2213.

  Off Sarich Point,
  44° 20'·4 N., 33° 31'·8 E. to 44° 20'·4 N., 34° 01'·7 E.
  Charts 2232, 2233
  Government of U.S.S.R.

In the Southern Approaches to the Kerch Strait (Kerchenskiy Proliv) (Kerch-Yenikale Strait),
44° 57′·8 N., 36° 29′·6 E.
Charts 2216, 2233, 2235.

Northern Approaches to Kerchenskiy Proliv (Kerch-Yenikale Strait),
45° 35′·2 N., 36° 42′·2 E.
Charts 2233, 2234.
Government of U.S.S.R.

Approaches to Berdyansk and Zhdanov,
46° 20′·0 N., 36° 46′·8 E. to 46° 44′·2 N., 37° 11′·5 E.
Chart 2234.
Government of U.S.S.R.
Approaches to Novorossiysk,
44° 31′·1 N., 37° 42′·9 E.
44° 30′· N., 37° 57′·4 E.
Charts 2245, 2235
Government of U.S.S.R.

7.13 (11) RED SEA, ARABIA, IRAQ AND IRAN.

* In the Gulf of Suez,
  29° 45′·0 N., 32° 32′·0 E. to 27° 30′·0 N., 34° 07′·0 E.
  Charts 3215, 2373, 2374, 2375, 7578.
  Scheduled for amendment 15th March 1983.

  In Approaches to Yanbu,
  24° 02′·6 N., 37° 45′·3 E. to 23° 54′·4 N., 38° 12′·2 E.
  Charts 327, 328.
  The Royal Commission for Jubail and Yanbu Kingdom of Saudi Arabia.

* In the Strait of Bab-el-Mandeb,
  12° 33′·0 N., 43° 27′·8 E. to 12° 55′·8 N., 43° 13′·1 E.
  Charts 1925, 143, 6.

* Off Ra's al Hadd,
  22° 31′ N., 60° 03′ E.
  Charts 38, 2851.

* In the Strait of Hormuz,
  26° 35′·0 N., 56° 32′·0 E.
  Charts 3956, 2888, 2837.

  Tunb-Farur (Jazīrat Tunb to Jazīreh-e Fārūr),
  26° 17′·0 N., 54° 30′·0 E. to 26° 15′·8 N., 55° 30′·0 E.
  Charts 2887, 2888, 2837.

* Between Zaqqum and Umm Shaif Oilfields,
  25° 06′·5 N., 53° 25′·0 E. to 25° 56′·6 N., 52° 59′·8 E.
  Charts 3733, 3952, 2889.
  Scheduled for implementation 1st March 1983.

* In the Approaches to Ra's Tanura (Tannūrah),
  27° 06'·5 N., 50° 42'·0 E. to 26° 40'·9 N., 50° 12'·1 E.
  Charts 3777, 3788.
  Amended width of Arrival Channel not yet IMO-adopted. See Admiralty NM 1370/82.

* In the Approaches to Ra's al Ju'aymah,
  26° 57'·0 N., 50° 13'·0 E. to 27° 11'·5 N., 50° 36'·0 E.
  Charts 3777, 3788.
  Remarks: See Admiralty Sailing Directions, N.P. 63.

7.14 (12) INDIAN OCEAN, PAKISTAN, INDIA, SRI LANKA, BANGLADESH AND BURMA.

* Off Dondra Head,
  5° 47'·0 N., 80° 35'·5 E.
  Charts 3265, 813, 828, 2898.

7.15 (13) MALACCA STRAIT, SINGAPORE STRAIT AND SUMATERA.

Port of Singapore—Designated Channels (inward and outwards),
1° 14'·2 N., 103° 42'·1 E.
Charts 2012, 2014, 2556, 2570.
1° 12'·0 N., 103° 50'·0 E.
Charts 1995, 2015, 2556.
Port of Singapore Authority.
Remarks: See Admiralty Sailing Directions, N.P. 44.

* At One Fathom Bank,
  2° 53' N., 100° 55' E.
  Chart 3946.

* In the Singapore Strait,
  1° 08' N., 103° 45' E.
  Charts 3947, 3833, 2598, 2570, 2556, 2569, 3831.

* At Horsburgh Light Area,
  1° 20' N., 104° 20' E.
  Chart 3831.

7.16 (14) CHINA SEA WITH ITS WEST SHORE AND CHINA.

Approaches to Hong Kong Harbour,
22° 15'·0 N., 114° 16'·0 E.
22° 14'·0 N., 114° 09'·0 E.
22° 13'·5 N., 114° 01'·2 E.
Charts 1917, 1918, 341, 342, 937, 938 ,3279.
Government of Hong Kong.
Remarks: See Admiralty Sailing Directions, N.P. 30.

Approaches to Shanghai.
31° 03′·0 N., 122° 18′·6 E.
31° 03′·5 N., 122° 23′·5 E.
Chart 1602.
Government of People's Republic of China.

7.17 (15) JAPAN.

Kurushima Kaikyō,
34° 07′·0 N., 132° 59′·7 E.
Chart 3604.
Government of Japan.
Remarks: Mandatory for all shipping.
          See Admiralty Sailing Directions, N.P. 42B.

Bisan Seto,
34° 18′·0 N., 133° 37′·4 E. to 34° 23′·9 N., 134° 13′·6 E.
Charts 1969, 3605.
Government of Japan.
Remarks: Mandatory for all shipping.
          See Admiralty Sailing Directions, N.P. 42B.

Akashi Kaikyō,
34° 37′·0 N., 135° 01′·0 E.
Chart 3614.
Government of Japan.
Remarks: Mandatory for all shipping.
          See Admiralty Sailing Directions, N.P. 42B.

Irako Suidō,
34° 33′·6 N., 137° 00′·2 E.
Chart 3650.
Government of Japan.
Remarks: Mandatory for all shipping.
          See Admiralty Sailing Directions, N.P. 42A.

Uraga Suidō,
35° 12′·5 N., 139° 46′·8 E. to 35° 24′·3 N., 139° 46′·6 E.
Charts 3360, 3548.
Government of Japan.
Remarks: Mandatory for all shipping.
          See Admiralty Sailing Directions, N.P. 42A.

Recommended and Voluntary Schemes.
Some traffic separation schemes recommended by Japanese government agencies and
several voluntary schemes are in use in Japanese waters. Where known, details are given
in Admiralty Sailing Directions. These schemes are not shown on Admiralty charts or on
the charts published by the Japanese Hydrographic Office.

7.18 (16) KOREA AND THE PACIFIC COASTS OF U.S.S.R.

Approaches to Masan,
35° 03′ N., 128° 40′ E.
Charts 3642, 1270.
Government of Korea.

Approaches to Inch'ŏn,
37° 20′ N., 126° 25′ E.
Charts 1065, 3366.
Government of Korea.

In the Approaches to the Gulf of Nakhodka (Zaliv Nakhodka).
42° 35′·0 N., 132° 55′·0 E.
Charts 3198, 2511.

* Off the Ostrovnoi Point (Mys Ostrovnyy),
42° 38′·0 N., 133° 33′·0 E.
Chart 2511.

Sōya Kaikyō (La Perouse Strait),
45° 47′·0 N., 142° 08′·5 E.
Charts 3341, 452.
Government of U.S.S.R.

* Off the Aniwa Cape (Mys Aniva) (Naka Shiretoko Misaki),
45° 55′·0 N., 143° 30′·0 E.
Chart 452.

Proliv Shanpberga (Shikotan Suidō),
43° 42′·0 N., 146° 30′·0 E.
Chart 452.
Government of U.S.S.R.

Proliv Yekateriny (Kunashiri Suidō),
44° 27′·0 N., 146° 43′·0 E.
Chart 452.
Government of U.S.S.R.

Proliv Friza,
45° 29′·0 N., 149° 10′·0 E.
Government of U.S.S.R.
Remarks: Not shown on Chart 4511. For details see Admiralty Sailing Directions,
N.P. 41.

Proliv Urup,
46° 20′·0 N., 150° 45′·0 E.
Government of U.S.S.R.
Remarks: Not shown on Chart 4511. For details see Admiralty Sailing Directions,
N.P. 41.

South of Ostrov Broutona,
46° 37'·0 N., 150° 50'·0 E.
Government of U.S.S.R.
Remarks: Not shown on Chart 4511. For details see Admiralty Sailing Directions, N.P. 41.

* In the Fourth Kuril Strait (Chetvertyy Kuril'skiy Proliv),
  Part 1. North of Ostrov Makanrushi,
        49° 55'·0 N., 154° 24'·0 E.
  Part 2. Off Mys Vasil'yeva,
        49° 52'·0 N., 155° 25'·0 E.
  Remarks: Not shown on Chart 4511. For details see Admiralty Sailing Directions, N.P. 41.

Approaches to Sovetskaya,
49° 05' N., 140° 25' E.
Government of U.S.S.R.
Remarks: Not shown on Chart 3340.

Mys Povoratnyy to Mys Opasnyy,
52° 30'·0 N., 158° 46'·5 E.
Government of U.S.S.R.
Remarks: Not shown on Chart 2388. For details see Admiralty Sailing Directions N.P. 43.

Avachinskaya Guba,
Part 1. Southern Appoach,
        52° 44'·5 N., 158° 45'·0 E.
Part 2. Eastern Approach,
        52° 48'·0 N., 158° 47'·5 E.
Government of U.S.S.R.
Remarks: Not shown on Chart 2388. For details see Admiralty Sailing Directions, N.P. 43.

7.19 (18) AUSTRALIA, AND PAPUA NEW GUINEA

* South of Wilson Promontory in the Bass Strait,
  39° 15'·0 S., 146° 15'·0 E. to 39° 11'·0 S., 146° 45'·0 E.
  Charts Aus 801, Aus 350, Aus 357, Aus 422, BA 1695A.

* In the Bass Strait,
  38° 44' S., 148° 15' E. to 38° 48' S., 148° 02' E.
  Charts Aus 357, Aus 358, BA 1695A, Aus 422, Aus 423.

7.20 (21) ALEUTIAN ISLANDS, ALASKA AND WEST COAST OF NORTH AMERICA, INCLUDING MEXICO.

Prince William Sound and Valdez Arm,
60° 16'·8 N., 146° 48'·6 W. to 60° 58'·5 N., 146° 47'·5 W.
Charts 3363, 3364.
Government of U.S.A.
Remarks: Scheme at present undergoing user evaluation.

Broughton Strait,
50° 37′·1 N., 127° 02′·7 W. to 50° 35′·8 N., 127° 00′·0 W.
Chart 3417.
Government of Canada.

Johnstone Strait,
50° 25′·1 N., 125° 58′·1 W. to 50° 22′·5 N., 125° 46′·4 W.
Charts 3333, 3260.
Government of Canada.

In the Strait of Juan de Fuca and its Approaches,
48° 28′·8 N., 124° 58′·6 W. to 48° 14′·2 N., 123° 28′·9 W.
Charts 2941†, 2689†.
Governments of Canada and U.S.A.

Off Discovery Island,
48° 22′·6 N., 123° 20′·0 W. to 48° 28′·6 N., 123° 11′·8 W.
Charts 1914, 2840.
Government of Canada.

Puget Sound to Rosario Strait,
47° 19′·5 N., 122° 27′·3 W. to 48° 45′·0 N., 122° 46′·4 W.
Charts 1792, 2840, 1947, 2689.
Government of U.S.A.
Remarks: Mandatory for all shipping.

Strait of Georgia,
48° 45′·0 N., 122° 46′·4 W. to 49° 19′·0 N., 123° 12′·0 W.
Charts 922, 576, 2840, 579, 2689.
Governments of Canada and U.S.A.
Remarks: Scheme at present undergoing user evaluation.

* Off San Francisco,
37° 45′·0 N., 122° 41′·5 W.
Chart 229

San Francisco Harbour and inner Approaches,
37° 46′·0 N., 122° 38′·0 W. to 38° 03′·5 N., 122° 17′·0 W.
Charts 591, 590.
Government of U.S.A.

* In the Santa Barbara Channel and in the Approaches to Los Angeles—Long Beach.
34° 20′·2 N., 120° 30′·3 W. to 33° 39′·7 N., 118° 17′·6 W.
33° 19′·7 N., 118° 03′·4 W. to 33° 37′·7 N., 118° 08′·8 W.
Charts 1082, 1063, 899.
Remarks: Currently being considered for amendment.

7.21 (22) WEST COASTS OF CENTRAL AND SOUTH AMERICA.

* In the Approaches to Antofagasta,
23° 38′·4 S., 70° 25′·9 W.
Charts 3077, 3071.

* In the Approaches to Quintero Bay,
  32° 44'·7 S., 71° 32'·6 W.
  Charts 1314, 3073.

* In the Approaches to Valparaíso,
  33° 01'·0 S., 71° 37'·3 W.
  Charts 1314, 3073, 3074.

* In the Approaches to Concepcion Bay (Bahía de Concepción),
  (i) Boca Grande 36° 35'·2 S., 73° 01'·4 W.
  (ii) Boca Chica 36° 36'·1 S., 73° 04'·2 W. to 36° 39'·0 S., 73° 04'·3 W. [Scheme now
      deleted—see Admiralty Notice to Mariners No. 1208 of 1983].
  Charts 1319, 3074.

* In the Approaches to San Vicente Bay (Bahía San Vicente),
  36° 44'·0 S., 73° 10'·2 W.
  Charts 1319, 3074, 3075.

7.22 (25) CARIBBEAN SEA, WEST INDIES AND THE GULF OF MEXICO.

Off Cabo San Antonio,
21° 43'·9 N., 85° 07'·2 W. to 22° 01'·0 N., 85° 07'·2 W.
Charts 3867, 1220, 2579.
Government of Cuba.
Remarks: Currently being considered for implementation.

Off La Tabla,
22° 19'·7 N., 84° 49'·9 W., to 22° 27'·9 N., 84° 42'·1 W.
Charts 3867, 1220, 2579.
Government of Cuba.
Remarks: Currently being considered for implementation.

Off Costa de Matanzas,
23° 23'·5 N., 81° 08'·0 W. to 23° 25'·0 N., 80° 53'.8 W. to 23° 23'·0 N., 80° 28'·0 W.
Charts 1217, 3866, 3867, 2579.
Government of Cuba.
Remarks: Currently being considered for implementation.

In the Old Bahama Channel,
22° 48'·4 N., 78° 45'·0 W. to 22° 35'·2 N., 78° 06'·4 W. to 22° 18'·9 N., 77° 39'·4 W. to
22° 09'·0 N., 77° 27'·8 W.
Charts 425, 2009, 3865, 3866, 2579.
Government of Cuba.
Remarks: Currently being considered for implementation.

Off Punta Maternillos,
21° 51'·2 N., 77° 06'·8 W. to 21° 47'·8 N., 77° 02'·8 W. to 21° 44'·2 N., 76° 54'·0 W.
Charts 3865, 2579.
Remarks: Currently being considered for implementation.

Off Punta Lucrecia,
21° 15'·0 N., 75° 42'·3 W. to 21° 11'·4 N., 75° 33'·4 W. to 21° 07'·0 N., 75° 25'·0 W.
Charts 3865, 2579.
Government of Cuba.
Remarks: Currently being considered for implementation.

Off Cabo Maysi,
20° 22'·8 N., 73° 58'·8 W. to 20° 05'·0 N., 73° 58'·8 W.
Charts 3865, 1266, 486, 2579.
Government of Cuba.
Remarks: Currently being considered for implementation.

In the Approaches to Galveston Bay,
29° 07'·75 N., 94° 22'·25 W. to 29° 18'·95 N., 94° 38'·65 W.
Charts 2831, 975, 3980,
Government of U.S.A.
Remarks: Currently being considered for implementation.
                 Proposed date for implementation, 1st October 1983.

7.23 (26) EAST COAST OF NORTH AMERICA, AND GREENLAND.

  * In the Approaches to Chesapeake Bay,
    36° 56'·2 N., 75° 57'·4 W.
    Charts 2843, 2861.

    Chesapeake Bay, off Smith Point.
    37° 54'·2 N., 76° 09'·8 W. to 37° 51'·4 N., 76° 09'·6 W.
    Charts 2846, 2848.
    Government of U.S.A.

  * Off Delaware Bay,
    38° 47'·3 N., 75° 02'·4 W. to 38° 47'·3 N., 74° 34'·6 W.
    38° 47'·3 N., 75° 02'·4 W. to 38° 27'·3 N., 74° 41'·8 W.
    Charts 2563, 2861.

  * Off New York,
    40° 30'·0 N., 69° 15'·0 W. to 40° 29'·2 N., 70° 14'·0 W.
    40° 27'·5 N., 73° 49'·8 W. to 40° 26'·0 N., 73° 05'·0 W.
    40° 27'·5 N., 73° 49'·8 W. to 40° 04'·0 N., 73° 17'·0 W.
    40° 27'·5 N., 73° 49'·8 W. to 39° 45'·7 N., 73° 46'·0 W.
    Charts 2755, 2860, 2492.
    Remarks: Eastern appoach off Nantucket, currently being considered for amendment.

  * In the Approaches to Narragansett Bay, Rhode Island and Buzzard's Bay, Massachusetts.
    41° 06'·0 N., 71° 23'·5 W. to 41° 25'·7 N., 71° 23'·5 W.
    41° 06'·0 N., 71° 23'·5 W. to 41° 24'·9 N., 71° 03'·9 W.
    Charts 2890, 2860, 2492.
    Remarks: Currently being considered for amendment.

* In the Approach to Boston, Massachusetts,
40° 49'·5 N., 69° 00'·0 W. to 42° 22'·7 N., 70° 40'·7 W.
Charts 1227, 3096, 2492, 2860.
Remarks: Currently being considered for amendment.

* In the Approaches to Portland, Maine,
43° 07'·8 N., 69° 55'·0 W. to 43° 31'·6 N., 70° 05'·6 W.
43° 24'·3 N., 69° 32'·7 W., to 43° 31'·6 N., 70° 05'·6 W.
Charts 2490, 3676, 2492.

Approaches to Bay of Fundy,
44° 22'·3 N., 66° 35'·2 W. to 45° 02'·8 N., 66° 08'·0 W.
Charts 352, 353, 1651.
Government of Canada.
Remarks: Mandatory for all shipping.
Changes to be made to this scheme.: date of implementation not yet announced.

Approaches to Halifax,
44° 25'·0 N., 63° 25'·0 W.
Charts 2410, 729, 1651.
Government of Canada.

* In the Approaches to Chedabucto Bay,
45° 23'·9 N., 60° 58'·8 W. to 45° 24'·2 N., 60° 27'·5 W.
Charts 2342, 729, 2727, 1651.

Gulf and River St. Lawrence,
48° 10'·0 N., 69° 28'·7 W. to 47° 30'·0 N., 60° 05'·0 W.
48° 10'·0 N., 69° 28'·7 W. to 51° 49'·0 N., 55° 41'·7 W.
Charts 1134, 307, 312, 779, 282, 284, 3335, 2034, 2727, 305, 1623, 1621, 232A, 232B,
324, 2516.
Government of Canada.

St. George's Bay,
45° 44'·5 N., 61° 31'·7 W. to 45° 53'·5 N., 61° 45'·5 W.
Charts 3383, 2034, 2727, 1651.
Government of Canada.

Placentia Bay,
46° 45'·0 N., 54° 45'·0 W. to 47° 46'·8 N., 54° 02'·2 W.
Charts 290, 232.
Government of Canada.

Hydrographic Department (*H*. 1226 77).

APPENDIX III

DEPARTMENT OF TRADE   MERCHANT SHIPPING NOTICE No. M.756

[*NOTE:* Now the Department of Transport]

KEEPING A SAFE NAVIGATIONAL WATCH

**Notice to Shipping Companies, Masters, Skippers, Officers and Seamen
of Merchant Ships and Fishing Vessels, and Nautical Schools**

8.01

1. There are at present four current Merchant Shipping Notices on Keeping a Safe Navigational Watch. These are:

   M.621—stressing the vital importance of ensuring that a proper lookout is kept AT ALL TIMES;

   M.685—giving the text of a Resolution A285 (VIII) adopted by the Inter-Governmental Maritime Consultative Organisation (IMCO) being a "Recommendation on basic principles and operational guidance relating to navigational watchkeeping";

   M.706—notifying the publication by IMCO in a booklet form as a saleable document of the Resolution A285 (VIII), and to recommend that this document be made widely available to seafarers, in particular that it should be prominently displayed on the bridge;

   M.708—notifying a slight amendment to Resolution A285 (VIII).

2. The Department of Trade has now decided to cancel all these notices, and to consolidate the recommendations in them by the following advice.

   (1) The Inter-Governmental Maritime Consultative Organisation (IMCO) has adopted Resolution A285. (VIII) "Recommendation on basic principles and operational guidance relating to navigational watchkeeping", and has published this Resolution in booklet form as a saleable document the text of which is also set out at the Appendix to this notice.

   (2) In view of the significant importance of this as it affects the maintenance of a safe navigational watch it is strongly recommended that this booklet be made readily available for perusal by all practising and trainee seafarers in the Deck Department, to whom the importance of gaining and maintaining a thorough knowledge of this recommendation is emphasised. It is specifically recommended that copies should be made available on board ships, at least one of which should be prominently displayed on the bridge, and that Masters and Skippers should ensure their watchkeepers are familiar with the contents. In this regard it is suggested that this recommendation could comprise a basic standing order for all Bridge Order Books, which could be

supplemented by the instructions of the company and the individual master. In addition candidates for all deck officer certificates of competency appearing for oral examination will be expected to have a thorough knowledge of this recommendation.

(3) Copies of the IMCO publication entitled "Recommendation on Basic Principles and Operational Guidance relating to Navigational Watchkeeping" may be obtained from the IMCO Secretariat, Publications Section, 104 Piccadilly, London W1V 0AE, at a price of 80p each (inclusive of packing and postage). All orders should include the appropriate remittance, and quote the sales reference "74.08.E".

(4) In conclusion the Department would stress the vital importance for maintaining a safe navigational watch that a proper lookout is kept AT ALL TIMES.

Department of Trade
Marine Division
London
April 1976   (MC 54/52/07)

[*NOTE:* IMCO is now IMO and its address is now as shown in para. 1.03, *ante.*]

8.02
APPENDIX A (to MERCHANT SHIPPING NOTICE No. M.756)

IMCO Resolution A.285 (VIII)—Recommendation on Basic Principles and Operational Guidance Relating to Navigational Watchkeeping

BASIC PRINCIPLES TO BE OBSERVED IN KEEPING A NAVIGATIONAL WATCH

The following principles shall be observed to ensure that a safe navigational watch is maintained:

(*a*) The master of every ship is bound to ensure that the watchkeeping arrangements are adequate for maintaining a safe navigational watch. Under his general direction, the officers of the watch are responsible for navigating the ship safely during their periods of duty when they will be particularly concerned to avoid collision and stranding.

(*b*) The basic principles including but not limited to the following shall be taken into account by all ships:

(i) **Watch arrangements**
The composition of the watch, including the requirement for look-out(s), shall at all times be adequate and appropriate to the prevailing circumstances and conditions.

When deciding the composition of the watch on the bridge the following points are among those to be taken into account:
(1) at no time shall the bridge be left unattended;
(2) the weather conditions, visibility and whether there is daylight or darkness;
(3) the proximity of navigational hazards which may make it necessary for the officer in charge to carry out additional navigational duties;

(4) the use and operational condition of navigational aids such as radar or electronic position-indicating devices and any other equipment affecting the safe navigation of the ship;

(5) whether the ship is fitted with automatic steering;

(6) any additional demands on the navigational watch that may arise as a result of special operational circumstances.

(ii) Fitness for duty

The watch system shall be such that the efficiency of the watchkeeping members of the crew is not impaired by fatigue. Accordingly the duties shall be so organised that the first watch at the commencement of a voyage and the subsequent relieving watches are sufficiently rested and otherwise fit when going on duty.

(iii) Navigational

(1) the intended voyage shall be planned in advance taking into consideration all pertinent information and any course laid down shall be checked;

(2) on taking over the watch the ship's estimated or true position, intended track, course and speed shall be confirmed; any navigational hazard expected to be encountered during the watch shall be noted;

(3) during the watch the course steered, position and speed shall be checked at sufficiently frequent intervals using any available navigational aids necessary to ensure that the ship follows the planned course:

(4) the safety and navigational equipment with which the ship is provided and the manner of its operation shall be clearly understood; in addition its operational condition shall be fully taken into account;

(5) whoever is in charge of a navigational watch shall not be assigned or undertake any duties which would interfere with the safe navigation of the ship.

(iv) Look-out

Every ship shall at all times maintain a proper look-out by sight and hearing as well as by all available means appropriate in the prevailing circumstances and conditions so as to make a full appraisal of the situation and of the risk of collision, stranding and other hazards to navigation. Additionally, the duties of the look-out shall include the detection of ships or aircraft in distress, shipwrecked persons, wrecks and debris. In applying these principles the following shall be observed:

(1) whoever is keeping a look-out must be able to give full attention to that task and no duties shall be assigned or undertaken which would interfere with the keeping of a proper look-out;

(2) the duties of the person on look-out and helmsman are separate and the helmsman should not be considered the person on look-out while steering; except in small vessels where an unobstructed all round view is provided at the steering position and there is no impairment of night vision or other impediment to the keeping of a proper look-out;

(3) there may be circumstances in which the officer of the watch can safely be the sole look-out in daylight. However, this practice shall only be followed after the situation has been carefully assessed on each occasion and it has been established without doubt that it is safe to do so. Full account shall be taken of all relevant factors including but not limited to the state of weather, conditions of visibility, traffic density, proximity of navigational hazards and if navigating in or near a traffic separation scheme. Assistance must be summoned to the bridge when any change in the situation necessitates this and such assistance must be immediately available.

(v) **Navigation with pilot embarked**
Despite the duties and obligations of a pilot, his presence on board does not relieve the master or officer in charge of the watch from their duties and obligations for the safety of the ship. The master and the pilot shall exchange information regarding navigation procedures, local conditions and the ship's characteristics.

(vi) **Protection of the marine environment**
The master and the officer in charge of the watch shall be aware of the serious effects of operational or accidental pollution of the marine environment and shall take all possible precautions to prevent such pollution particularly within the existing framework of existing international regulations.

OPERATIONAL GUIDANCE FOR OFFICERS IN CHARGE OF A NAVIGATIONAL WATCH

Introduction

1. This document contains operational guidance of general application for officers in charge of a navigational watch, which masters are expected to supplement as appropriate. It is essential that officers of the watch appreciate that the efficient performance of their duties is necessary in the interest of safety of life and property at sea and the avoidance of pollution of the marine environment.

General

2. The officer of the watch is the master's representative and his primary responsibility at all times is the safe navigation of the vessel. He must at all time comply with the applicable regulations for preventing collisions at sea (see also paragraphs 23 and 24).

3. The officer of the watch should keep his watch on the bridge which he should in no circumstances leave until properly relieved. It is of especial importance that at all times the officer of the watch ensures that an efficient look-out is maintained. In a vessel with a separate chart room the officer of the watch may visit this, when essential, for a short period for the necessary performance of his navigational duties, but he should previously satisfy himself that it is safe to do so and ensure that an efficient look-out is maintained.

4. There may be circumstances in which the officer of the watch can safely be the sole look-out in daylight. However, this practice shall only be followed after the situation has been carefully assessed on each occasion and it has been established without doubt that it is safe to do

so. Full account shall be taken of all relevant factors including but not limited to the state of weather, conditions of visibility, traffic density, proximity of navigational hazards and if navigating in or near a traffic separation scheme.

When the officer of the watch is acting as the sole look-out he must not hesitate to summon assistance to the bridge, and when for any reason he is unable to give his undivided attention to the look-out such assistance must be immediately available.

5. The officer of the watch should bear in mind that the engines are at his disposal and he should not hesitate to use them in case of need. However, timely notice of intended variations of engine speed should be given when possible. He should also keep prominently in mind the manoeuvring capabilities of his ship including its stopping distance.

6. The officer of the watch should also bear in mind that the sound signalling apparatus is at his disposal and he should not hesitate to use it in accordance with the applicable regulations for preventing collisions at sea.

7. The officer of the watch continues to be responsible for the safe navigation of the vessel despite the presence of the master on the bridge until the master informs him specifically that he has assumed responsibility and this is mutually understood.

Taking over the watch

8. The officer of the watch should not hand over the watch to the relieving officer if he has any reason to believe that the latter is apparently under any disability which preclude him from carrying out his duties effectively. If in doubt, the officer of the watch should inform the master accordingly. The relieving officer of the watch should ensure that members of his watch are apparently fully capable of performing their duties and in particular the adjustment to night vision.

9. The relieving officer should not take over the watch until his vision is fully adjusted to the light conditions and he has personally satisfied himself regarding:

    (a) standing orders and other special instructions of the master relating to the navigation of the vessel;

    (b) the position, course, speed and draught of the vessel;

    (c) prevailing and predicted tides, currents, weather, visibility and the effect of these factors upon course and speed;

    (d) the navigational situation including but not limited to the following:

        (i) the operational condition of all navigational and safety equipment being used or likely to be used during the watch;

        (ii) errors of gyro and magnetic compasses;

        (iii) the presence and movement of vessels in sight or known to be in the vicinity;

        (iv) conditions and hazards likely to be encountered during his watch;

        (v) the possible effects of heel, trim, water density and squat on underkeel clearance.

10. If at the time the officer of the watch is to be relieved a manoeuvre or other action to avoid any hazard is taking place, the relief of the officer should be deferred until such action is completed.

Periodic checks of navigational equipment

11. The officer of the watch should make regular checks to ensure that:
  (*a*) the helmsman or the automatic pilot is steering the correct course;
  (*b*) the standard compass error is established at least once a watch and when possible, after any major alteration of course. The standard and the gyro compasses should be frequently compared; repeaters should be synchronised with their master compass;
  (*c*) the automatic pilot is tested in the manual position at least once a watch;
  (*d*) the navigational and signal lights and other navigational equipment are functioning properly.

Automatic pilot

12. Officers of the watch should bear in mind the need to station the helmsman and to put the steering into manual control in good time to allow any potentially hazardous situation to be dealt with in a safe manner. With a vessel under automatic steering it is highly dangerous to allow a situation to develop to the point where the officer of the watch is without assistance and has to break the continuity of the look-out in order to take emergency action. The change-over from automatic to manual steering and vice versa should be made by, or under the supervision of, a responsible officer.

Electronic navigational aids

13. The officer of the watch should be thoroughly familiar with the use of electronic navigational aids carried, including their capabilities and limitations.

Echo-sounder

14. The echo-sounder is a valuable navigational aid and should be used whenever appropriate.

Navigational records

15. A proper record of the movements and activities of the vessel should be kept during the watch.

Radar

16. The officer of the watch should use the radar when appropriate and whenever restricted visibility is encountered or expected and at all times in congested waters having due regard to its limitations.

17. Whenever radar is in use, the officer of the watch should select an appropriate range scale, observe the display carefully and plot effectively.

18. The officer of the watch should ensure that range scales employed are changed at sufficiently frequent intervals so that echoes are detected as early as possible and that small or poor echoes do not escape detection.

19. The officer of the watch should ensure that plotting or systematic analysis is commenced in ample time, remembering that sufficient time can be made available by reducing speed if necessary.

20. In clear weather, whenever possible, the officer of the watch should carry out radar practice.

Navigation in coastal waters

21. The largest scale chart on board, suitable for the area and corrected with the latest available information, should be used. Fixes should be taken at frequent intervals; whenever circumstances allow, fixing should be carried out by more than one method.

22. The officer of the watch should positively identify all relevant navigation marks.

Clear weather

23. The officer of the watch should take frequent and accurate compass bearings of approaching vessels as a means of early detection of risk of collision; such risk may sometimes exist even when an appreciable bearing change is evident, particularly when approaching a very large vessel or a tow or when approaching a vessel at close range. He should also take early and positive action in compliance with the applicable regulations for preventing collisions at sea and subsequently check that such action is having the desired effect.

Restricted visibility

24. When restricted visibility is encountered or suspected, the first responsibility of the officer of the watch is to comply with the relevant rules of the applicable regulations for preventing collisions at sea, with particular regard to the sounding of fog signals, proceeding at a moderate* speed and he shall have the engines ready for immediate manoeuvres. In addition, he should:

(a) inform the master (see paragraph 25);

(b) post look-out(s) and helmsman and, in congested waters, revert to hand steering immediately;

(c) exhibit navigation lights;

(d) operate and use the radar.

It is important that the officer of the watch should have the manoeuvring capabilities including the "stopping distance" of his own vessel prominently in mind.

Calling the master

25. The officer of the watch should notify the master immediately under the following circumstances:

(a) if restricted visibility is encountered or suspected;

(b) if the traffic conditions or the movements of other vessels are causing concern;

---

*The Regulations for Preventing Collisions at Sea, 1960, presently in force, using the words "moderate speed".

The International Regulations for Preventing Collisions at Sea 1972, expected to come into force in 1976, use the words "safe speed".

[*Note:* The 1972 Rules are now in force.]

(*c*) if difficulty is experienced in maintaining course;

(*d*) on failure to sight land, a navigation mark or to obtain soundings by the expected time;

(*e*) if land or a navigation mark is sighted or a change in soundings occurs unexpectedly;

(*f*) on the breakdown of the engines, steering gear or any essential navigational equipment;

(*g*) in heavy weather if in any doubt about the possibility of weather damage;

(*h*) in any other emergency or situation in which he is in any doubt.

Despite the requirement to notify the master immediately in the foregoing circumstances, the officer of the watch should in addition not hesitate to take immediate action for the safety of the ship, where circumstances so require.

Navigation with pilot embarked

26. Despite the duties and obligations of a pilot, his presence on board does not relieve the officer of the watch from his duties and obligations for the safety of the ship. He should co-operate closely with the pilot and maintain an accurate check on the vessel's positions and movements. If he is in any doubt as to the pilot's actions or intentions, he should seek clarification from the pilot and if doubt still exists he should notify the master immediately and take whatever action is necessary before the master arrives.

The watchkeeping personnel

27. The officer of the watch should give the watchkeeping personnel all appropriate instructions and information which will ensure the keeping of a safe watch including an appropriate look-out.

Ship at anchor

28. If the master considers it necessary a continuous navigational watch should be maintained. In all circumstances, however, the officer of the watch should:

(*a*) determine and plot the ship's position on the appropriate chart as soon as practicable and at sufficiently frequent intervals check when circumstances permit, by taking bearings of fixed navigational marks or readily identifiable shore objects, whether the ship is remaining securely at anchor;

(*b*) ensure than an efficient look-out is maintained;

(*c*) ensure that inspection rounds of the vessel are made periodically;

(*d*) observe meteorological and tidal conditions and the state of the sea;

(*e*) notify the master and undertake all necessary measures if the vessel drags the anchor;

(*f*) ensure that the state of readiness of the main engines and other machinery is in accordance with the master's instructions;

(*g*) if visibility deteriorates notify the master and comply with the applicable regulations for preventing collisions at sea;

(*h*) ensure that the vessel exhibits the appropriate lights and shapes and that appropriate sound signals are made at all times;

(*i*) take measures to protect the environment from pollution by the ship and comply with the applicable pollution regulations.

8.03

DEPARTMENT OF TRADE   MERCHANT SHIPPING NOTICE No. M.997

[*NOTE:* Now the Department of Transport]

BRIDGE MANNING, WATCHKEEPING AND THE COMMAND OF FISHING VESSELS

Notice to Owners and Skippers of Fishing Vessels

This Notice supersedes Notice No. M.865

1. The investigation of groundings and collisions involving fishing vessels continues to reveal that one or more of the following were important contributory factors—

(*a*) an unqualified man in charge of the watch;

(*b*) only one man on watch;

(*c*) a poor lookout being kept;

(*d*) divided command.

2. Owners and Skippers are therefore strongly urged to ensure that on any fishing vessel there is the appropriate number of crew members who are capable of taking charge of the watch and that such watchkeepers are suitably experienced. Where there is no statutory requirement for the carriage of certified officers then the man in charge of the watch should have the necessary knowledge and skill satisfactorily to keep a safe navigational watch. (Training for watchkeeping is an important element in acquiring the necessary competence.) The need for a competent watchkeeper is self evident when making a landfall, navigating close to the coast, in dense traffic and in restricted visibility or severe weather conditions. However casualties still occur where the man in charge of the watch is an unqualified deckhand who is seriously deficient in knowledge of navigation, in the use of the navigational aids normally available on fishing vessels and in a knowledge of the Collision Regulations.

3. Casualties also continue to occur when there is only one man on watch. Even if the watchkeeper is certified there will be occasions when he will be unable successfully to cope with the steering, the navigation and the keeping of a proper lookout. In addition a man on watch alone can fall asleep or suffer some mishap which results in the wheelhouse being left unattended. A number of casualties arising from this cause could have been avoided by the presence of a second man in the wheelhouse.

4. It is appreciated that the nature of certain fishing operations, for example those involving inshore vessels, is such that crew members are often fatigued by long hours of work and lack of sleep. In these circumstances it is easy for a lone watchkeeper to fall asleep particularly during the hours of darkness. It is also appreciated that the size of the crew of the smaller inshore vessels may not be sufficient to permit a two-man watch, or that the wheelhouse may not be large enough to comfortably accommodate two men. In these circumstances it is

essential that the single watchkeeper is fit enough to take charge of the watch but Skippers should endeavour, where possible, to have two men on watch during the hours of darkness, in restricted visibility, in severe weather conditions and when navigating close to land.

5. With an increasing number of fishing vessels of all types being fitted with an automatic pilot, attention is drawn to the recommendations on the use of this equipment in Merchant Shipping Notices M.756, Keeping a Safe Navigational Watch and M.864, Use of Automatic Pilot and the Changeover from Automatic to Manual Control. It is recommended that in any fishing vessel fitted with an automatic pilot, a watch alarm should also be incorporated in that system. The watch alarm should be designed to provide a timed, manually reset, audible alarm which will operate at all times when the associated automatic pilot is in the auto steering mode. The alarm will be required to be fail safe in the event of autopilot power failure and to be interference proof in that any attempt to prevent its proper operation must inhibit automatic pilot operation. In larger vessels where there would normally be three men in the watch the provision of an automatic pilot and watch alarm should not be used as a reason for reducing the complement of the watch when the automatic pilot is being used.

6. Whatever the competence of the man in charge of the watch and the number of men on watch, it is absolutely essential that a proper lookout is kept at all times. Recent casualties include examples of fishing operations being carried out with no one in the wheelhouse in restricted visibility; no one on watch at night when a vessel was at anchor in the open waters of the North Sea; a single watchkeeper engaged in non-essential conversation on VHF; a single watchkeeper spending too much time in the engineroom; and, even with the wheelhouse properly manned, neither watchkeeper looking astern or in a direction abaft the beam resulting in a vessel being run down by an overtaking vessel.

7. A poster emphasising the importance of maintaining a proper lookout on fishing vessels exhibited in Department of Trade Marine Offices and copies are available from these offices for display in appropriate positions on board fishing vessels and on owners' premises. However, it is also necessary to draw to the attention of all concerned the importance of safe navigation and the priority it should receive in the organisation of work on board all types of fishing vessels particularly when proximity to the land or to other vessels demands increased vigilance.

8. There have also been a number of casualties involving fishing vessels where a crew member employed by virtue of his experience in fishing techniques has been in virtual command of the vessel notwithstanding the presence on board of a certificated Skipper. Attention is drawn to the need to ensure that an appropriately qualified Skipper is *in command* of the vessel and that experts in fishing techniques do not go beyond their role as advisers, thereby giving rise to a divided command with its attendant hazards. Where a certificated Skipper and/or Second Hand is required to be carried on a United Kingdom fishing vessel that person is required to act in that capacity in accordance with the Merchant Shipping (United Kingdom Fishing Vessels: Manning) Regulations 1980 (SI 1980 No. 1227).

Department of Trade
Marine Division
London WC1V 6LP
November 1981

8.04

DEPARTMENT OF TRADE   MERCHANT SHIPPING NOTICE No. M.1020

[*NOTE:* Now the Department of Transport.]

KEEPING A SAFE NAVIGATIONAL WATCH ON BOARD
FISHING VESSELS

Notice to Owners, Operators, Skippers, Mates and Crews of Fishing
Vessels, and to Nautical Schools

The Inter-Governmental Maritime Consultative Organisation (IMCO) has adopted Resolution A.484(XII) "Basic Principles to be Observed in Keeping a Navigational Watch on board Fishing Vessels" relating to the principles to be observed in order to ensure that a safe navigational watch is maintained.

2. The basic principles are reproduced in the Annex to this Notice and should be observed by all concerned.

3. Candidates for all fishing certificates of competency will, with effect from 1 June 1982, be expected to have a thorough knowledge of the content and application of the basic principles.

Department of Trade
Marine Division
London WC1V 6LP
May 1982

ANNEX

BASIC PRINCIPLES TO BE OBSERVED IN
KEEPING A NAVIGATIONAL WATCH ON BOARD
FISHING VESSELS

1. These basic principles are to be observed by skippers and watchkeeping personnel to ensure that a safe navigational watch is maintained at all times.

2. The skipper of every fishing vessel is bound to ensure that watchkeeping arrangements are adequate for maintaining a safe navigational watch. Under the skipper's general direction, the officers of the watch are responsible for navigating the vessel safely during their periods of duty when they will be particularly concerned with avoiding collision and stranding.

3. The basic principles, including but not limited to the following, should be taken into account on all fishing vessels. However, very small fishing vessels may be excluded from fully observing the basic principles. References to the wheelhouse should, in such vessels, be construed as meaning the position from which the navigation of the ship is controlled.

4. En route to or from fishing grounds

4.1 Arrangements of the navigational watch

4.1.1. The composition of the watch should at all times be adequate and appropriate to the prevailing circumstances and conditions and should take into account the need for maintaining a proper look-out.

4.1.2 When deciding the composition of the watch the following factors, *inter alia*, should be taken into account:

4.1.2.1 at no time should the wheelhouse be left unattended;

4.1.2.2 weather conditions, visibility and whether there is daylight or darkness;

4.1.2.3 proximity of navigational hazards which may make it necessary for the officer in charge of the watch to carry out additional navigational duties;

4.1.2.4 use and operational condition of navigational aids such as radar or electronic position-indicating devices and any other equipment affecting the safe navigation of the vessel;

4.1.2.5 whether the vessel is fitted with automatic steering;

4.1.2.6 any unusual demands on the navigational watch that may arise as a result of special operational circumstances.

4.2 Fitness for duty

4.2.1 The watch system should be such that the efficiency of watchkeeping personnel is not impaired by fatigue. Duties should be so organised that the first watch at the commencement of a voyage and the subsequent relieving watches are sufficiently rested and otherwise fit for duty.

4.3 Navigation

4.3.1 The intended voyage should, as far as practicable, be planned in advance taking into consideration all pertinent information and any course laid down should be checked before the voyage commences.

4.3.2 During the watch the course steered, position and speed should be checked at sufficiently frequent intervals, using any available navigational aids necessary, to ensure that the vessel follows the planned course.

4.3.3 The officer in charge of the watch should have full knowledge of the location and operation of all safety and navigational equipment on board the vessel and should be aware and take account of the operating limitations of such equipment.

4.3.4 The officer in charge of a navigational watch should not be assigned or undertake any duties which would interfere with the safe navigation of the vessel.

4.4 Navigational equipment

4.4.1 The officer in charge of the watch should make the most effective use of all navigational equipment at his disposal.

4.4.2 When using radar the officer in charge of the watch should bear in mind the necessity to comply at all times with the provisions on the use of radar contained in the applicable regulations for preventing collisions at sea.

4.4.3 In the cases of need the officer of the watch should not hesitate to use the helm, engines and sound signalling apparatus.

4.5 Navigational duties and responsibilities

4.5.1 The officer in charge of the watch should:

4.5.1.1 keep his watch in the wheelhouse which he should in no circumstances leave until properly relieved;

4.5.1.2 continue to be responsible for the safe navigation of the vessel despite the presence of the skipper in the wheelhouse until the skipper informs him specifically that he has assumed that responsibility and this is mutually understood;

4.5.1.3 notify the skipper when in any doubt as to what action to take in the interest of safety;

4.5.1.4 not hand over the watch to a relieving officer if he has reason to believe that the latter is obviously not capable of carrying out his duties effectively, in which case he should notify the skipper accordingly.

4.5.2 On taking over the watch the relieving officer should satisfy himself as to the vessel's estimated or true position and confirm its intended track, course and speed and should satisfy himself as to the vessel's estimated or true position and confirm its intended track course and speed and should note any dangers to navigation expected to be encountered during his watch.

4.5.3. Whenever practicable a proper record should be kept of the movements and activities during the watch relating to the navigation of the vessel.

4.6 Look-out

4.6.1 In addition to maintaining a proper look-out for the purpose of fully appraising the situation and the risk of collision, stranding and other dangers to navigation, the duties of the look-out should include the detection of ships or aircraft in distress shipwrecked persons, wrecks and debris. In maintaining a look-out the following should be observed;

4.6.1.1 The look-out must be able to give full attention to the keeping of a proper look-out and no other duties shall be undertaken or assigned which could interfere with that task.

4.6.1.2 The duties of the look-out and helmsman are separate and the helmsman should not be considered to be the look-out while steering except where an unobstructed all-round view is provided at the steering position and there is no impairment of night vision or other impediment to the keeping of a proper look-out. The officer in charge of the watch may be the sole look-out in daylight provided that on each such occasion;

4.6.1.2.1 the situation has been carefully assessed and it has been established without doubt that it is safe to do so;

4.6.1.2.2 full account has been taken of all relevant factors including, but not limited to:
—state of weather
—visibility
—traffic density
—proximity of danger to navigation
—the attention necessary when navigating in or near traffic separation schemes;

4.6.1.2.3 assistance is immediately available to be summoned to the wheelhouse when any change in the situation so requires.

4.7 Protection of the marine environment

4.7.1 The skipper and the officer in charge of the watch should be aware of the serious effects of operational or accidental pollution of the marine environment and should take all possible precautions to prevent such pollution particularly within the framework of relevant international and port regulations.

4.8 Weather conditions

4.8.1 The officer in charge of the watch should take relevant measures and notify the skipper when adverse changes in weather could affect the safety of the vessel, including conditions leading to ice accretion.

5. Navigation with pilot embarked

5.1 Despite the duties and obligations of a pilot, his presence on board does not relieve the skipper or officer in charge of the watch from their duties and obligations for the safety of the vessel. The skipper and the pilot should exchange information regarding navigation procedures, local conditions and the vessel's characteristics. The skipper and the officer of the watch should co-operate closely with the pilot and maintain an accurate check of the vessel's position and movement.

6. Vessels engaged in fishing or searching for fish

6.1 In addition to the principles enumerated in section 4, the following factors should be considered and properly acted upon by the officer in charge of the watch:

6.1.1 other vessels engaged in fishing and their gear;

6.1.2 safety of the crew on deck;

6.1.3 adverse effects on the safety of the vessel and its crew through reduction of stability and freeboard caused by exceptional forces resulting from fishing operations, catch handling and stowage, and unusual sea and weather conditions;

6.1.4 the proximity of offshore structures with special regard to the safety zones;

6.1.5 wrecks.

6.2 When stowing the catch, attention should be given to the essential requirements for adequate freeboard and adequate stability at all times during the voyage to the landing port taking into consideration consumption of fuel and stores, risk of adverse weather conditions and, especially in winter, risk of ice accretion on or above exposed decks in areas where ice accretion is likely to occur.

8.05
DEPARTMENT OF TRADE   MERCHANT SHIPPING NOTICE No. M.834

[*NOTE:* Now the Department of Transport.]

OBSERVATION OF TRAFFIC SEPARATION SCHEMES

**Notice to Owners, Masters, Skippers and all concerned with the
Navigation of sea-going vessels**

This Notice supersedes Notices No. M.645, M.669 (in part) and M.793

1. Rule 10 of the 1972 International Regulations for Preventing Collisions at Sea (which came into force on 15 July 1977) governs the conduct of all ships using Traffic Separation Schemes which have been adopted by the Inter-governmental Maritime Consultative Organization (IMCO).

2. The Rule is reproduced as an Annex to this Notice. It has given rise to a number of questions and the Department therefore considers it desirable to draw attention to some of its provisions:

Application

Paragraph (a). It is important to note that the Rule only applies to schemes which have been adopted by IMCO; in other schemes local regulations may apply, and these may modify not only Rule 10 but also in some cases other Steering and Sailing Rules. Before entering a traffic separation scheme, therefore, the relevant volume of Sailing Directions, as well as the chart in use, should be consulted.

A full list of Schemes, both those adopted by IMCO and those laid down by national administrations, is published each year in Admiralty Annual Notice to Mariners No. 17; changes and additions are promulgated by Notices which are published in the Weekly Edition of Admiralty Notices.

Procedure within a Traffic Lane

Paragraph (b) and (c). All vessels using a traffic lane must conform to the essential principles of routeing: if they are following the lane they must proceed in the general direction of traffic flow and if they are crossing it they must do so as nearly as practicable at right-angles to that direction. The same procedure applies to vessels which are within a lane for purposes other than passage through or across it, such as vessels engaged in fishing, if they are making way; it is appreciated that such vessels cannot always maintain a steady course and speed but their general direction of movement must be in accordance with this principle. Any substantial departure from this direction by any vessel is only allowed if it is required by overriding circumstances such as the need to comply with the other Steering and Sailing Rules or because of very bad weather conditions. Particular attention is drawn to the requirement that vessels which must cross a traffic lane shall do so at right angles. Crossing at right-angles keeps the time a crossing vessel is in the lane to a minimum, and leads to a clear encounter situation with through vessels.

Inshore Zones

Paragraph (d). This paragraph requires through traffic which can safely do so to use the appropriate traffic lane rather than the inshore zone. Its purpose is to reduce the number of head-on encounters in inshore zones. It does not preclude through vessels under stress of weather from seeking the protection of a weather shore, nor does it impose any specific behaviour on ships in inshore zones, so vessels in such zones must continue to look out for other traffic heading in any direction.

Anchoring within a Separation Zone

Paragraphs (e) and(g). The question has arisen as to whether a vessel which needs to anchor because for example of an engine breakdown or because of bad visibility may do so in a separation zone. In the Department's view this would be a seamanlike manoeuvre and is allowed under paragraph (e)(i).

Fishing Vessels

Paragraphs (*b*), (*c*), (*e*) *and* (*i*). Vessels fishing within a traffic separation scheme are considered to be using the scheme and must therefore when working in a traffic lane conform to the essential principles laid down in paragraphs (*b*) and (*c*) of the Rule and discussed above. When fishing in a separation *zone* they may follow any course. The requirement that vessels fishing must not impede through traffic means that they must not operate in such a manner that they, or their gear, seriously restrict the sea room available to other vessels within a lane. They should make every endeavour whilst fishing to avoid interfering with traffic; but if nonetheless risk of collision with another vessel develops then the normal steering and sailing rules apply.

Sailing Vessels and Small Craft

Paragraph (*j*). Similarly, sailing vessels and small craft of less than 20 metres (65 feet) in length are to avoid interfering with the flow of through traffic; but, again, if risk of collision does develop the normal steering and sailing rules apply. No specific mention is made in the Rule of a sailing vessel having an auxiliary engine, but it is the Department's view that if such a vessel cannot follow proper routeing procedures under sail because of light or adverse winds, then she should make use of her engine in order to do so.

3. Traffic Separation Schemes are usually sited where there is a heavy concentration of shipping. Mariners are therefore reminded of the particular importance of strictly adhering to Rules 5 to 8 which refer to Look-out, Safe speed, Risk of Collision and Action to Avoid Collision. Mariners are also reminded that except where there are special local rules to the contrary the other Steering and Sailing Rules—those of Section II when vessels are in sight of one another and that of Section III in restricted visibility—apply within a scheme just as elsewhere at sea. Through vessels do *not* have any priority over crossing or joining traffic.

Signal—YG

4. The Department of Trade considers it important that any vessel observed in a traffic separation scheme which appears to be navigating otherwise than in accordance with the established principles for such schemes is advised of the fact at the time. A special signal exists for this purpose: the two letter signal YG meaning "You appear not to be complying with the traffic separation scheme".

The master of any vessel receiving this signal by whatever means should take immediate action to check his course and position and any further steps which appear to him appropriate in the circumstances.

This signal is now embodied in Part VI of the International Code of Signals.

Department of Trade
Marine Division
London WC1V 6LP
February 1978

[*NOTE:* Annex not printed. IMCO is now IMO.]

8.06

DEPARTMENT OF TRADE   MERCHANT SHIPPING NOTICE No. M.1029

[*NOTE:* Now the Department of Transport.]

NAVIGATION IN THE DOVER STRAIT

**Notice to Owners, Masters and all concerned with Navigation of
Seagoing Vessels**

This Notice supersedes Notice No. M.869

1. The Dover Strait and its approaches are among the busiest shipping lanes in the world and pose serious problems for safety of navigation. The traffic separation scheme there and its associated inshore traffic zones have been designed to assist seafarers to navigate these waters in safety. The Department wishes, therefore, to emphasise the need for careful navigation in the area and for proper use to be made of the traffic separation scheme and its associated inshore traffic zones. This will help to prevent not only loss of life and ships, but also the pollution that can be caused by a stranding or collision particularly when a laden tanker or other vessel carrying a noxious cargo is involved.

2. On 1 July 1982 amendments were made to the Dover Strait Traffic Separation Scheme. For details of these amendments mariners should consult the relevant Notice to Mariners and amended charts and publications issued by the Hydrographic Department. However the basic changes to the scheme can be summarized as follows:

   (i) Creation of a separation zone over the Sandettie Bank.

   (ii) Widening of the Deep Water Route by moving the central separation zone between the SW and NE-bound lanes to the northwestward.

   (iii) Introduction of a new separation zone along the southern side of the NE-bound lane in the Sandettie area.

   (iv) Introduction of limits at each end of the English and French inshore traffic zones.

   (v) Changes in the separation zones to the west of the Varne.

3. The Department particularly wishes to draw to the attention of mariners the introduction of limits to the inshore traffic zones. Though the number of collisions in the Dover Strait and its approaches has declined since the introduction of the traffic separation scheme and its application becoming mandatory for all ships in 1977, a large percentage of subsequent collisions have occurred in the English inshore traffic zone. One of the factors relating to these collisions is the density of two way traffic in the zone. Much of this traffic has resulted because the lack of definition of the extent of the zone has meant Masters have been unsure of their position in relation to the application of Rule 10(d) of the International Collision Regulations in deciding whether they are "through" vessels or not.

4. The amended scheme defines the limits of the inshore traffic zones. The French inshore traffic zone lies between Cap Griz Nez in the north and a line drawn due west, south of Le Touquet in the south. The English inshore traffic zone now extends from a line drawn from the western end of the scheme to include Shoreham to a line drawn due south from

South Foreland. These explicitly defined end-limits to the inshore traffic zones are shown on the Admiralty charts. It is the Department's view that any vessel which commences its voyage from a location beyond one limit of the zone and proceeds to a location beyond the further limit of the zone and is not calling at a port, pilot station or destination or sheltered anchorage within the zone is a "through" vessel and for the purposes of Rule 10(d) should, if it can safely do so, use the appropriate traffic lane of the adjacent traffic separation scheme, unless some abnormal circumstance exists in that lane.

5. In addition, although Rule 10(b)(iii) requires vessels normally to join and leave a traffic lane at the termination of the lane, it does permit a vessel to join a lane from the side at a small angle to the general direction of traffic flow. Consequently vessels bound south west from a port in the English inshore traffic zone and vessels which have disembarked their pilots within the zone are advised to join the south west lane as soon as it is safe and practicable to do so. All vessels are advised to keep clear of boundary separation lines or zones in accordance with Rule 10(b)(ii); failure to observe this rule has been one cause of repeated damage to the CS.2 (now CS.4) buoy. As shown on charts this buoy is now protected by an "area to be avoided" by all classes of ships.

6. Use of the traffic separation scheme in accordance with Rule 10 of the International Collision Regulations does not in any way alter the over-riding requirement for vessels to comply with the other rules in the International Collision Regulations. In particular it is pointed out that vessels do not by virtue of using the traffic lanes in the general direction of the traffic flow, enjoy any privilege they would not have elsewhere. In addition, vessels using the traffic separation scheme are not relieved of the requirement to proceed at a safe speed, especially in condition of restricted visibility.

7. The Channel Navigation Information Service (CNIS) carries out continuous radar surveillance of the Dover Strait area. Broadcasts, giving navigational information to shipping, are made by Dover Coastguard on Channel 10 VHF in English and by Gris Nez Traffic on Channel 11 VHF in French and English. The Department draws the attention of mariners to the services provided and recommends them to listen to the broadcasts.

8. In addition, a large number of vessels navigating through the area contact the Information Service and the Department welcomes the growth of such reporting-in as conducive to safety of navigation. Attention is drawn in particular to the Ship Movement Reporting (MAREP) scheme which provides for voluntary reporting by certain vessels. The details of this and other CNIS services are contained in the Admiralty List of Radio Signals Vol. 6 and the English Channel Passage Planning Guide (Ad. Chart No. 5500) with any changes in the service being promulgated in Notices to Mariners.

9. Merchant Shipping Notice No. **M.834** draws attention to observance of traffic separation schemes in general.

Department of Trade
Marine Division
London WC1V 6LP
July 1982

8.07

Department of Trade   Merchant Shipping Notice No. M.895

[*NOTE:* Now the Department of Transport.]

THE APPLICATION OF THE INTERNATIONAL REGULATIONS FOR PREVENTING COLLISIONS AT SEA 1972 TO DYNAMICALLY POSITIONED VESSELS AND THE DANGERS TO DIVERS OPERATING FROM SUCH VESSELS

Notice to Shipowners, Masters and Officers of Merchant Ships and Fishing Vessels

1. The attention of mariners is drawn to the special limitations imposed on Dynamically Positioned Vessels by the nature of their work and the need for them to operate in sea conditions as favourable as possible. Further, these vessels when operating in the diving support mode are required to hold position most accurately often very close to the legs of platforms. In the event of movement of the vessel, which may be due, for example, to the wash of a passing ship, risk of serious injury to the divers and/or damage to the vessel or platform could occur.

2. In view of these considerations, mariners are requested to give as wide a berth as possible to vessels displaying the signals required by [Rule 17*] paragraphs (*b*) and (*d*) as applicable of the International Regulations for Preventing Collisions at Sea 1972, as set out in Schedule 1 to the Collision Regulations & Distress Signals Order 1977 (SI 1977/1978). If they are unable to pass at least ½ mile-clear, they should reduce speed when navigating near such vessels. To assist in identification Dynamically Positioned Vessels should also use the single letter "A" of the International Code of Signals using any method of signalling which may be appropriate.

3. It is also recommended that a Dynamically Positioned Vessel should, before commencing diving operations, ascertain that no other vessel is operating in its immediate vicinity. The vessel should also broadcast on the appropriate frequencies a navigation warning to all ships indicating the nature of its operation and such broadcast should be repeated at intervals whilst the operation is in progress. Additionally the vessel should ensure that the broadcasts are acknowledged by the appropriate coastal radio station who will rebroadcast them in their routine schedules.

4. Attention is also drawn to the provisions of Rule 36 of Schedule 1 to the Collision Regulations & Distress Signals Order 1977 which enables a vessel to make signals to attract the attention of another vessel to alert her to a danger which may exist.

Department of Trade
Marine Division
London WC1V 6LP
September 1979

*[*NOTE:* This is printed as Rule 17 but appears to be a misprint for Rule 27. The references to the Collision Regulations and Distress Signals Order 1977 should now be read as references to the Merchant Shipping (Distress Signals and Prevention of Collisions) Regulations 1983, S.I. 1983, No. 708.]

8.08

DEPARTMENT OF TRADE   MERCHANT SHIPPING NOTICE No. M.870

[*NOTE:* Now the Department of Transport.]

IDENTIFICATION SOUND SIGNALS FOR PILOTAGE VESSELS IN RESTRICTED VISIBILITY

Notice to Shipowners, Shipmasters and Seamen and Others concerned with Foreign-going and Home-Trade Merchant Ships and Fishing Vessels

This Notice supersedes Notice No. M.537

1. Rule 35(i) of the International Regulations for Preventing Collisions at Sea, 1972, which became operative on 15 July 1977 reads:

"A pilot-vessel when engaged on pilotage duty may, in addition to the signals prescribed in paragraphs (a), (b) or (f) of this Rule sound an identity signal consisting of four short blasts".

2. In the United Kingdom the practice has been for some pilotage authorities to have their own distinctive sound signals for the identification of their pilot vessels in conditions of poor visibility. Pilot vessels in Trinity House pilotage districts have, since 1 September 1965 sounded four short blasts in these conditions.

3. In view of the permissive signal of four short blasts for pilot-vessels provided in Rule 35(i) the Department asked all the pilotage authorities in the United Kingdom whether they would wish to replace their existing local signal by the signal of four short blasts provided for in the Collision Regulations. The consensus of opinion was in favour of adopting the signal of four short blasts.

4. The signal of four short blasts should be now be introduced in most ports where it is being adopted; however, some pilotage authorities will not be able to introduce it until their bye-laws are amended. Nevertheless, pilotage authorities for Sunderland and some pilotage authorities in the Bristol Channel consider special identification to be essential in their areas and will continue to use their existing identity signals.

5. Certain harbour authorities make provision for the use of the sound signal "H" (four short blasts) to indicate lack of manoeuvrability or not under command. To avoid any misunderstanding in the use of "H" by pilot vessels, the Department has recommended to all concerned that the sound signal "D" (a long blast followed by two short blasts) should instead be used to indicate lack of manoeuvrability or not under command. It is hoped that most harbour authorities will use this signal.

6. The Department has advised the authorities concerned that where any changes are made to existing signals, an appropriate notice to mariners should be issued.

Department of Trade
Marine Division
London WC1V 6LP
January 1979

INDEX